Myths & Hitches

2

MISCONCEPTIONS, FALLACIES & FALSE BELIEFS

about

**Heroes & Villains
Wars & Revolutions
Disasters**

Don M. Ferry

DEDICATION

To my wife Olivia, our children Gia, Rica and Dondi, our sons-in-law Bill and Manley, and all our grandchildren, and to those friends and associates who have supported us in this endeavor.

ACKNOWLEDGMENT

The author is highly indebted to his wife Olivia for editing the greater portion of this work, and to his son Dondi for his contributions to the cover design of the book.

TABLE OF CONTENTS

PREFACE

This is the second volume in the series entitled *Myths & Hitches*, a comprehensive collection of misconceptions and fallacies culled from popular lore. Arrayed in its pages are more than 300 items of information in several genres, from *heroes and villains* to *wars and revolutions* to *disasters*. What they convey may seem ordinary, but only in the sense that most everything in this world is ordinary. In fact, they are a cut above common trivia, owing to a feature that makes them uniquely engaging: each is a pseudo-fact, a lie dressed up as a truth, a belief that's flawed to the gills. People love trivia because they entertain, and trivia debunked can do no less—like a pratfall, which signifies nothing except that it's amusing. A pratfall deflates the pompousness of human behavior, while a fallacy exposed deflates the pomposity of human knowledge.

Many profess to debunk for a higher purpose: to enhance education and promote general literacy by eliminating errors and fallacies from the vast reservoir of popular information. It's an ideal, of course, but in raising the bar, it turns what should be a fun-filled exercise into something truly demanding and, at times, hardly feasible. Very often, the lie to be excised may have already become entrenched as myth, a myth even more wholesome and beguiling than the truth. For instance, was it history's loss but literature's gain that Longfellow (intentionally or not) fiddled with the facts concerning Paul Revere's ride on that fateful night of April 18 in 1775? Would the reputation for flamboyance of golden age pirates, so dear to Hollywood, suffer from the finding that they preferred marooning to walking the plank as punishment for their victims? And—pardon the pun—would the apple look or feel any different if it were shown that, contrary to Civil War lore, it did not figure in Lee's surrender to Grant?

We share in the ideal, too, but only where, by exposing the untruth, we are able to ferret out the corresponding truth. When we fail, as we often do, we can only take comfort in Von Goethe's words: "It is easier to perceive error than to find truth, for the former lies on the surface and is easily seen, while the latter lies in the depth, where few are willing to search for it." Sadly, even the few who do decide to search 'in the depth' find out soon enough that truth has many faces, that "what is true by lamplight is not

5

always true by sunlight." For truth may vary as to place: the ancient Roman writer Suetonius often failed to agree with his Greek counterpart Plutarch on significant details, making the study of Greco-Roman history thoroughly confusing to one who is not a pupil of either. Truth may also vary as to time, a phenomenon that that archetype of reference books, the Encyclopedia Britannica, makes evident whenever it comes out with a new edition to update or revise an earlier one. In a sense, the 'untruths' presented in this book are just versions of the truth, which means that, unless we are sure of our grounds, there is no need to impose the ideal by banishing them from popular lore as falsehoods.

Still, while we aim primarily to entertain, we hope to leave the message that the inability or difficulty of finding the truth is no license to falsify it. Information, essential or not, deserves to be reported accurately or not at all, and the historian, journalist, screenwriter, artist and blogger who care enough for what they do must keep that trust. The way information is handled in a society impacts ultimately on that society's respect for truth as a value on which all other values must rest.

Don M. Ferry

N.B.: The above has been lifted essentially from the preface of a similarly themed book, *Untruths and Nothing But* (Infinity Publishing, 2009), by the author. Some of the contents of that book have been expanded, reorganized and carried over into this volume of *Myths & Hitches* as well as into three other volumes of the series (*Myths & Hitches 1, 3* and *4),* all available in eBook format. Please refer to the end of each volume for a detailed list of the topics covered. —DMF

Heroes
&
Villains

1

Days Of Guns And Bosses

On Gangsters and G-Men

"You can get much farther with a kind word and
a gun than you can with a kind word."

•

Al Capone

1. Bringing Out the Dead Files

Myth! Hoover demonstrated his hands-on leadership of the FBI by making the most number of personal arrests.

This may be why, as a biographer once observed, none of the eight presidents Hoover served could fire him during the unprecedented 48 years he lasted in his job, and he was an American idol on the day he died. But Hoover never really made an arrest in his life, which was not unusual, since no FBI director ever did. People tend to remember Hoover as Mr. FBI himself, quietly masculine, sharp with his sleuthing, and skillful with a gun. Yet the Director never conducted an investigation, and according to a top aide, he didn't even know how to use a gun. It didn't help his macho image any that he was a life-long bachelor who was inseparable from his companion, FBI deputy director Clyde Tolson. In a 1993 best seller, Tolson was branded as Hoover's lover in a closely guarded homosexual relationship.

Even at the macro level, Hoover is touted to be a highly intelligent administrator whose decisions were based on a vast reservoir of personal knowledge. This, a critic notes, is just too much to expect of a man who never once left America while he was in charge of the FBI, and didn't know first hand what was happening with the rest of the world during his tenure. According to most of Hoover's biographers, the underpinnings of his vast personal and official power consisted of only two things: one was *records*, which he used effectively to empower, neutralize or destroy, and the other was *publicity*, which he manipulated so well that he succeeded in institutionalizing not only the FBI but also himself.

The rumor is that when Hoover died, President Nixon sent government troops to seize his secret files, which had the low-down on the private lives of politicians and celebrities. Nixon, it is added, could have used the records to maneuver his way back into a position of political power after Watergate, but he chose not to. A contrary rumor is that Hoover's secretary had the files destroyed in the weeks following her boss' death with the full knowledge of the Bureau's new director, L. Patrick Gray III.

The first story is highly unlikely, and the second is only partly true. What really happened is that, acting on Nixon's orders,

Attorney General Richard Kleindienst, in the company of his assistant Gray, summoned Assistant to the Director John Mohr and instructed him to secure Hoover's private office. Mohr did, but neglected to tell Kleindienst that the FBI's most secret files were kept by Hoover's long-time secretary, Miss Helen Gandy, outside of his office. A few hours after Hoover's death, Miss Gandy, without anyone's consent or knowledge, shredded the files that she thought were personal. She then divided the rest between Deputy Associate Director Mark Felt and Deputy Director Clyde Tolson.

Gray, before and after he replaced Hoover as FBI director, had gone after the 'secret files' in earnest but couldn't find any. He was so convinced by the various explanations given him that all he could tell reporters in his first press conference was, "(T)here are no dossiers or secret files. There are just general files…"

---

2. The Forest for the Trees

Myth! Hoover waged a life-long crusade against organized crime, which made him one of the foremost authorities on the subject.

Hoover's views were God's gospel when it came to the subject of crime. He knew everything there was to know about criminals and conspirators, particularly those he branded 'public enemies'. Once the discussion shifted to organized crime, however, even his own associates would shake their heads in disbelief. For Hoover would consistently maintain there was no such thing as organized crime at any level.

Insiders believe this idiosyncrasy stemmed from Hoover's obsession with keeping the Bureau's reputation for integrity and efficiency intact. The Director didn't want the Bureau slowed unnecessarily by cases involving crime lords who were hard to pursue and prosecute. Moreover, the FBI had no informants to penetrate closed societies like the Mafia, particularly since Hoover was not keen on training ethnic undercover agents or using them except in 'communist conspiracy' cases. Finally, there was the danger of Hoover's scrupulously principled agents being corrupted by organized crime.

10

Personal but no less credible reasons have also been advanced, including the rumor that Hoover did not want to cause trouble for powerful politician friends who were under the influence of the syndicates. Hoover himself was quite close to a number of mob figures, notably New York crime boss Frank Costello, with whom he did not want to trigger any major confrontation.

3. Brotherhood of Hoods

Myth! Organized crime in Hoover's time was a highly centralized operation managed by a grand Mafioso.

At one extreme of the crime spectrum is Hoover's disclaimer about organized crime. At the other is the warning issued by the Kefauver hearings in the early 1950s about the existence of the Mafia as a single, threatening entity. The image summoned up has been that of a highly centralized criminal organization, with a structured hierarchy and links to a Sicilian secret society.

The supreme head is called by various names: the grand Mafioso, the Godfather, the boss of bosses. The 'US Mafia' is perceived as a franchisee that exercises loose, albeit unified, supervision over various semi-independent subsidiary operations in the big American cities. A criminal investigator worth his salt knows all this is myth. The Mafia is not and has never been a single, monolithic organization, and to speak of it as "the Mafia" is a mistake. Senator Kefauver, the experts say, "merely assumed its existence" and "did not prove it." In the US, there is no central organization, only local 'mafias', that is to say, as many fully independent operations as there are major cities, each extending its powers as far as the boundaries of the city or district in which it has established an exclusive presence. The links between the Mafia groups in different cities have always been weak, and when one transcends its boundaries, the other Mafia outfits usually challenge it.

The belief that the Mafia is an Italian import is pooh-poohed by many writers, who say it is wrong to think that Italians who had learned and perfected the rudiments of criminal behavior at home organized the US system. There is no evidence that most of those who joined Mafia gangs in America had belonged to Mafia groups

11

in the homeland or that they had ever been engaged in criminality in Italy. The claim that the entry of Sicilian immigrants in the 1890s marked the beginning of organized crime in the country is patently false. According to Shenkman, "there was organized crime in America before 'the Mafia' appeared, and it's likely organized crime will continue to exist in this country if 'the Mafia' disappears."

There was indeed a Mafia that existed in Sicily, but it was totally unlike the one in the US and could not have been transplanted to America. The Italian version was part of the legitimate society that performed both legal and illegal services, and was a by-product of the Sicilian land tenancy system. The Mafiosi were once mercenaries who eventually took over from the landlords and established a patron-client relationship with the peasants to both protect and exploit them. Many duly became peasant bandits with patriotic and family loyalties after fleeing to the hills during the Arab conquest of Italy in the ninth century. This accounts for why the word 'mafia', or place of refuge, is of Arabic rather than Italian origin.

---

4. Blood and Wine

Myth! Al Capone was the biggest outlaw to come out of Prohibition.

Movie actors James Cagney and Edward G. Robinson made a career out of portraying Prohibition mobsters who built criminal empires on illicit trade in liquor. Al Capone, one of the most popular models for gangster films since the 1930s, is perceived to be the biggest of these 'little Caesars'. However, Norman Clark (*Deliver Us from Evil*, 1976) challenges the Hollywood myth by maintaining that Capone was not Prohibition-made and "would have surfaced as a major criminal whether liquor was legal or not." Organized crime didn't really originate with Prohibition, as some people believe, since major criminal gangs were already thriving in New York and Chicago at the turn of the century and long afterwards, when liquor became a restricted item of commerce. Capone was into organized crime even before the advent of Prohibition, and before he went public in the 1920s with a series of shake-ups in the 'Mafia' culminating in the St. Valentine's Day Massacre. Like his rivals Dion O'Banion and George 'Bugs' Moran, 'Scarface' Al made his money in gambling and prostitution, not liquor, although Clark contends it is an error to attribute this gangster's rise to any one phenomenon. Capone's reason for being, according to the same author, was the subcultures "indigenous to the massive urban growths such as New York or Chicago," and which took advantage of "an institutionalized commerce in illegal goods and services".

If one must know, the biggest outlaw to come out of Prohibition was not as well recognized as Al Capone. Called the 'King of Bootleggers', Emanuel Kessler was pushed into the limelight only when a federal grand jury indicted him for masterminding a 'rum plot' involving the disappearance of thousands of cases of whiskey and champagne. At his sentencing in 1923 for liquor violations and tax evasion, the courtroom was filled to overflowing by men described by court attendants as the "cream of the bootlegging craft."

5. Touch Me Not

Myth! **The FBI was Capone's bugbear, the agency that brought about the convictions ending his criminal career.**

Elliot Ness, looking every bit like a Hoover hound, was the crime fighter nonpareil in the wild and woolly '20s. Robert Stack felt honored portraying him on TV in the 1950s, saying he was deeply touched by the incorruptibility and bravery of the man. In 1987, Kevin Costner revived the Ness image in an exciting film performance as one of Brian de Palma's *The Untouchables*.

The real Ness, as it turns out, was a US Treasury agent and not an FBI man, a fact that neither the series nor the movie bothered to make clear. Undoubtedly, this was to take advantage of the FBI's higher profile and larger appeal to the public. In the series, Ness was luminous fighting alongside FBI men, who were the perceived nemeses of Prohibition mobsters. In real life, it was different. The FBI was a 1935 carryover from the eleven-year-old Bureau of Investigation (BI), which J. Edgar Hoover headed as its first and last director. As the BI, it had hardly made a ripple during the bootlegging years, and in the FBI format would not come of age until after Prohibition, when Ness' principal quarry, Al Capone, was no longer active.

The Costner film seems a bit more accurate, particularly as it correctly attributes to the Treasury Department Capone's conviction on income tax evasion charges in 1931, after he had completed a one-year sentence in 1930. However, it lapses into error with the suggestion that, on the same occasion, the Department, through Ness, brought about the 'downfall' of Capone's infamous enforcer Frank Nitti. One ridiculous sequence shows Ness shoving Nitti to his death from the roof of a tall building. Actually, after being convicted of big-time extortion in 1943, long after the Untouchables had disbanded, Nitti chose to commit suicide to avoid going to jail.

Many popular sources, including the Kostner film, assume that the Treasury Department or the FBI had something to do with Capone's earlier conviction in 1929, which put him in a Philadelphia jail for one year on suspicion of complicity in the St. Valentine's Day Massacre. But more reliable biographers say that, to avoid retaliation from rival gangs victimized by that infamous event, Capone himself engineered his arrest, trial, and sentencing on weapons charges, the whole procedure taking a mere 16 hours and 35 minutes. It was no secret that the mobster spent a safe and comfortable term in his cell complete with luxuries that he negotiated with his friendly jailers.

Yet another cinematic error shows Ness coming face to face with Capone in the courtroom during the latter's 1931 trial. Few realize that, in real life, no physical confrontation occurred between the two at this or any other time. Indeed, except for his unsuccessful 1928 investigation of Capone for income tax evasion, the off-screen Ness was never involved with the mobster, much less with his eventual prosecution in 1931 and his 11-year imprisonment at Alcatraz afterwards. The IRS' top investigator Frank J. Wilson under the direction of Elmer Irey, the agency's chief law enforcement officer, provided the spadework for the Treasury's effort to bring down the curtain on the crime lord.

This was not the only time Irey's group had solved a crime and been shoved aside by the FBI, thanks to Hoover's penchant for headline hogging. In the 1932 Lindbergh kidnapping case, gold certificates that Irey had required to be included in the ransom money were eventually found in the possession of Richard

Hauptmann and used in his conviction. Charles Lindbergh later told Irey that had it not been for him and his boys, the kidnapper would not have been caught. As usual, when Hoover overheard the compliment, he immediately instructed his publicity department, Crime Records, to make sure that Irey's participation would not be mentioned in any of the Bureau's records.

6. Shooting from the Mouth

Myth! The notorious gang leader 'Machine Gun' Kelly invented the term 'G-men' to describe his FBI captors.

In the film *Machine-Gun Kelly* (1958), the title character is a bank robber who is given his nickname by the police and the public because of his skill in using a machine gun, which he slings over his shoulder and fires indiscriminately while making good his escape. The real George 'Machine Gun' Kelly had this fearsome reputation as well, and his involvement with the Shannon gang in the highly publicized 1933 kidnapping of oil man Charles Urschel helped put him in the FBI order of battle as a public enemy. The FBI tracked the gang to its Texas hideout and rounded up all except Kelly and a cohort, who were later captured and sent to prison for life.

Many historians love to point out that, far from being the crime legend he was touted to be, Kelly was a promotions job by Kathryn Shannon, his wife, who gifted her drunkard husband with the weapon and advertised him through calling cards and word-of-mouth as a fearless crook who was often away robbing banks. She invented his expertise with a machine gun, beclouding the fact that the amiable crook never killed anyone nor fired his weapon in anger. When the underworld started calling the small-time hood "Popgun" Kelly in obvious contempt, she countered by devising the sobriquet "Machine Gun" Kelly. George's only noteworthy crime was the Urschel kidnapping, of which Kathryn was the real mastermind and for which she was also imprisoned for life.

J. Edgar Hoover proudly related the FBI version of 'Machine Gun' Kelly's capture in a 1946 issue of the *Tennessee Law Review*. According to Hoover, when the FBI cornered Kelly in a Memphis, Tennessee, farm in 1933, the fugitive, realizing he was going nowhere, threw up his hands and shouted, "Don't shoot, G-men, don't shoot." Some wordsmiths believe this was how the word "G-men," short for "government men," was coined, and why it has been applied to FBI agents in particular. The myth was dramatized in the 1959 James Stewart starrer *The FBI Story* and referenced in the 2011 film *J. Edgar*. But others, aware that employees of the federal government were already called G-men by the media at the time of Kelly's capture, accuse J. Edgar Hoover of fabricating the story to promote the image of the Bureau. The lie, they say, is evident from contemporary accounts of Kelly's capture in the gangster's bungalow by Memphis police officers under the command of W. J. Raney. There was no FBI agent in sight, and what Kelly told his captors came out in the national press as, "Okay, boys, I've been waiting for you all night." Whether or not Hoover was correct, it is almost certain the term did not originate from Kelly or his wife, but from Ireland, where it was commonly used as early as the 1920s to refer to the Dublin Metropolitan Police.

7. Red for Danger

Myth! Hoover competed for media mileage with public enemies of every kind, including John Dillinger, the fugitive who was set up for the FBI by a mysterious 'lady in red'.

According to the story most people hear, Anna Sage Miller, a 42-year-old Romanian-born madam of an Indiana brothel whom the government was trying to deport, went to Melvin Purvis, head of the FBI Chicago office, and offered to set up her friend and customer, John Dillinger, in return for her freedom. Sage told Purvis that on the night of July 22, 1934, she would accompany Dillinger to a movie at the Biograph Theater in Chicago, wearing a red dress to set her apart. As planned, the woman in red came out of the theater at 10:30 p.m. in the company of the gangster and his lover, Mrs. Rita Keele, and Purvis and his men moved in and gunned Dillinger down as he attempted to reach for a weapon.

Myth busters say ridding this account of Dillinger's demise of its many errors is like rewriting history. They point out, first, that it was not Sage but Det. Sgt. Martin Zarkovich of the East

Chicago, Indiana, Police Department who arranged the deal between her and the FBI. Second, it was not Rita Keele who accompanied Dillinger and Sage to the movie, but his girl friend, Polly Hamilton, a 26-year-old waitress who had been Zarkovich's own lover in the past. Third, it was Polly, not Anna, who was wearing the bright 'red' dress, although she knew nothing about the set-up. Finally, the dress was really orange, and only looked red because of the bright lights of the movie marquee.

8. Your Friendly Hoover Man

Myth! Hoover amply rewarded his trusted agent Melvin Purvis for his role as "the man who shot Dillinger."

For orchestrating the FBI operation that led to the killing of John Dillinger, special agent Melvin Purvis earned his niche in history as "The Man Who Shot Dillinger." Originally, the title had meant Purvis fired the gun that brought down Dillinger. Media gave him sole credit although it was not clear who and how many lawmen out that night shot the notorious outlaw. The concept changed abruptly when a jealous J. Edgar Hoover, in an effort to minimize Purvis' role, revealed that it was really a group effort, the declaration remaining official even after investigation showed FBI agent Charles Winstead most likely fired the fatal gun. Hoover would later take Purvis out of his key assignments and renege on the deal with Sage, who was eventually deported.

Acting on information Anna Sage Miller and other whistle blowers provided him, Purvis and 15 of his men had staked out the theater in which Dillinger was seeing the Clark Gable movie *Manhattan Melodrama*. When the outlaw emerged, they pursued him as he tried to pull a .38-caliber pistol from his belt and flee toward an alley. Before he could fire a shot, three bullets hit him, two in his chest and one in the back of his neck. He died within minutes but no one, not even Purvis, could tell which was the fatal bullet and which FBI gun delivered it.

Purvis became public hero number one in the mid-1930s despite absence of proof that he was the man who shot Dillinger. What makes it even more surprising is that he did not conform one bit to the image of the FBI agent that Hoover assiduously molded and planted in the minds of most Americans. Purvis had been turned down for a job at the State Department when he walked over to the Department of Justice and applied for the position of special agent. Very slight in build and just a shade under five feet tall, 'Little Mel' failed to meet the minimum weight and height requirements of the Bureau. He totally lacked experience and, except on that particular occasion, had not traveled once outside his home state of South Carolina. Contrary to a well-publicized myth that no candidate was ever accepted into the Bureau or received advancement during employment through political connections, Purvis made it on the recommendation of a powerful Southern senator who was a good friend of his father's. In less than six years, Purvis had been put in charge of the FBI's second-most-important field office, Chicago.

Not long after the Dillinger affair, Hoover, afraid that Purvis was overshadowing him, drove his once favorite agent out of the Bureau. Purvis reportedly committed suicide, using a gun his fellow agents had given him at his retirement party. Later investigations showed, however, that he accidentally shot himself while retrieving a bullet jammed in the pistol, the incident occurring twenty-five years after he had left the FBI.

9. The Last Wave

Myth! **The worst crime wave ever to beleaguer the FBI occurred in the Midwest during the 1930s.**

The 'Midwestern crime wave' may have been the progenitor of two American institutions—the Hollywood gangster film and the FBI—but it was not a crime wave at all. It consisted of the run-of-the-mill antics of John Dillinger, Baby Face Nelson, Alvin 'Creepy' Karpis, Ma Barker, George 'Machine Gun' Kelly and 'Pretty Boy' Floyd, all small-time hoods many cuts removed from the big-city gangs and criminal syndicates of the Prohibition era. Because of the desperate times, they caught the public fancy by appearing to be Robin Hoods who robbed from the rich to benefit the poor. Floyd, for instance, endeared himself to farmers and homesteaders hit hard by the Depression by stealing or destroying loan and mortgage records during his robberies. The press had a heyday reporting their crimes, chases and escapes, glamorizing these exploits "like a continuing serial at the Saturday matinee."

The 'wave', which began in 1933, was of very short duration, being practically over in 1934. It was restricted to a limited area, with most of the crimes occurring in only seven states: Missouri, Illinois, Indiana, Ohio, Wisconsin, Minnesota and Iowa. The events themselves would have easily slipped into oblivion had they not been exaggerated and manipulated by the publicity-conscious J. Edgar Hoover to promote himself and the FBI.

10. Barrow & Parker, Bank Specialists

Myth! Among those riding the Midwest crime wave of the 30s were big-time bandits Bonnie and Clyde, whose glamorized exploits provided romantic appeal to the golden age of outlaws.

One of the most romanticized criminal duos were Bonnie Parker and Clyde Barrow, whose glamorization began with Bonnie's decision to write to the newspapers about their exploits and submit her maudlin poetry for publication. It is said that when the couple died under a hail of police bullets outside Gibsland, Louisiana, just one day before Clyde's 25th birthday, not a few lovers heaved a collective sigh of regret.

The first Hollywood movie about the two, Fritz Lang's *You Only Live Once* (1937), was made three years after the fact, while the best—Arthur Penn's critically praised *Bonnie and Clyde* (1967)—came thirty years later. A 1992 TV movie with the somewhat misleading title "Bonnie & Clyde: The True Story" is a youth-oriented reworking of the legend showing the tandem as teenagers.

One writer's description of the real Parker and Barrow is a revelation on how Hollywood big bucks can transform the lowest of criminals into bigger-than-life figures: "They were inept thieves, their targets were penny-ante (Barrow had started out as a chicken thief), and their love life was bizarre." Their clumsily executed robberies of small, unprotected banks in hick towns could only yield them petty cash at high costs. They thought nothing about using hostages as shields against police bullets, and

19

snuffed out fourteen lives with brutality and nonchalance, each a spur-of-the-moment action that involved almost no risk. The perverse pair often shared the same lovers, meeting their well-deserved fate when a colleague Clyde helped escape from jail betrayed them to the police.

11. The Caged Bird Wouldn't Sing

Myth! Robert F. Stroud was a gentle and erudite convict called "The Birdman of Alcatraz" because of his interest in birds while imprisoned in Alcatraz.

Robert F. Stroud's popular nickname, "Birdman of Alcatraz," is also the title of the 1962 movie about this man's extraordinary life as a convict. Burt Lancaster plays Stroud as a lowly educated genius who, while spending time in Leavenworth, kills a prison guard, but has his death sentence commuted to solitary confinement for life through political intervention solicited by his mother. He suffers the physical and mental torture of being alone, until at some point during his stretch, he provides his own therapy by taking an interest in birds. He delves into both the theoretical and practical aspects of ornithology, and develops a remarkable expertise in this science that eventually helps soften his anti-social attitudes.

However, aside from the fact that many of its sidelights are not real incidents, the movie fails to explain why Stroud, despite his accomplishments, could not get a parole. Obviously, it could not reveal the truth that the flesh-and-blood Stroud, whose correct nickname was "Bird Doctor of Leavenworth," was a psychopath who had to be kept almost continuously in solitary confinement under heavy guard because of his dangerously erratic behavior. His two books on ornithology may have been an accomplishment in itself, but they were basically plagiarisms of limited merit, and after this short-lived creativity, he languished for another 22 years in Leavenworth before it was decided to move him to Alcatraz for better handling and control. He spent the next 21 years of his life on the Rock until he died from a massive heart attack in 1963. But contrary to what the film shows in an effort to justify its title, at no time during his incarceration at Alcatraz did Stroud ever have birds or show any interest in them.

Stroud could have become a plain bird doctor, without the damning label of Leavenworth or Alcatraz, had he committed his first crime—simple manslaughter—at a much later date. As it was, Stroud, barely 19 and below voting age, was slammed into the federal poker because Alaska, where it happened, was still federal territory. The state penal system could have paid closer attention to the man's talents and, without the corrupting influence of large-scale prisons, managed his rehabilitation and early parole.

---

12. Halloween Perennial

Myth! The earliest 'slasher' films with a Halloween setting inspired the real-life murder of a boy who bit into an apple stuffed with razor blades.

School and police authorities join parents in telling their kids to be wary of strangers on Halloween night, and to watch out especially for tampered treats that may contain razor blades, needles, poison, or drugs. Sociologists say this concern is unwarranted, because the horror of Halloween is just another urban legend based largely on hearsay and exaggerated reporting. Two researchers came out with this surprising conclusion after reviewing all the Halloween-related stories published by four city newspapers between 1958 and 1984. They found 76 reported incidents, of which many turned out to be unverifiable or fake and none in which death or serious injury resulted.

No one is sure how the legend got started, or why it became so widespread and well accepted. The two researchers thought it was a necessary consequence of the well-publicized police investigation of the seven deaths caused by cyanide-laced Extra Strength Tylenol sold in the Chicago area, exacerbated by the wave of Hollywood 'slasher' films starting with the now classic *Halloween* (1979). Actually, the links are too tenuous to warrant an opinion. The Tylenol incident did not occur on a Halloween and had nothing to do with that holiday. The only authentic Halloween murder on record happened before the earliest of the 'slasher' films and was committed *en famille* rather than by a stranger. Eight-year-old Timothy O'Bryan of Houston, Texas, died on Halloween night in 1974 after eating a package of Pixie Stix candy tainted with cyanide. The boy's father, Ronald Clark O'Bryan, perpetrated the murder for insurance by inserting the poison candy into Timmy's bag after the latter had returned from trick-or-treating.

13. Tweedy Man in Nasty Situation

Myth! The infamous Boss Tweed of Tammany Hall escaped while serving time for corruption, but a Thomas Nast cartoon led to his recapture.

The falsities woven about political kingpin William M. Tweed were enough to send him crashing down from his perch as boss of New York City's Democratic organization. Tweed was accused of having used fake leases, padded bills, false vouchers and other devices to plunder the city of a sum estimated to range between 30 and 200 million dollars. Being politically motivated, this was all grossly exaggerated, of course, and although repeatedly indicted for fraud, Tweed could not be convicted for lack of direct evidence. Finally, a case for misdemeanor—failing to audit claims against the city—was railroaded before a biased judge and jury, and this succeeded.

Popular lore remembers the blatant charges but not the fact that Tweed had initiated innumerable worthwhile reforms during his long career as a public servant. Consequently, few are aware that the original sentence of 12 years in prison was reduced to one year, and his $12,750 fine to $250. Unfortunately, upon his release from jail, his persecutors had him rearrested as a defendant in a civil suit to recover ill-gotten wealth and confined to the debtor's prison of the era. He escaped and worked his way to Cuba and then to Spain, but according to a now legendary report, he was identified by a Spanish officer from a newspaper cartoon by Thomas Nast, which mistakenly suggested that he was a kidnapper of children. Actually, while passing through Cuba, a low-level American consul had already tagged Tweed and American authorities had arranged for his arrest in Spain.

22

14. Big, Maybe, but Stainless, No

Myth! Speaking in behalf of organized crime, the high-profile racketeer Meyer Lansky once said, "We're bigger than U.S. Steel."

That classic paean to organized crime in America—"We're bigger than US Steel"—is generally credited to Meyer Lansky, a big-time celebrity racketeer. He murmured what sounded like it in 1962 as a passing commentary while watching a television program on the subject of organized crime with his wife. The whisper was caught by FBI microphones tapping his hotel suite, but for some reason the tape was never submitted as evidence in Lansky's indictment.

Using FBI files as his source, Lansky biographer Robert Lacey writes that the famous phrase has never been proved to be Lansky's. It was a paraphrase of an agent's report of what he thought he'd heard from the tape, and when released to media, it was transformed into a direct quote by Life, Time, and many other publications. The colorful Lansky became the model for some cinematic characters, one of whom remarked in *The Godfather II*: "Michael! We're bigger than U.S. Steel!" However, the gangster denied making the quote, and Lacey himself doubts he ever did.

15. Bank Jobs and Cash Flows

Myth! Asked why he robbed banks, the notorious hold-up artist Willie Sutton replied, "Because that's where the money was."

Willie Sutton, who died at the age of 79, was called "The Actor" by his associates because of his penchant for using actor's make-up, garb and disguises when robbing banks. He was also known as the "wiley" Sutton who engineered many spectacular prison escapes. But he never fired a gun during any of his escapades, admitting that his fear of the electric chair was too great. The civic-minded man responsible for surrendering Sutton to the authorities was assassinated without the bank robber knowing anything about it. The rub-out was ordered by Mafia man Albert Anastasia, who had seen the victim being interviewed on TV and had screamed before gang members, "I can't stand squealers! Hit that guy!" The police agreed that Anastasia, who had no association whatever with Sutton, only acted on whim.

Sutton's explanation for robbing banks had an earthy wisdom to it: "Because that's where the money was." He supposedly gave the answer to a reporter who asked why the publicity-conscious crook chose this prosaic way to crime. Sutton later confessed in his autobiography: "I never said it. The credit belongs to some enterprising reporter who apparently felt a need to fill out his copy." He added: "I can't even remember when I first read it. It just seemed to appear one day, and then it was everywhere." But Sutton liked the phrase so much he entitled his memoir *Where the Money Was*.

16. Top Goon

Myth! **The FBI's J. Edgar Hoover invented the words 'Public Enemy No. 1' for the highest ranked in the agency's 'Most Wanted' list of fugitives.**

Popular belief notwithstanding, it was U.S. Attorney General Horace Cummings who thought up the inglorious tag and applied it to the then current national peeve John Dillinger in the 1930s. Hoover would later use the label on Alvin 'Old Creepy' Karpis in the press preparatory to his capture, but the former Ma Barker cohort was obviously undeserving of it and was only given the honor (or dishonor) to enhance the Director's own reputation.

In those days, there could be one or several Public Enemies No. 1, or none at all, as what happened when the press stopped using the term after the 1930s. And there was no Public Enemy No. 2 or other lower designation. A vestige of early Rome, the phrase 'public enemy'—without any number attached to it—came into popular usage in America as early as the 1920s in connection with the activities of Al Capone and later as the title of a 1931 James Cagney movie. Later as 'public enemies', it would describe

24

Dillinger and his gang in a 2009 Hollywood crime thriller with the actor Johnny Depp portraying the notorious villain.

Neither 'public enemy' nor 'Public Enemy No. 1' ever became an official designation, unlike the 'FBI's Ten Most Wanted', a list widely publicized to warn the populace about the nation's most dangerous outlaws and to obtain information and public cooperation for catching them. Wanted lists remain a consistent feature of the US justice system today, but the 'FBI's Ten Most Wanted' is as much a misnomer as 'Public Enemy No. 1' was. Besides the fact that no ranking is assigned to the enumeration, there have been years when the list contained less than ten names and other years when it contained more, as in 1991, when it had 16.

II

The Long Arm Of The Law

On International Law Enforcement

*"In crime, as in love, there are only
those who do, and those who don't dare."*

•

Francois Vidocq

1. The World is his Beat

Myth! Victims of international crimes seek relief from Interpol, a police agency with law enforcement functions that transcend national boundaries.

What happens when a terrorist perpetrates his crime in one jurisdiction and escapes to another? Most victims believe they have a savior in waiting in the Man from Interpol. Except for an identity that's shrouded in mystery, this character is likened to the best international operatives of fiction, such as Matt Helm, Derek Flint and James Bond.

Here's sad news for those who hanker for the glamorous life of an Austin Powers as well as those who desperately want his assistance. Interpol is not a public institution, as many believe, nor is it franchised to operate as a legally constituted international agency. It is a private organization subscribed to by police agencies of over 100 nations and funded by them with dues and donations. It has no police force of its own, and neither Interpol nor any of its employees is equipped with a law enforcement function. 'The Man from Interpol' as a freewheeling detective who moves from country to country, operating wherever he wants and making arrests from Hong Kong to New York, is a false image imparted to the public by films and television. According to Jack Higgins (*Great Cases of Interpol*, 1982), "Interpol does not transcend the activities of an individual nation's police force."

Interpol is limited to only one aspect of police work, if it may be called that, which is to provide information, or access to information, by way of guidance or assistance to a member nation's police force in the pursuit of a specific case, activity or person. Each member country has a national central bureau staffed by its own police officers and closely tied to Interpol's General Secretariat in St. Cloud, near Paris. While the actual police business in any given case is carried out by the police of that country, Interpol offers support by acting as a clearinghouse for information, providing technical assistance and serving as a major communication link between the bureaus.

Since problems may arise from acts that are criminal in one place but not in another, Interpol is allowed to operate only in certain clearly defined areas. Thus, drug trafficking, art theft, bank robbery, counterfeiting, forgery and smuggling may have transnational implications and come under the purview of the Interpol. On the other hand, international terrorism and most crimes against the state are excluded, being ostensibly political in nature.

2. Le Jeune Air

Myth! The French Foreign Legion is a refuge for fugitives, ex-convicts, exiles and other kinds of riffraff.

The spate of Hollywood adventure films in the 1930s featuring the French Foreign Legion accounts for the mystique that continues to surround this military organization. The typical film tends to suggest that, because of the harshness of the discipline and the environment under which the Legion operates, it is able to attract mostly riffraff, convicts, exiles and the like, whose motivation to serve is only as good as the reprieve that is granted them from prosecution or other forms of criminal justice. In classics like *Morocco* (1930) and *Beau Geste* (1939), the Legion's contingents are commonly characterized as devil-may-care types who are assigned very difficult and oftentimes suicidal missions.

Despite such foreboding film titles as *Legion of the Doomed* (1958), none of these depictions has a basis in fact. According to the Britannica, the Legionnaire is "more likely to be a European professional soldier who prefers fighting with the legion to garrison duty with his own army." He is not required to destroy his identity and his past when he joins the outfit, and although he is generally allowed to use a pseudonym, this is to protect his privacy from his comrades rather than from the Legion itself. He may opt for anonymity only for a lawful reason, and any taint of a criminal record is reason enough for his extradition to the proper authorities by the Interpol and the Deuxeme Bureau.

Although the Legion owes absolute loyalty to France, the recruit is not made to take an oath to serve that country, as is generally supposed. His vow, rather, is to serve the Legion, which is suggested by the unofficial motto, *Legio Patria Nostra* ("The legion is our fatherland"). Nevertheless, the legionnaire becomes eligible for French citizenship after serving one enlistment of five years with good conduct.

3. Changing Lanes

Myth! **Francois Vidocq, the colorful founder of the French Sureté, is one of France's greatest criminologists and poets.**

Francois Eugène Vidocq was both a criminal expert and an expert criminal during his lifetime. This dual qualification was what prepared him for the job of founding the Sureté. As France's most wanted criminal in his early years, he was always in and out of prison, repeatedly making daring escapes and becoming a master of disguise in his efforts to remain free. To clear his name permanently, he offered to become a police informer, then joined the force as a detective, until in 1812, he used his diverse criminal experience to establish the French Sureté. Hiring only ex-convicts as detectives, Vidocq was paid a commission for every arrest, and this sometimes caused him to overstep his bounds. But on the whole he acquired a reputation for being relentless, swift and successful. By 1820 he had shaped the bureau into a 30-man team of experts, most of them reformed criminals, and reduced the crime rate in Paris by 40 per cent.

However, despite Vidocq's acclamation as the father of modern criminology and of the French police, and as the first private detective, critics doubt that the hundreds of bizarre adventures he crammed into his memoirs are all authentic. Be this as it may, the first book on crime he wrote in 1827 influenced generations of fictional sleuths, from Poe's C. Auguste Dupin to Agatha Christie's Hercule Poirot. Victor Hugo epitomized him in *Les Miserables*, first as the fugitive Jean Valjean and later as the great manhunter Inspector Javert, thus becoming one of the few men to have both the hero and the villain in a novel modeled after him.

Francois Vidocq should not be confused with another French paragon of reformation, the criminal Francois Villon, who also switched over to the good side in time to become one of the country's greatest poets.

4. Treading the Yards

Myth! Britain's national police force is called Scotland Yard.

Scotland Yard referred originally to a plot of land in London on which stood the guesthouse of the King of Scotland. It later became the address of the London police force, and remained so until it was assigned as the name of the force toward the end of the nineteenth century.

Now as then, Scotland Yard is not a national police force, nor is it a special branch for handling difficult or significant cases. As the police force for the London metropolitan area, it is one of the many local police units encompassed by the British law enforcement system.

There is a popular misconception that Scotland Yard operates on the same level as the FBI, which is a national or federal police force. It is believed that if the FBI is empowered to enter into an investigation once a crime has 'crossed' state boundaries, so is Scotland Yard liable to be called into a case of which one or some elements span the British Isles. The truth is that no national police exists for the British Isles, or on a lesser scale for the United Kingdom or even Great Britain or England. The closest is MI-5, but this is a branch of the military, not the police. The British law enforcement system consists of many police forces and as many decentralized administrative operations, except for common services preempted by the Home Office for better cooperation between the forces, e.g., training, research, laboratories, wireless depots, and central and regional records.

Scotland Yard is the most significant of Britain's local police forces because it serves the London Metropolitan area. But the Yard is not a special or other branch of any larger police force, as it is the London outfit itself, and the idea that it is a special London unit quite apart from the regular Metropolitan Force is simply an evocation of the mythical phrase "call in Scotland Yard" so often heard in the movies. The distress call does mean, however, that the Yard has a team of experienced detectives who are available to provincial or colonial forces for dealing with difficult crimes, and other local forces can call them for assistance in the investigation of murder.

5. London Nightsticks and Bobby Pins

Myth! The London bobby does police work of all types without the benefit of firearms.

Unlike police in most other countries, the vast majority of British police officers—and the London bobbies especially—do not carry firearms on standard patrol. As the Britannica puts it, "The London policeman carries only a small baton; the New York City policeman carries a large-caliber revolver and a baton; the Paris policeman carries a small-caliber semi-automatic pistol, a baton and a leaded cape; and the Cairo (Egypt) policeman carries a submachine gun or automatic rifle." People presume the London boy in blue is more adept than any of the others at using his baton or billy, since this is the only weapon he can use in a city that counts as one of the most complex in the world. It should be remembered that the British capital has produced at one time or other Rippers and Bluebeards, homicidal football fans, IRA bombers, and, if Hollywood is to be believed, even werewolves.

The Britannica is off the mark, however, when it suggests that the bobby is never armed. For one, the small nightstick has been replaced by an Extendable "Asp" or fixed Monadnock PR-24 baton and a CS/PAVA spray. More significantly, plagued by a sharp rise in gun violence, London police have resorted increasingly to firearms since the 1980s. Even before, when the icon of the unarmed bobby was at its brightest, firearms were never out of his reach, whether in the street or on special assignment. During that era, a good percentage of the London police force were qualified in the use of handguns, and there were hundreds who were rifle marksmen. More so today, when most London police stations have guns on hand if needed. Many carry guns or use rifles for various purposes, e.g., members of the Special Branch in charge of important visitors keep themselves armed as a matter of course, and police constables guarding embassies do the same on occasions.

Actually, the British Transport Police is the only police force in the country without firearms officers, relying as it does on the local territorial force should an armed incident occur on the railways.

31

6. Les Condés de France

Myth! **A policeman in France is called *gendarme*.**

The regular police in France are called 'police', not 'gendarmes'. The latter term refers to a special military unit that does surrogate police work in certain designated areas.

The literal English translation of gendarme is "armed people", which is probably why most everyone thinks this familiar French word means 'policeman' in France. It is erroneously used to refer to the members of France's Police Nationale, a combination of the Prefecture of Police of Paris and the Sureté Nationale, which perform regular police functions throughout the land. The correct name for these members is *police*, which, except for a slightly different pronunciation, is the same word used for their US counterparts.

The real *gendarmes* belong to France's second national police force, the Gendarmerie Nationale, which, strictly speaking, are not policemen but soldiers who are formed in strictly disciplined units and quartered in barracks. Each military area they cover is under the command of a general, and the minister for the armed forces directly controls the central headquarters. However, while the Gendarmerie are considered military personnel, they are also as much a police organization as the Police Nationale. They undertake police work along certain main roads and in country districts and towns with less than 10,000 inhabitants. Some of them are even appointed to the judicial police and empowered to inquire into and deal with all types of crime.

7. Years of the Pig

Myth! **The street parliamentarians of the 1960s coined the word 'pig' as a term of abuse for policemen.**

"Pig!" was one of the most common epithets heard during mass marches and rallies in the US of the 1960s. Embittered protesters engaged in the struggle for civil rights and peace in Vietnam

32

hurled the insult generally at the police, who stood out as hated symbols of the Establishment and its authority. The idea was obviously to liken law enforcers, who were considered dumb, dirty and condescending, to a "grunting, mindless herd, swinish in its attitudes and behavior."

Popular belief notwithstanding, the invective was not coined by the street parliamentarians of that turbulent decade, although how they came up with it is not clear. Among thieves in England, 'pig' was a term of abuse for policemen as long ago as the early nineteenth century. Later in the same century, it had even acquired a rather specific connotation, that of a policeman's spy, an informer or 'stool pigeon', whom the London underworld also called "noses." This was apparently in reference to the habit—common with both the animal and its human counterpart—of 'nosing around'. But 'pig' did not originate with the English, either. The earliest use of the word was many centuries before, by the Israelites against the police authority of the Roman Empire during their period of captivity.

Most of the other nicknames for policemen have not been as derogatory. About the time the word 'pig' began to be used in England, the home secretary, Sir Robert Peel, caused the establishment of the Metropolitan Police Force, earning for its members the nickname 'peels' and 'bobbies'. More than a hundred years earlier, English policemen had been called 'cops', which many believe was a slang derivation from the copper buttons they wore, but was actually taken from the Latin word *capere*, meaning to seize or capture.

8. Rough Stuff in the Blue Lodge

Myth! 'Third degree' is a police procedure taken from the initiation rites of third degree Masons.

The term 'third degree', sometimes associated with the classification of murder according to its gravity ('murder in the first degree', etc.), is actually part of the esoterica of the Order of Free and Accepted Masons. The rules of this organization provide that one must hurdle three 'degrees of proficiency' before he can qualify as a full-fledged member. Each degree is a ritual that tests the candidate for knowledge obtained from previous degrees or through study. In the third degree, the atmosphere is secretive, inquisitorial and mildly physical, with symbols and shadows interplaying in an apocryphal crime drama that the neophyte is required to enact. The effect is more awesome than any of the standards set in the previous two degrees, and is probably what accounts for the impression that the 'third degree' method of police investigation, which seeks to extract information from a witness through deceit, intimidation and sometimes violence, is of Masonic origin.

The Masonic phrase dates to 1772 and its police use to 1880. However, it is quite unfair to compare the initiation for third-degree Masons with the brutal police procedure that has been outlawed in most modern jurisdictions. Those who have gone through the Masonic ritual readily admit that even teenagers and old men will have little difficulty dealing with its physical and psychological challenges. The two senses of the phrase 'third degree' may be etymologically related, but this is no indication that the violence implicit in third-degree methods of interrogation is a heritage of Masonic practice rather than of police roguery.

It is obvious both Masonic and police concepts of 'third degree' derive primarily from the use of the word 'degree' as a measure of importance, severity or intensity, 'third degree' being higher than 'first' or 'second degree'. Still, considering their relative dates of origin, the police term is more proximate and therefore more likely related to later phrases such as 'third degree burns' (France ca. 1832) than to the rituals of Masonry. The public's association of the police procedure with the known types of felonies also seems inappropriate. Most anywhere in the US and other legal jurisdictions, murder in the first degree is more serious than murder in the second, and there is no murder in the third. Other felonies might fall under a 'third degree' category, but as in the case of murder, where the severity of the offense is measured in reverse, these would be the least serious in the penal system. Examples of third-degree felonies would include elder abuse, assault and battery, drug possession, driving under the influence, child molestation, arson, transmission of pornography, embezzlement, theft, and fraud.

III

Way Of The Gun

On Western Outlaws and Gunslingers

"At least two-hundred men have been killed
in Lincoln County during the past three years,
but I did not kill all of them."

•

Billy the Kid

1. The Far Country

Myth! The Old West was rooted in lawless violence.

In Palisade, Nevada, in the 1870s, it was usual for incoming train passengers to witness gunplay on the grounds near the local station. The fight, however, was only staged by actors to bring in tourists who expected this kind of violence in the American West.

In reality, gunfights were very rare in Palisade or elsewhere in the western US. Despite the popular myth, the West was actually safer and more peaceful than the congested, government-dominated cities in the East. The false image of the frontier as a place of violence has been developed mostly by Hollywood hype, from Edison's *The Great Train Robbery* (1903) to Sam Peckinpah's *The Wild Bunch* (1969). The scripts of most of the early cowboy films were based on the penny novels and the Wild Bill West Show.

As one writer notes, many more people have died in Hollywood Westerns than ever died on the real frontier, Indian wars considered apart. The most infamous cow towns in Kansas—Abilene, Dodge City, Ellsworth, Wichita, and Caldwell—were not as bad as they have been projected to be, with records indicating that between 1870 and 1885, just forty-five murders occurred in all of them. In their most violent years, Dodge City had only five killings, Deadwood in South Dakota four, and Tombstone five. Paul Kirchner mentions a study showing that in Aurora, Nevada, a town of over 5,000 mostly single young males, muggings and other forms of physical violence were rare, and rapes and bank robberies were nil. Duels were legal, but these were mostly between drunks defending their honor. The OK Corral shoot-out in Tombstone became famous because town boosters deliberately overplayed the drama to attract new settlers. The 'Showdown on Front Street' seen in a typical western movie or TV program did not usually happen, as people were more likely to be shot in ambush under cover of night. Ironically, some western towns became notorious from the presence not of outlaws and troublemakers but of their own law officers.

36

2. Five in the Body, One in the Foot

Myth! The posse and the sheriff, like the five-pointed lawman's badge, originated in the Old West.

The two greatest symbols of law enforcement in US history are the sheriff and his star.

While the star is indigenous to the American West, the sheriff isn't. Sheriffs were in place in England long before America was discovered—back as far as the Norman Conquest in 1066—and would be transplanted in Canada, Scotland, and Northern Ireland as well. The concept arrived in the American West with the posse, or *posse commitatus*, an ancient English institution consisting of the shire's force of able-bodied private citizens summoned to assist in maintaining public order. The word 'sheriff' is a combination of *shire* and *reeve*, which in Old England meant county and head of a county, respectively.

If it is difficult to find in print or on film a sheriff's badge that is not shaped like a star, so also in real life. The belief originating in primitive and medieval societies is that the star possessed many magical powers, foremost being the power to guard against danger and control evil forces. As the symbol of guardianship, the star was the logical choice to represent the office of sheriff, and it became the hologram of many American comic superheroes. It is said that the sheriff or marshal had a five-pointed star and his deputy used a six-pointed one, but this was more theoretical than real. There was probably this distinction in the beginning, until it became acceptable for a lawman of whatever rank to wear any configuration provided his designation was clearly engraved on the badge.

3. Tastes Like Dirt

Myth! Gunslingers of the Old West originated the phrase 'bite the dust'.

Allegorically, the phrase 'bite the dust' is applied to a whole range of characters—from the defeated politician and the beaten athlete, to the bankrupt businessman and the jailed outlaw. Because Indians and cowboys who are shot off their mounts in Western movies are said to "bite the dust," the belief is that it was originally cowboy lingo.

In fact, the American cowboy was one of the last to use the expression—if he ever used it. The equivalent "bite the ground" first appeared in Homer's *Iliad*, Book II, lines 417-18, and seems to have been a popular Greek metaphor for inglorious death in battle. Later, it became common in England, where the almost literal translation of William Cowper (1838), Vol. I, page 49, read: " . . . his friends, around him, prone in dust, shall bite the ground." One of the earliest applications by an American can be found in a poem by William Cullen Bryant (1870), a New Yorker famous for writing *Thanatopsis*. Bryant wrote: "...his fellow warriors, many a one, fall round him to the earth and bite the dust." Even earlier than Bryant was Carl J. Andersson, a British explorer in South Africa, who wrote in his *Lake Ngami* (1856), page 363, that one of his characters, a hunter, "had made numerous lions bite the dust."

Regrettably, the expression is losing its punch from overuse. Modern slang has now so greatly reduced its force that it implies little more than to suffer disaster of moderate degree.

4. The Deadliest Guns are Live

Myth! The successful gunfighter of the Old West shot from a holstered position and was always the first to get his gun out of its holster.

Wyatt Earp, who became a consultant to movie productions about the Old West, decried the way Hollywood cowboys handled their gun on screen. Despite his advice, Western movies have stuck to their myth. For instance, we still see gunfighters shooting from the hip when, according to Earp, the gun should be fired at about the level of the waist, arm extended with elbow half bent. This helps bring the muzzle of the gun close to the aiming line. In *Insultingly Stupid Movie Physics* (2007), author Tom Rogers shows with the use of geometry that the misalignment between the muzzle and the aiming line by a mere 2 inches will cause the bullet to miss by a foot a target 10 feet away. Factors like recoil, bullet drop due to gravity, hand tremors and misalignment of the body's many joints will make missing even more likely.

The former lawman is quoted by author Stuart Lake as saying that the successful gun handler took the time to aim, and was not always the first to get his gun out of its holster. Modern cinema has shown more sense in portraying city crime fighters, who are made to assume a careful two-handed aim at eye level instead of the fast one-hander that rarely shoots straight in real life.

Earp also maintained that 'fanning' the gun and shooting two guns at once looked spectacular on the screen, but were wasteful and ineffective when done in actual practice. The movies would have us believe Butch Cassidy's crony, the Sundance Kid, had this talent, but it's doubtful that he ever used it in real emergencies. Experienced gunfighters often carried two shooters, one in reserve, but fanning one or both or using them simultaneously was only good for exhibition purposes.

The descriptive term 'six-shooter' was somewhat of a misnomer for the early models of 'the gun that tamed the West'. The weapon had chambers for six bullets, but since the sixth chamber was loaded with a dummy bullet or else kept empty, it could be fired only five times before a full reload. Especially for revolvers that were modified for hair-trigger sensitivity, it was common to leave the hammer resting on the empty or dummy chamber to avoid the embarrassment of accidentally shooting one's self in the foot or thigh. Needless to say, this precaution was necessary only while the gun was in its holster, and did not have to be observed when reloading during a firefight.

5. Off the Wall and Into a Hole

Myth! Leading his violent gang into South America, Butch Cassidy met a suicidal end fighting Bolivian soldiers with his cohort The Sundance Kid.

The 1969 film *Butch Cassidy and the Sundance Kid* tells us Butch was the head of the legendary outlaw group called the Wild

Bunch (*aka* the Hole-in-the-Wall Gang). The Western Outlaw-Lawman History Association begs to differ, saying that the real leader was Harvey Logan, alias Kid Curry, who would later commit suicide rather than face capture after a train robbery near Parachute, Colorado, in 1903.

Butch's myth begins with his name. This was George Parker in the records of the Pinkerton Agency and Robert Leroy Parker, the eldest son of Maximillian and Annie Parker, in the US census of 1880. Sam Peckinpah's 1969 *The Wild Bunch* throws no light on Butch's identity; that film is about a fictional gang led by a character named Pike Bishop, and its story of aging outlaws who, in 1913, decide to pull one last robbery before they retire is nowhere near Butch's experience. The violence of the real-life Wild Bunch was directed mostly at inanimate objects, such as mailbags and train safes, and until late in his life, Cassidy personally preferred intimidation to force and apparently killed no one. Logan himself killed only four men, all in street duels and none in pursuit of the gang's activities, while the Sundance Kid (Harry Longbaugh), reputedly one of the fastest guns during his time, displayed his dexterity mainly at exhibitions. Some deaths may have occurred indirectly in carrying out the gang's plans, but other than this, the only gunfight Butch and Sundance are said to have got into was the one in which they died.

The final scene of the 1969 movie is a freeze-frame of the two characters leaping towards a contingent of Bolivian soldiers and presumed death. This Hollywood interpretation of what many people believe happened during a robbery in 1908 or 1909 somewhere in Bolivia, possibly San Vicente, vies with the versions found in popular literature. In one such version, Butch killed the captain of the soldiers, then used his last two bullets to keep himself and the wounded Sundance from being taken alive. In another, the Kid died from the soldiers' fire and Butch used his last bullet on himself. A third version gives full credit to the Bolivian cavalry for their deaths, while a fourth claims Sundance was killed in the shoot-out but Butch managed to survive.

Butch's sister, then in her 90s, contradicted all these stories in a 1976 biography entitled *Butch Cassidy, My Brother*. In the book, she claimed Butch came home to Utah to visit his father and family in 1925, years after his reported death in South America. During that visit, Butch allegedly told her that the two men killed by the Bolivian soldiers were intentionally misidentified by one of his friends to give Butch an opportunity to bury his past and go straight. According to the same book, Butch died of pneumonia in the fall of 1937 somewhere in the Northwest, and was buried by his family in a secret place. Sundance was reported to have rejoined his mistress and lived quietly in Wyoming until 1956. It was later hinted that the man with Butch that fateful day in Bolivia was not really Sundance but his best friend Elzy Lay.

6. Precocious Young Gun

Myth! Billy the Kid killed 21 men by the time he was 21 years old.

Billy the Kid did not come from Texas but was born in New York City on Nov. 23, 1859, and died at Fort Sumner, New Mexico Territory, on July 15, 1881. It was shortly after attaining the young age of eighteen that Billy emerged as a reckless boy gambler and gunslinger with the name William H. Bonney, but dubbed 'The Kid' because of his youth and size. Few are aware William H. Bonney was also an alias: 'William H.' was borrowed from Billy's stepfather, while 'Bonney' (or 'Bony' or 'Bonnie') was the name of a man reputed to be his real father. There were also times the outlaw called himself Kid Antrim, after his mother, whose maiden name was Antrim. Hank the Kid would have been more appropriate because his real name—the one he was born with and by which he had been known until his first killing—was Henry McCarty.

Arthur Penn's 1958 movie, *The Left-Handed Gun*, made a case out of Billy the Kid being left-handed, but in reality he was not. According to a researcher, "a reversed photographic plate used to produce the only picture of Billy known to exist made it appear that way." It is also not true that Sheriff Pat Garrett was the only lawman to put the young outlaw in check. Sheriff Perfecto Armijo of Bernalillo County in New Mexico arrested Billy in 1880 some months before Garrett did.

We are told that Billy the Kid killed 21 men, one for every year of his life, and was a psychopathic murderer who was vicious, unpredictable and indiscriminate in his killing habits. Apparently, this was part of the wild talk that only started after his last few hectic days on earth. However disturbed young Billy might have been, evidence shows his victims were a mere handful—three men killed for sure, and probably three or four more. There is no record he ever robbed banks or trains, or had his name put on 'most wanted' posters, or engaged in gunslinging duels.

A possible reason for Billy's exaggerated reputation is that he started his violent career quite early. He was only fifteen when he figured in a robbery of a store in Silver City, New Mexico, and eighteen when, having fled to Arizona Territory, he killed his first man in a brawl. After that, he was in and out of trouble, until a leader in New Mexico's notorious Lincoln County War hired him. He may have been innocent of the fatal shooting of a lawman, but from this he emerged as the teen-aged fugitive leader of a gang of rustlers and killers.

Caught by Sheriff Pat Garrett and sentenced to hang, Billy was on his way to his execution when he managed to kill the two armed deputies guarding him while he was chained hand and foot. His spectacular escape under almost impossible conditions made Billy the Kid a living legend overnight—and the undeserving suspect in every murder in New Mexico.

7. Bat Strikes Out

Myth! **Bat Masterson had 22 notches on his gun (for the number of victims he killed) before dying in a shootout.**

Bat Masterson had a reputation that preceded him wherever he went, from Dodge City through the boomtowns of the West. But it was highly exaggerated, and so was the news that he was killed in a shoot-out. The gambler and lawman retired to become a sportswriter at the San Francisco Morning Telegraph, where he was found slumped over his desk one morning, dead from a heart attack.

It is claimed he was called Bat because he was such an excellent shot that he could kill a bat on the wing with his pistol. The better view, however, is that he earned his nickname from using his cane more often than his gun, by thrashing or tripping up drunkards and troublemakers with his 'bat' at the saloons he frequented.

His speed on the draw was remarkable, but the only times he displayed this skill were at public exhibitions. Although he has been credited with 30 to 40 killings, 22 of them supposedly notched on his gun, records indicate that Bat killed only two men, both of them in self-defense—Sgt. Melvin King in 1876 and Jack Wagner in 1878. Besides, no gunfighter notched his gun for any purpose, as he would have been ill-advised to do so. Serration on a gun handle, particularly of heavy recoiling hand jobs, can injure one's hand. Masterson himself started the myth that outlaws did it in the old days, by recounting that when he retired to New York, a local gun collector constantly pestered him for one of his frontier-day Colts. Just to get it over with, he went to a gun shop and bought an old Colt, then cut 22 notches in the handle and sold it to the collector for a fantastic profit.

8. Roving Hood of the West

Myth! Robert Ford was executed for the murder of Jesse James, despite the claim that Ford's victim was only a James look-alike.

Jesse James became a legendary figure after his death, a sort of Robin Hood of the Wild West even though his robberies benefited no one outside his group. According to some studies, he started his life of errancy more as a political outlaw than as a social criminal, an ex-Confederate seeking vengeance on the federal authorities and former Unionists responsible for killing many of his associates during the Civil War. This may be so, but in his teenage years, he was already an enthusiastic follower of William Quantrill and 'Bloody' Bill Anderson, notoriously cruel guerillas who thought nothing of killing unarmed Union troops and scalping and dismembering their bodies. After these leaders were eliminated, James joined the Younger Gang, participating in a remarkable string of robberies from Iowa to Texas and from Kansas to West Virginia for no other reason than personal gain.

When Jesse was 22, he robbed the Daviess County Savings Association in Gallatin, Missouri, in the process killing a cashier whom he thought was a former militia officer. This self-proclaimed attempt at revenge, and his daring escape through the middle of a posse shortly afterward, put his name in the newspapers for the first time. His emergence as the most famous of the former guerrillas turned outlaw was parlayed to the utmost with the help of John Newman Edwards, a Kansas City editor then campaigning to return former Confederates to power in Missouri. Edwards made Jesse a symbol of Confederate defiance of Reconstruction through his elaborate editorials and favorable reporting, often times giving false information to throw law enforcement off the bandits' trail. The breakup of the Youngers provided some respite to the outlaw's career, but in 1879 at the age of 31, he recruited his own gang and returned to crime.

It is said that on the morning of April 3, 1882, Robert Ford, who was visiting Jesse James in his house on the outskirts of St. Joseph, Missouri, shot Jesse while the latter was standing on a chair and dusting a picture on the wall. This popular account of Jesse's demise was challenged for a long time by the claims of Rudy Turilli, a recognized authority on the James Brothers. In 1948 Turilli presented a 100-year-old man named J. Frank Dalton before some surviving friends and acquaintances of the gunslinger, and they all affirmed that Dalton was the real Jesse James. Dalton testified that Ford, who was really Jesse's first cousin, killed another outlaw, a Jesse James look-alike named Charlie Bigelow, to protect Jesse from bounty hunters and to share with the other conspirators the $10,000 reward on Jesse's head. While Ford was quickly brought to trial and sentenced to death, the governor, who was also in the know, pardoned him two hours later.

Dalton died on August 16, 1951, just short of his 104th birthday, and lies buried in Granbury, Texas. Turilli's allegation was not successfully disputed until September 1995, when DNA taken from the remains of the man shot by Ford and tested against living members of the James clan proved without doubt that it was indeed Jesse James.

---

9. The Coach that Turned into a Bank

Myth! Wells Fargo, founded by Westerners to ply the New York-San Francisco overland route, was the stagecoach service highway bandits loved to rob.

We know Wells Fargo for the ubiquitous San Francisco bank that it is today, and for the stagecoach empire in the West that it once was. And also as the patsy of stage coach robbers during Wyatt Earp's time.

Actually, this is not a case of a coach turning into a bank. The bank was established independently in 1851 and sold in 1905, and owes its present powerful position in the finance world to other than its founders. The stagecoach, on the other hand, came a few years later—in 1857, to be exact—to provide regular ancillary transportation and mail services to the bank's clientele particularly in the mining industry. As early as 1852, stagecoach operations were mainly on a subcontracted basis between New York and San Francisco via the Isthmus of Panama. However, contrary to what this implies, stagecoaches were used only on the isthmus, and the rest of the route was by sea.

Although the name Wells Fargo is intimately associated with the history, folklore and development of the American West, its founders, Henry Wells (1805-1878) and William Fargo (1818-1881), were dyed-in-the-wool Easterners who lived in New York. Since forming the company in 1852 after the gold rush, Wells went west just one time, while Fargo never ventured from his New York home.

Wells Fargo did not become the largest stagecoach network in the United States through internal expansion. Rather, it did this by absorbing the Pony Express and, more substantially, the great Southern Overland Mail Company in 1866. It amalgamated with the Adams Express in 1918 as the American Railway Express Company, paving the way for its transition from stagecoach to transcontinental train.

The coach was never held up during all the time it was under the protection of the Earps. But from 1875 to 1883, it was the favorite target of arguably the most colorful (and misconceived) bandit the West has ever seen, the English-born Charles Earle Bowles, *aka* Black Bart. With a knapsack over his head to hide his face and armed with a shotgun that he never once fired, the gentlemanly Bowles, acting alone and on foot (he was terrified of horses), committed 28 successful robberies against Well Fargo stagecoaches during that period. Part of the Black Bart legend is his habit of leaving a poem he had composed at the site of each crime, but in truth he did this only on his fourth and fifth

45

robberies. He would not have been identified and captured if Wells Fargo detectives had not traced a bloodied handkerchief that he dropped on his last try to a laundry near his home in San Francisco. Black Bart's six-year prison term (he was convicted only for his 28th robbery) was reduced to four for good behavior, after which he disappeared and was never heard of again.

10. Why Wyatt was at the Fight

Myth! **Wyatt was leading a deputized group to enforce the law against the Clantons when the Gunfight at the OK Corral erupted.**

No other incident in the history of the American West is as beclouded in misconception as the century-old Gunfight at the OK Corral. The shootout is often described as a morality play in which good clashes with evil, implying that one side or the other was honorable. The little known truth is that every single player, from both the Earp and the Clanton side, brought a deadly weapon and an unsavory reputation to the occasion.

Although the three Earp brothers and Doc Holliday (a fourth Earp, Warren, portrayed in the film *My Darling Clementine* as one of those killed, was actually absent) were led by Virgil, who was the town marshal, it was Wyatt, his deputy, who would assume legendary proportions by coming out of the gunfight unscathed. The testimony of many eyewitnesses that the Earps had gunned down the Clantons without provocation was obviously a canard in light of the fact that three of the four in the Earp group were wounded. The shootout was over in 30 seconds, which is one-tenth the time it took to show the sequence in the 1957 film *Gunfight at the OK Corral*.

The fight was a prearranged duel between two gangs that wanted control of Tombstone, beginning with Ike Clanton hurling a challenge at the Earps to meet him and his gang at the OK corral. The Clantons posted themselves and waited, and were the first to go for their guns. Not all used shotguns, as is often claimed, and accounts saying that two—Ike Clanton and Tom McLaury—were not armed have no basis. Some depictions would show only two of the Clantons as armed and the shootout occurring almost face-to-face, as if the Earps chose to pounce upon unwitting opponents rather than fight an even duel. Historians believe the truth to be somewhere between this and the description given in Stuart Lake's biography.

One version of the shootout claims the Earps had tried to arrest the Clantons before the fireworks started, but this sounds like an attempt by Earp apologists to cloak the duel with a mantle of legality. The fact is that Virgil Earp, though he was a federal marshal, was not wearing his badge at the time of the shooting, and neither was Wyatt as his deputy. The others—Morgan and Doc Holliday—were not law officers nor were they deputized for the purpose.

In a manner of speaking, it was the Clantons who had the law on their side, namely, Tombstone sheriff Johnny Behan, whose hate for Wyatt drove him to sympathize with the Clanton gang. Before the fight, Behan falsely informed the Earps that he had disarmed the Clantons, and afterwards tried to facilitate the escape of Billy Claiborne and Ike Clanton from the fight scene.

Behan's attempts to arrest Wyatt after the shootout were rebuffed, and a coroner's jury refused to hold the Earps and Holliday for the death of the cowboys. Later, thinking he was the only witness to the gunfight, Behan testified against Wyatt's group at the Cochise County grand jury sitting at Tombstone. But not even the Earps' non-appearance at the hearings could restore Behan's damaged credibility, and the evidence on the whole was insufficient to charge Wyatt and his group with responsibility for the incident.

11. It Wasn't OK, Doc

Myth! The famous showdown between the Earps and the Clintons occurred inside the OK Corral.

The name 'Gunfight at the OK Corral' is supposed to tell us where the famous showdown between Wyatt Earp's group and the Clanton gang was held, but it's misleading. The gunfight in Tombstone, Arizona Territory, on October 26, 1881, actually took place in a vacant lot next to Camillus Fly's photographic studio, which was ninety feet east of the OK Corral's back entrance.

Stuart Lake described the whole incident based on data provided by Wyatt, but no one is certain which of the two gave the wrong location. What is significant is that the name has stuck, and Tombstone, now a tourist town, has reportedly corrected the discrepancy by enlarging the OK Corral to encompass the actual battle site.

It is said that the gunfight at the OK Corral ended in another prominent part of Tombstone—Boot Hill—meaning that Boot Hill, which was a cemetery, became the final resting place of those who lost out in that famous duel. In Old West parlance, Boot Hill is a metaphor for dying in a shootout.

12. The Path to Dusty Death

Myth! Doc Holliday died on the side of the Earps in the Gunfight at the OK Corral.

Contrary to the movies' depiction that Doc Holliday died at the OK Corral, he breathed his last on his sickbed six years after the shoot-out and fourteen years after his doctor had told him he would die of tuberculosis within a year. Holliday was not himself a doctor but a dentist who began drifting in the west in search of drier climes for his consumption, and who would acquire a name more for surviving his physical ailment than for fighting in the legendary skirmish. He and Frank McLaury shot at each other, and while Frank was hit in the heart, the latter's last bullet hit Doc's hip-holster, glanced, and shaved a strip of skin from his back.

The ones who met their ends at the OK Corral were Frank and Tom McLaury and Billy Clanton, all belonging to the Clanton Gang, and those wounded were Holliday and Virgil and Morgan Earp. Later, friends of the Clantons killed Morgan with a sniper bullet and crippled Virgil with a shotgun blast. Wyatt countered by gunning down Frank Stilwell and Indian Charlie, his suspects in the ambush of his brothers. Obviously, that part about Morgan dying on the spot at the OK Corral and gasping the words, "I guess you were right, Wyatt, I can't see a damn thing," in affirmation of his brother's denial of an afterlife is another fallacy in the colorful retelling of the event.

13. Tinhorn Star

Myth! Wyatt Earp was the quintessential US marshal of the Old West.

As may be expected, the book and the movies detailing Wyatt Earp's career omit some of the thorny points, e.g., in 1871 he was indicted for horse stealing; as a policeman in Wichita, Kansas, in 1874, he was caught pocketing the fines he collected; he was later dismissed from the force for fighting with a politician; and the first man he killed was a drunken cowboy. Besides his victims at the Gunfight and three others he gunned down without much of a fight, Wyatt claimed to have dispatched Curly Bill Brocious and Johnny Ringo. This despite historians who insist that Curly was alive after a decade and Ringo committed suicide.

Contrary to the title of Stuart N. Lake's 1931 book, *Wyatt Earp: Frontier Marshal,* Wyatt was never a marshal, for the highest he could manage was deputy marshal, a position he exploited without too many scruples. A Tombstone resident once called him a "tinhorn outlaw operating behind a badge," and many others would regard the Earp brothers' zealous enforcement of the law in Tombstone, which led to the famous Gunfight, as "due more to protecting their own casino interests than dedication." Even in Los Angeles, where Wyatt eventually settled and became a Hollywood consultant, he was once charged with vagrancy and conducting a bunco operation.

14. Craven Idol

Myth! Wild Bill Hickok single-handedly defeated the notorious McCanles Gang.

Wild Bill Hickok was first made famous in 1861 by an article in Harper's New Monthly Magazine recounting how he had fought a whole gang of outlaws and secessionists led by a man named McCanles. Hickok had succeeded in killing six of them with the six bullets in his gun and the remaining four with a knife, and still managed to survive despite being riddled with bullets and stab wounds.

The article completely ignored the finding at Wild Bill's trial that McCanles was neither an outlaw nor a rebel, nor that he had a gang, and that he was, in fact, a respectable businessman trying to collect money from Hickok's employer named Wellman. He had gone to Wellman's ranch, accompanied by his 12-year-old son and two employees, to demand a settlement, and while arguing with Wellman in his yard, he had noticed Hickok stepping inside the house and lurking near a window. When McCanles yelled at Hickok to come out, Hickok shot him through the curtain and also fired at his two companions, although it was more probable the latter were killed by Wellman and his men.

The lone survivor in McCanles' group was the boy, whereas none on Wild Bill's side was even wounded. The prosecution asked why a father would bring his son along if his intention were to commit mayhem, and also presented evidence that the victims were unarmed. Nonetheless, the jury accepted Wild Bill's plea of self-defense and acquitted him on the ground of insufficiency of evidence.

Born James Butler Hickok, it is rarely explained why the nickname he later acquired and by which he became famous is Bill. Some say Bill had nothing to do with a second name or an alias, but was a derivative of another nickname he had—'Duck Bill', for his long nose and protruding lip. The truth is, when still a young man, 'Wild Bill' decided to scrap the name James and replace it with William, from his father. Thereafter, William, with its diminutive Bill, was what he signed in all his correspondences and the only name he asked both friends and detractors to call him by.

15. Calamity was a Woman

Myth! Wild Bill Hickok and the notorious bandit queen Calamity Jane were lovers.

Martha Jane Canary was nicknamed 'Calamity Jane' because of her reputation as a jinx. This legendary woman is glamorized—sometimes as a bandit queen, which she wasn't—in several

Hollywood movies, ranging from the 1953 musical starring Doris Day to the 1995 western *Wild Bill* featuring Ellen Barkin. All of the portrayals on film as well as those on television tend to obscure Calamity Jane's incompatible roles in real life as tomboy and prostitute. On the one hand she affected male dress, a six-gun and a tough image, and on the other she offered her body to the frontier riff-raff to assuage her poverty.

It is not clear if Calamity Jane ever consorted with the outlaw Sam Bass, as one of her movies would have us believe, but it is well known that when another gunslinger, Wild Bill Hickok, died, she mourned him for life as if she had been his sweetheart. She displayed a public obsession for the dead cowboy, despite little evidence that she was anything more than a casual acquaintance. At age 51, she was buried next to Hickok in accordance with her last wish, believing the lie told her by sympathetic friends that the day she chose for the burial was the anniversary of his murder.

16. A Hand to Die For

Myth! Wild Bill Hickok's unlucky 'dead man's hand' consisted of a pair of black aces and a pair of red eights.

Soon after its foothold in the American West, poker became the centerpiece in a famous controversial killing—that of the notorious gunslinger Wild Bill Hickok. Both history and the cinema have muddled up some of the evidence from the Hickok crime scene, one of which was the definition of the so-called "dead man's hand," the unlucky poker combination Wild Bill was holding when Jack McCain shot him from behind in a Deadwood, South Dakota saloon in 1876. The cards that half-spilled from Wild Bill's grasp when he fell from his stool (there were no chairs in those days) vary with most accounts, but the consensus is that these were two pairs of black aces and eights—not one pair black and the other red, as the 1939 film *Stagecoach* would suggest— and the fifth card was a jack of diamonds. Contrary to the legend, there was no superstition attached to the hand at the time, the combination of black aces and eights becoming unlucky only on account of Hickok's death.

51

Wild Bill, who had a strong sense of caution, preferred to sit against a wall, except that on this occasion he sat with his back to a door. Although movie portrayals tend to show him with his back to the front door, what really happened was that he was facing the front door as usual, while a rear door was standing open. The assassin didn't come in through this rear door, as is sometimes alleged, but casually through the front door in full view of Wild Bill. Walking to the bar, he sauntered around to a point a few yards behind his victim, where he swiftly drew his .45-caliber Colt and fired once.

17. Bison Bill and the Indians

Myth! For killing more than a hundred Indians, William Cody became the model for Ned Buntline's fictional Buffalo Bill.

There are two Buffalo Bills, one real and the other fictional. The real Buffalo Bill, known at times by his birth name William Cody, bids strongly as the model for the fictional character created by Ned Buntline.

Buntline was the originator of dime novels, writing about his cowboy hero in over 400 of them. Cody is widely regarded as Buntline's inspiration for the Buffalo Bill saga, although he was apparently just a showman and, on the side, a bison hunter in the true West that he traveled. Despite being one of the best shots in the West, Cody's reputation as a gunslinger was pure fiction. It was only in the novels that Buffalo Bill resorted so often to gunfire.

Even as an Indian scout, Cody did not kill many Indians, as his Wild West show boasted. He was already old when his estranged wife revealed that he had been wounded in combat with Indians only once—a scalp wound from the Sioux—and not 137 times, as he claimed. The legend that he single-handedly killed Yellowhand, the Cheyenne chief, might be true, but in the case of another famous chief, Tall Bull, he kept changing so many of the details of their supposed encounter that the story became suspect. Finally, he confessed to a newspaper that the real killer of Tall Bull was a Lieutenant Hayes, although other sources reported that it was Major Frank North. Incidentally, North would have been the basis for the dime novel idol had he not declined Buntline's offer, which eventually went to Cody.

The real Buffalo Bill got his name from shooting buffalo, not from riding on a buffalo while shooting Indians. Cody may not have killed many Indians, but as a champion hunter, he killed thousands of buffaloes, almost single-handedly wiping out the animal to feed railroad workers constructing the Kansas Pacific Railway in 1876-78. Ironically, it was Cody's Wild West show that later spread the news of the buffalo's dwindling numbers and helped save it from extinction.

Coming now to the fictional Buffalo Bill, when Ned Buntline was asked who his real-life model for the character was, he did not point to Cody but to himself. It turns out he had a perfectly good reason for the self-praise, although it was not too obvious. Buntline was 'a battered customer, who had weathered adventures as fantastic as his own novels'. He had been a cabin boy, a duelist, a killer, an explorer, a leader of the Astor Place riot of 1849, a member of the Know Nothing Party, and a Civil War veteran. Buntline's first Buffalo Bill novels were, in fact, based on his own experiences as a trapper and soldier in the West.

Naturalists say Cody should have been called Bison Bill and not Buffalo Bill. Semantically speaking, none of the more than 4,000 animals Cody bagged in a single season, or the record 69 he shot in one day, was a buffalo. What was then popularly called buffalo is actually bison, which is different from the real buffalo, a beast of burden common to Asia and Africa.

53

IV

Tramps And Thieves

On Shady Characters

"Listen to them. Children of the night.
What beautiful music they make."

•

Count Dracula

1. Something Wrong with the Count

Myth! **Count Cagliostro cut a figure that was the pure embodiment of evil.**

The name Count Cagliostro has become suggestive of someone sinister and evil because its owner, Giuseppe Balsamo, was thought to have a truly despicable reputation. This confidence artist par excellence wove such a dark mystique about him that people thought he was the devil himself.

However, it may not be fair to regard Balsamo, who assumed the cognomen when he married a countess, as deserving of opprobrium when others who were truly evil are often held in awe. He might have been a charlatan and an exhibitionist, but he was far from evil and was in fact a charitable man. The Count only pretended to be dark and sinister to create a desired effect for his acts as a harmless necromancer. Touring Europe in the eighteenth century, he entertained his audience with a display of occult knowledge, magic tricks, chemical marvels, medicine and mystic powers. True, he was also a hoaxer and a liar—the historian Thomas Carlyle called him "the king of liars" and "the most perfect scoundrel"—but he used the black arts basically to give pleasure rather than pain. And in the few times he stole, almost all of his victims were the corrupt royalty, unlike, say, P.T. Barnum, who was low enough to bother with ordinary people.

Cagliostro's downfall came when he got involved with the Cardinal de Rohan in the theft of a diamond necklace intended for Queen Marie Antoinette. He was likely the least guilty, but his partner and mistress went against him, and he was convicted while the rest of the accused, including the Cardinal, were acquitted. Because of his intimidating presence and the bad publicity he almost always generated, Cagliostro, many historians believe, became the ideal scapegoat to take the rap for the Cardinal. They agree that he was not a bad person, and was condemned mostly out of jealousy and unfounded suspicion. Unfortunately, he had the gall to be interested in the occult and the supernatural at a point in history when this was frowned upon by the Church.

2. Hatchet Job

Myth! Lizzie Borden took an axe / And gave her mother forty whacks / When she saw what she had done / She gave her father forty-one.

Even before the trial of Lizzie Borden on the charge of hacking her parents to death with a hatchet in 1892, the children of Fall River, Massachusetts, where the murders happened, began chanting the now famous refrain. Though ingenious in a cruel sort of way, the inventor of the rhyme obviously had no handle on his axe (!). For one thing, the victim Abby Borden was not Lizzie's real mother but her estranged stepmother. For another, Abby suffered 19, not 40, blows from a hatchet, which is not the same as an ax. Lizzie's father, Andrew, was killed with only one whack of the hatchet, after which the murderer dealt nine more blows to make sure he was dead. Finally, the whole doggerel lost its essence and even became possibly slanderous when Lizzie was fully acquitted based on only sixty-six minutes of deliberation.

Long after the acquittal, Edmund Pearson suggested in two books that Lizzie did do it. Refuting him was a reporter and crime writer, Edward D. Radin, who wrote in *Lizzie Borden: The Untold Story* (1961) that Pearson gave undue credence to the circumstantial evidence linking Lizzie to the killings but ignored those in her favor. Radin tagged the Bordens' maid, Bridget Sullivan, as the most logical suspect, although she was not even arrested despite being the only other person in the house with the family.

3. Surly Czar

Myth! Ivan IV was called the Terrible because of his dreadful temper and savage nature.

The Russian czar Ivan IV Vasilievich was called the Terrible because, according to his legend, he was just that—terrible. He amused himself by throwing pets from the towers of the Kremlin, and killed people, including his son, with his own hands. He tortured thousands of citizens, indulged in long drinking bouts, and had seven wives (not including a girl who died from a heart attack on learning he had picked her for his third wife). It was claimed that he exterminated the whole city of Novogorod when he heard it was conspiring to defect to neighboring Lithuania.

The fact, of course, is that 'terrible' as part of Ivan's title did not mean savage or dreadful or disagreeable. It was a mistranslation of the word *grozny* in his Russian title, Ivan Grozny, meaning Ivan the Awful, or awe-inspiring. Ivan was the first tsar and one of the most reform-minded, an eloquent and able executive whose temper and cruelty were not unusual for his day and age and whose royal behavior was not any more wicked than that of most other monarchs of the period. It is true that in a fit of anger, he struck his 27-year-old son in the head with his iron-tipped staff, killing him, but this was clearly accidental. The reason he committed depredations against his own people, notably the citizens of Novogorod, during his seven years reign of terror, was to flush out the ambitious and ruthless boyars, the princes hostile to his rule. The other grossly unpleasant stories told about him were mere rumors that his enemies most likely spread at home and abroad.

Ivan, it is said, ended up becoming one of the most peaceful hermits ever, spending the last few years of his life doing nothing but meditating and praying in solitude and self-denial. He died shorn as a monk—he simply collapsed on March 18, 1854 while playing chess—and was buried in a monk's robes.

---

4. Hardcore Practitioner

Myth! **The graphic sex and violence of today's Hollywood films are no match to those depicted in the Marquis de Sade's novels or in his real-life escapades.**

The Marquis de Sade (real name: Donatien Alphonse François) lent his name to the aberrant behavior called sadism, which he not only practiced but also wrote about in such celebrated works of fiction as *Justine* (1791). However, his deeds, for which he was first imprisoned in 1763 when he was 23 and newly married, were not really as savage as the scenes depicted in his novels, and the latter, in turn, are no more repulsive than the graphic sex and violence of today's Hollywood films. De Sade vented his imagination mostly on prostitutes, but never to the point of killing them, and since they were paid for the purpose, even rape seems technically doubtful.

His life became a series of jailing, escapes and scandals, interrupted only by a respite during the French revolution when he showed a gentler nature as secretary of the Revolutionary Section of Les Piques in Paris and a delegate to visit hospitals in that city. He wrote several patriotic addresses, and during the Reign of Terror saved the lives of his father-in-law and the latter's wife even though they had been responsible for his various imprisonments. His writings personally offended Napoleon, and caused his final arrest and detention at the lunatic asylum at Charenton, where he died.

De Sade's works are today regarded in a different light in the literary world. In the 19th century, they were read underground and mainly by writers and artists who found in de Sade "a sense of freedom and a poetic testing of experience and imagination." But in the late 20th, they can be found on open shelves alongside highly reputable classics, with many critics (notably the Britannica) finally agreeing that they "belong to the history of ideas and mark an important moment in the history of literature."

5. Nobody Loves Lucy

Myth! **Lucrezia was the worst of the Italian Borgias, earning a reputation for evil as a notorious intriguer who poisoned many of her enemies and lovers.**

Many of the things we know about Lucrezia Borgia are pure fiction. First, the Borgias, of whom Lucrezia was one, were actually surnamed Borja, since they were Spaniards, not Italians. Second, their monstrous reputation, which equated them with evil, was exaggerated, the product of rumors spread by the Romans because they resented a Spanish family controlling the papal throne. And third, unlike her brother Cesare and their father Rodrigo, who probably deserve the opprobrium heaped on the family by history, Lucrezia was a much-maligned lady, courtesy of the historian Guicciardini and a host of discredited Neapolitan satirists.

Lucrezia was, according to her own letters, a model of domesticity, her real problem being "an insipid, almost bovine, good nature." More pawn than principal, and far from being the murdering type, she was much less deserving of her reputation than Caterina Sforza, a harsh town administrator suspected of being behind a rather incompetent plot to poison the pope. And Catherine de' Medici proved even more arrant as the mastermind of the St. Bartholomew's Day massacre in 1572. Lucrezia is popularly believed to have conspired in the murder of her husband Alfonso di Bisceglia in order to protect the incestuous relationship she was carrying on with Cesare (and at other times with Rodrigo). But in fact, Cesare had openly admitted to killing Alfonso in retaliation for an unsuccessful assassination attempt against him. Historians specializing in that era are agreed that all the charges against Lucrezia bear no relation to the truth, and that this linguist and poet who devoted herself to works of charity was actually beloved by the people of Ferrara when she died at age 39.

---

6. Having a Ripping Time

Myth! Jack the Ripper's official identity is kept hidden because of his royal connections.

British media have suggested that Jack the Ripper was either Sir William Gull, Queen Victoria's royal physician, or Edward, duke of Clarence, the Queen's grandson and heir to the throne. But officially, the identity of this most infamous of serial killers has remained elusive.

Jack the Ripper, who brutally murdered five prostitutes in London's East End in 1888, left tantalizing clues that the police were never able to solve. At first theorizing that a doctor had done the killings because of the way the bodies had been cut up, investigators placed at least three MDs at the top of the list of suspects. But later they added other professionals, including Sir Arthur Conan Doyle's own favorite suspect, an unidentified midwife.

The medical theory was given a royal flavor when a Jack the Ripper series in 1988 hosted by Britain's Thames TV categorically named Sir William Gull, Queen Victoria's royal physician, as the Ripper. However, this was soon dismissed as a red herring to divert public suspicion from a much bigger royal suspect. Speculation on the British royal started with a witness account of a 'well-dressed' man talking to the last victim shortly before her death, and on this flimsy evidence, a writer in 1970 concluded that the Ripper was Prince Albert Victor, known as Prince Eddy (Edward, Duke of Clarence), the grandson of Queen Victoria and heir to the throne of England. Gossip and media, including movies and television, have conspired to give some semblance of fact in the popular mind to the idea that Edward's deteriorated mental state, caused by syphilis, compelled him to commit the murders. Arrayed against these, however, are well-written articles that question the plausibility of the Duke's involvement, and on balance, experts agree there is no convincing evidence to support the royal theory.

---

7. Mad Monk

Myth! Gunshot wounds caused the violent death of Rasputin.

Rasputin, a semiliterate Siberian miracle healer, performed his healing powers on the hemophiliac son of Czar Nicholas II and Alexandria, and thereafter became unofficially the most powerful man in the Russian Empire outside of the royal family. Worried that this power was beginning to corrupt and weaken the Czar's regime, two nobles in the palace at St. Petersburg—Prince Felix Yusupov, husband of the Czar's niece and a notorious transvestite, and Vladimir Purishkevich, an adviser to the Czar—decided to act.

Yusupov invited Rasputin to his house at midnight on December 29, 1916, with the intention of poisoning him with cyanide-laced cake and wine. When Rasputin felt no ill effects, this prompted Yusupov to shoot him in the back. After a doctor had pronounced him dead, Rasputin suddenly got up, tore an epaulette from Yusupov's shoulder, and ran after both Yusupov and Purishkevich, managing to break down a door that the fleeing pair had locked after them. In the courtyard, Purishkevich shot Rasputin twice, and when his victim collapsed, he continued to kick him in the head while Yusupov beat it with a steel rod. Making sure he was dead, they bound Rasputin's hand and dumped him into a hole in the ice of the Neva River. When his body was recovered, the autopsy revealed that he had freed one of his hands from the ropes just before he drowned.

8. Out for Blood

Myth! The fictional character Dracula is patterned after a figure of Eastern European folklore.

Not many who have read Bram Stoker's book or seen the Bela Lugosi film classic realize that a historically significant person served as the model for Dracula. This was Vlad Dracul, who became a Romanian national hero after he waged a war of terror against the Turks. Dracul, or Drakul, meaning either "dragon" or "devil," was a ruling member of the Bassarab dynasty of Walachia, which is now a province of Romania. The words "devil" and "vampire" are interchangeable in many languages, thus the association of Dracula with vampirism. Stoker, who was not a German, as most people think, but an Irish writer whose full name was Abraham Stoker, was engaged in research at the British Museum when he chanced upon sources of Eastern European folklore involving Vlad Drakul. On the advice of a professor from the University of Budapest, he transplanted his model to Schassburg, Transylvania, a place steeped in vampire lore, and came up with Count Dracula.

Stoker found Drakul's myth convincing, probably unaware that it was actually molded by the reality of his crueler son Vlad Tepes, also called Vlad the Impaler. Tepes, the Prince of Walachia, would have been a more appropriate model for Dracula considering his singular claim to infamy: he destroyed some 100,000 of his subjects and enemies by impaling them and drinking their blood. Some historians mistakenly believe it was Tepes who became one of Romania's patriots after fighting the Turks and capturing Budapest; in fact, the honor belongs to the less perverted Drakul. The boyars of Romania, never forgetting Drakul's brutal reign, assassinated him, but when the Turks later surged across the Danube, his countrymen realized they had lost a true defender of Christianity against the Ottoman Empire, and hailed him as a national hero.

V

Cloak And Dagger

On Notable Spies and Traitors

"All of Britain could not slay me. Can you, lads?"

•

Benedict Arnold

1. Cracker Jacks at Work

Myth! **The first time Germany's Enigma encrypting system was broken was by the British shortly before the end of World War II.**

The British raised a collective howl when the Hollywood film *U-571* was released in 2000 showing a group of US Navy submariners capturing a Naval Enigma machine from a German U-boat. According to Wikipedia, "the real *U-571* was never involved in any such events, was not captured, and was in fact sunk in January 1944, off Ireland, by (the) Royal Australian Air Force. The real *U-570* was captured almost intact by the Royal Navy in 1941, although not before her crew had destroyed almost all the secret materials on board." A protesting Tony Blair, along with other MPs, declared the film "an affront" to British sailors because of its depiction of Americans as being the first to capture a Naval Enigma machine, which, with its associated code books, was needed to decrypt the Nazis' secret communication system during World War II. In the real world, the feat was accomplished on May 9, 1941 when the HMS *Bulldog* of the Royal Navy under the command of Captain Joe Baker-Cresswell overwhelmed the German U-boat U-110. The U.S. Navy scored its first and only seizure of a Naval Enigma machine off a U-boat in June 1944, when the Allies were already reading Naval Enigma routinely.

It has been pointed out, nevertheless, that the real achievement in the Allies' relentless campaign to defeat Hitler's formidable message-coding system was not the capture of the first Naval Enigma machine (the hardware) but the successful unraveling of the encryption processes (the software) that the machine, among other elements, helped to establish. As Wikipedia notes, breaking the messages enciphered by Enigma was almost impossible even if the code breaker had a working copy of the device as long as he didn't know the right combination of initial electric and mechanical settings, which the Nazis cleverly changed from time to time. The task required the combined efforts and talents of brilliant mathematicians, code breakers, intelligence officers and communications experts, all deeply familiar with the language and mentality of the Germans and their radio operating procedures.

Equally if not more significant were the counterpart machines, nicknamed "Bombe", which provided electro-mechanical computing power that helped shorten the process of deciphering the Enigma messages. The Bombe technology was developed by Alan Turing for the British, but it was actually preceded by the Polish version, called Bomba, in 1938. In fact, as early as December 1932, the Polish were the first to break Germany's military Enigma ciphers, and in Warsaw five weeks before the outbreak of World War II in 1939, they presented their Enigma decryption techniques and equipment, including Bomba, to French and British military intelligence. *Enigma*, a 2001 British film about the code breaking efforts of England's Bletchley Park in that war, took its turn to be criticized for not mentioning the Polish cryptanalysis foundation on which subsequent British code breaking became dependent for success.

It is sometimes said that the Enigma machine, reputedly the greatest intelligence device to come out of World War II, was neither Allied nor Axis because its inventor was the Dutchman Hugo Alexander Koch. But the more rightful claimant appears to be the German engineer Arthur Scherbius who, at the end of World War I, brought out patents independently (and perhaps ahead) of Koch, retired Koch's own patents after purchasing them, and made the machine operational. The Nazis polished Enigma for a military use and remained convinced during most of World War II that its encoding system, which could garble a message into any one of a possible ten sextillion different codes, was absolutely unassailable. Beyond mere suspicions that their intelligence services could not prove, Hitler's people were unaware that the Poles, the British and the French were singly or jointly succeeding in cracking Enigma, by altering or reconstructing the machine and deciphering its code.

US Colonel William F. Friedman is generally reputed to have broken the Japanese code with the use of Enigma, but it was actually the genius of civilian cryptanalyst Harry Larry Clark that triggered the American breakthrough. Ironically, while the newly found intelligence on the Japanese failed to anticipate the attack on Pearl Harbor, it was put to good use against the Germans in the Normandy invasion. Significant information on Nazi fortification in France in 1943 was squeezed out of the contents of a secret message sent to Tokyo by a Japanese diplomat after he had toured German defenses on the French coast.

2. Spies in the Closet

Myth! Homosexuals in general do not make effective spies.

Gays are generally branded as security risks for many reasons, none of which holds water. The most obvious—that homosexuals are emotionally weak and open to blackmail—is disputed, and correctly so, by historians who argue that "heterosexuals can just as easily be lured into 'honeypot' sex traps and blackmailed—even more so when they are married." The myth is that most homosexual spies are 'femme' or not tough, but in fact, "these (are) very hard men (with) minds like steel traps and the ability to betray friends, family and country to advance their political goals." Their unorthodox sexual preferences force them from puberty to live secret lives, which makes them far more prepared mentally and emotionally for deception and social hypocrisy, both vital ingredients in the making of an excellent spy. Moreover, "because of their basically feminine nature, gays are remarkably loyal and dependable, are far more sensitive than 'straights', and can more readily sense nuances in a situation that help them avoid danger, traps and other entanglements. "

It is no wonder, says an analyst, that the most brilliant spies in history have been homosexuals. Three of the Cambridge Four—Guy Burgess, Donald MacLean and Anthony Blunt—were confirmed homosexuals working in the highest echelons of the British government while doing undercover work for the Soviets. At the height of their spying days, beginning after their induction into the Communist Party and graduation from Cambridge in the 1930s, Burgess was a high-ranking member of British Intelligence who helped establish the CIA, MacLean was First Secretary at the British Embassy in Washington, DC, and Blunt was the knighted Surveyor of the King's Pictures and Art Professor at the University of London. Their collective work as conspirators is believed to have impacted to a large degree on Soviet decision-making in erecting the Berlin Wall, initiating the Korean War, and developing the Russian H-bomb.

Curiously, some of those who have criticized gays involved in Communism or espionage as immoral, weak-minded and untrustworthy, such as the notoriously homophobic J. Edgar

Hoover of the FBI and Roy Cohn of the HUAC, were reputed to be homosexuals themselves.

3. Crosswords of the Times

Myth! The two most effective methods of secret transmission during World War II were the crossword puzzle and the postage stamp.

Strict censorship of communications by belligerent nations has promoted ingenious ways of transmitting secret messages. But lacking any official records showing otherwise, the claim that the crossword puzzle and the postage stamp were two of the most mundane items used successfully to convey coded information in World War II is obviously untrue.

In 1944, several issues of the Daily Telegraph, a London newspaper, featured crossword puzzles in which some of the answers were exactly the same as the code words for implementing the Normandy attack. The five beach code words "Omaha," "Utah," "Gold," "Sword," and "Juno" appeared in the puzzles within a period of several weeks preceding the invasion. Even "Overlord," the code name coined by Churchill for the entire operation, came up, along with "Neptune" and "Mulberry." The authorities became concerned, but their investigation proved that it was all a coincidence, though one of the strangest on record

Even more impressive than the crossword puzzle is the postage stamp, the clandestine use of which allegedly originated in the Civil War and since then has been tried in all wars, including the Vietnam War. In a classic story, an American prisoner in a Japanese camp wrote home after a long hiatus, and in the typewritten letter provided a clue that prompted the recipient to steam off the stamp, revealing the grisly message, "They've cut off my hands." This urban legend has no real foundation, and crumbles in light of the fact that, in modern wars, POWs and soldiers on both sides have no need for stamps because of franking privileges granted by international convention.

4. The I in Intrepid

Myth! The head of British intelligence in the western hemisphere during the greater part of World War II was 'The Man Called Intrepid'.

Nigel West cites some fallacies in William Stevenson's book *A Man Called Intrepid*, which was written as the real-life story of Sir William Stephenson, the virtual head of British Intelligence (known as British Security Coordination, or BSC) in Canada and the Americas between 1940 and 1945. Not the least is the claim that Stephenson was code-named Intrepid at the instance of Churchill. This is highly unlikely, says West, since Intrepid was a matter of public record in Washington as the name of the organization and not of its Director. Stephenson was assigned the secret code-number 48100 by British intelligence, while INTREPID was the cable address duly registered for BSC (its office was located in the Rockefeller Center at 630 Fifth Avenue) with Western Union and the State Department pursuant to a requirement of American law for all foreign government agencies. Apparently, it would have made more sense if Stevenson had called his hero The Man From Intrepid.

According to West, a number of accomplishments credited to Stephenson by the book are all false. For instance, it was chronologically impossible for Stephenson to have recruited the famous spy called Madeleine, and there is no real evidence that he was involved in the assassination of Reynard Heydrich. He did not coin the word "Top-secret Ultra" for decrypts coming from the Enigma machine, as it was the Naval Intelligence Division that adopted the term for these decoded items in June 1941, more than twelve months later. And he could not have kept FDR informed on the German military situation after the evacuation of Dunkirk inasmuch as the Wehrmacht's Enigma code would only be broken in 1942.

Needless to say, Stevenson's mistakes should not denigrate from the overall accomplishments of Sir William, among which are the key role he played in the creation of the CIA; the setting up of the first training school for clandestine wartime operations in Canada and North America; and the establishment and operation of the British Security Coordination in New York City as an umbrella organization for various British intelligence services throughout the Americas. A British knighthood and the Presidential Medal for Merit (the highest civilian award in the US at the time), among other awards, attest to the deeds of this wartime hero, who is rightly known as "The Quiet Canadian" rather than as "The Man Called Intrepid."

5. They Talked to the Wind

Myth! The employment of Navajo 'windtalkers' by the US Marine Corps in World War II marked the first time a Native American language was applied in military communications.

The Navajos from Arizona, Colorado, New Mexico and Utah had a language that was totally incomprehensible to anyone who had not lived among them and studied it in depth. In 1942, it was estimated that only some 28 non-Indians could understand what Navajos said, and none of them was German or Japanese. Hence, to confuse the Japanese who were listening in on US Marine Corps radio transmissions in the Pacific during World War II, the Corps employed more than 300 Navajos as radio code talkers. By the end of the war, there were 420 Navajos dispensing messages to American troops, not one of which could be read by any method outside their own.

But, contrary to allegations, this was not the first time the US used an American Indian language to send and receive coded messages. In World War I, American troops in Europe had been having difficulty transmitting their messages without the Germans breaking their code. When an inventive American officer thought of using a little-known language as a code, one that the Germans could not possibly know, he settled on the language of the Choctaw Indians. The officer recruited eight Choctaws, who provided American forces with a perfect conduit for their secret orders.

To avoid a repetition of their World War I experience, Germany sent philologists to America after the war to study the dialects of the Indian tribes. But they still could not help the

Japanese in World War II because, for all the depth and breadth of their work, they missed the Navajos somehow.

---

6. Moles in the Field

Myth! The CIA as the most secretive and operational of spy organizations has many more field agents than home office personnel.

In *The Invisible Government*, their 1964 book about the American intelligence community, David Wise and Thomas B. Ross point out that the CIA, the principal cog in "this interlocking, hidden machinery," is not invisible at all. Most everybody knows where it is. Despite the atmosphere of secrecy that surrounds the building at Langley, Virginia, a foreign agent would not have the slightest difficulty finding CIA headquarters. A standard map of Washington shows the site in clear detail, and public transportation in the area always announces the CIA as part of its scheduled route. Also, most everybody knows what it is. Because it's written about, spoofed, filmed and plastered on the Internet more times than any other spy agency, the CIA's doings, both real and fictional, are familiar even to the citizens of the remotest third world countries.

Another fallacy about the CIA is that its agents are the most traveled spies in the world. They are seen as sowing intrigue from the corporate jungles of Europe to the tropical jungles of Asia, organizing or overthrowing banana republics faster and oftener than United Fruit did. All these may be true to an extent, but with one important distinction: the greater part of a CIA operation is done at its Langley, Virginia, home. It is estimated that less than 5 per cent of the work force are involved in spying or covert operations; the rest are essentially white collar types who sit behind desks and computers reading and interpreting materials and shuttling them between points. The data analyzed are from all sources, printed and electronic, but the least used method of bringing them in is by operatives.

7. Laughing his Way to the Gallows

Myth! **The notorious Nazi propagandist Lord Haw-Haw was revealed to be a Briton named William Joyce.**

At the end of World War II, the British arrested forty-year-old William Joyce, a Ph.D. candidate from King's College, London, and hanged him for treason. The charge: Joyce was the notorious Nazi propagandist Lord Haw-Haw who had spent much of the war broadcasting in English for Berlin.

Historians doubt Joyce was the real Haw-Haw, and even if he were, they say Joyce should not have been executed as a traitor. For one, he was not British but American, passing himself off in Europe as a British citizen and traveling on an improperly issued British passport. For another, while it might have been foolhardy of him to pretend to be Lord Haw-Haw, his broadcasts were not real propaganda, as they were based on scripts that, though widely regarded as false, were in fact mostly true. The information they disseminated was culled from British newspapers that had been obtained within twenty-four hours of their publication.

In any case, the Brooklyn-born Joyce could not have been the same broadcaster that an English professor dubbed "Lord Haw-Haw" and journalists sometimes called "Oxford Accent," since this shadowy figure had been announcing from Berlin even before Joyce got there. It was not known who Lord Haw-Haw really was, but many listeners in England were already aware at some point that Joyce's was not the voice they had come to hate. Unfortunately, Joyce made the mistake of appropriating it after his arrival in Germany, where, having found himself stranded at the outbreak of the war, he had decided to embark on a radio career to sustain himself.

8. Square Pegs in the Oval Office

Myth! **Benedict Arnold was the first American patriot and highest-ranking American official to commit treason against the United States.**

71

It is not the name Benedict Arnold that should bring to mind stories of the first high-ranking American patriot to become a spy for the British. There is evidence that Charles Lee (1731-1782), an American general who distinguished himself in the defense of Charleston early in the Revolution, committed treason ahead of Arnold. Lee was captured and held by the British for fifteen months, during which time he was believed to have offered his captors a plan for defeating his countrymen. Later, he was court-martialed and broken of command for ordering a confused and nearly costly retreat at the Battle of Monmouth.

Still, the earliest known high-ranking traitor in the American Revolution, though he was not in the military, was Dr. Benjamin Church, a respected physician from Boston and the first Surgeon General of the United States. He had been appointed in 1775 owing to his powerful credentials as a patriot zealot, having been the first on hand to treat the wounded after the Boston Massacre. There was no inkling that he was an enemy spy until coded documents he was transmitting to the British were intercepted. He was only three months into his position when he was tried, convicted and sentenced to life imprisonment, spared of the hanging that an irate George Washington thought he deserved.

If a case can be made for treating former Union officials or military officers who later entered active service in the Confederacy as traitors to the United States, the name of rebel general Robert E. Lee would be on the list. It must be remembered that Lee was once a commander of West Point like Arnold. However, overshadowing—and outranking—Lee and all others in similar situations is John Tyler, a former president of the United States. Tyler was William Henry Harrison's running mate in 1840, and when Harrison died in 1841, he assumed his place as president for the next four years. Twenty years later, he joined the South when it seceded from the Union. He died in 1862 in the service of the Confederacy as the elected Virginia representative to that government's House of Representatives, and was buried with full honors by the rebels. This earns Tyler the ignominy of being the only ex-president to renounce the US and to serve an enemy government until his death.

9. A Column too Many

Myth! General Emilio Mola, a Franco stalwart during the Spanish Civil War, invented the term 'fifth column'.

'Fifth column' refers to a group or organization of persons who act secretly within a city or country to further the interests of an outside enemy, and a fifth columnist is a secret agent. The expression, which arose in 1936, is popularly attributed to General Emilio Mola (1887-1937) in the Spanish Civil War. It is said that Mola, a stalwart of the rebel leader Francisco Franco, was leading four columns of armed insurgents against the Spanish capital of Madrid when he told foreign journalists that he had a "fifth column" within the city. What he really meant was that he had another group of sympathizers and active partisans waiting to assist in overthrowing the city's defenses by sabotaging the Loyalists from the rear.

How Emilio Mola got the credit no one knows, but it was really Lieutenant General Quepo de Llano, famous as the 'broadcasting general' during the Spanish Civil War, who introduced the term. In the early days of the war, de Llano was heard airing a threat to the Loyalist forces in Madrid: "We have four columns on the battlefield against you and a fifth column inside your ranks." This was the first recognition in modern warfare of organized forces behind the battle lines ready to sabotage the defense of a position.

10. Stirrings Underground

Myth! Spy novelist John Le Carré coined the word 'mole' to describe an enemy undercover agent.

John Le Carré, author of 'cold war' bestsellers in the spy genre, is the reputed originator of the word 'mole' to describe an undercover agent working in the enemy camp. The popular novelist was one of the first to bring to light the underground activities of secret agents and double agents operating during the uneasy peace that followed World War II. He created the tragic figure of Leamas in *The Spy Who Came in From the Cold*, and his prototypical British spy, George Smiley, in *The Honorable Schoolboy*.

Though the word 'mole' appears liberally in the earlier Le Carré novel *Tinker Tailor Soldier Spy*, the author uses it best in reference to Smiley's favorite agent, the Honorable Schoolboy himself, Jerry Westerby. But the spy term is not an original in any of Le Carré's Cold War thriller collection. A news feature in the New York Times of February 7, 1984, focusing on the extensive library of spy literature belonging to intelligence officer Walter L. Pforzheimer, suggested the existence of a rare Elizabethan manuscript that proved the earliest known usage of the term was by Francis Bacon in one of his unpublished works in the 17th century.

11. Returning a Coat?

Myth! At his deathbed, Benedict Arnold became penitent and restored his allegiance to the United States.

Benedict Arnold is perhaps the most despised figure in American history, but he may not entirely be without sympathizers in the country that he renounced. Despite his name being a synonym for traitor, rumor has it that he restored his allegiance to the United States just before he died, in a manner worthy of Frank Capra's most patriotic film. After achieving the status of legend, the rumor has even registered as truth in some collections of quotes and anecdotes.

The story is that when he was about to die, he put on his old American uniform, saying, "Let me die in my American uniform in which I fought my battles. God forgive me for ever putting on any other." As one debunker puts it, "Nice story—if it were true, but it isn't. All the evidence suggests it not only didn't happen but couldn't have happened." After Arnold's death, his wife wrote that he was delirious during his last three days and was entirely unable to swallow or speak.

12. Mission Implausible

Myth! Among all US enforcement agencies, the FBI caught the most number of spies during World War II.

When newspaper headlines shouted "FBI Captures 8 German Agents Landed by Subs," not many knew it was one more propaganda ploy to promote the FBI as the foremost spy catcher in the US during the war years. Hoover hid the real story—that of George John Dasch, one of the agents, surrendering and then turning in the others—from even the President.

In fact, the FBI never caught a spy during Hoover's time, notwithstanding the reputation established for them as spy catchers. He did write once in the Reader's Digest (April 1946), in a piece entitled "The Enemy's Masterpiece of Espionage," that in August 1941, the FBI caught a young Balkan playboy who had just arrived in the US, having in his possession a letter with a microdot on the envelope. Under a special magnifying glass, the dot revealed voluminous writing, part of which was an entire Nazi questionnaire asking for specific information on Pearl Harbor. Hoover failed to mention that this spy was a British double agent named Dusko Popov, who came to the US at the instance of British Intelligence precisely to confer with the FBI chief about the microdot. To show his spite for the British (he suspected them of supporting Wild Bill Donovan, his rival at the OSS), he chased Popov out of the country and back to England. Popov would eventually become Ian Fleming's model for James Bond.

Hoover later wrote FDR claiming credit for the discovery of the microdot. One of several enclosures to the letter was a translation of the microdot's contents omitting entirely the section on Hawaii and Pearl Harbor.

VI

Days Of The Jackal

On Famous Assassinations

"It is better to be violent, if there is violence
in our hearts, than to put on the cloak of
non-violence to cover impotence."

·

Mahatma Gandhi

1. He loved Twinkies but hated Milk

Myth! The assassin of San Francisco Mayor George Moscone legally proved that his capacity had been diminished by his addiction to Twinkies.

On November 27, 1978, Dan White, a former San Francisco Supervisor, brutally shot and killed the city's progressive Mayor George Moscone and a current Supervisor, the openly gay Harvey Milk. The motive was clear: White was angry at Moscone for refusing to reappoint him to his just-resigned Board of Supervisor's seat, and at Milk for intensively lobbying against the reappointment.

San Francisco, long regarded as one of the most politically sedate and tolerant cities of the US, was shocked into a new reality by the twin murders. Equally shocking was the subsequent conviction of White for voluntary manslaughter, a much lesser crime than first-degree murder and one that sent the indictee to a 5-year jail term (after parole) in lieu of the electric chair. The totally unexpected turn of events led to rioting among the city's large gay community and the eventual abolition by the state of California of certain laws relating to diminished capacity as a mitigating circumstance in homicide. Apparently, the jury had swallowed hook, line and sinker the claim of White's lawyers— the soon-to-be called "Twinkie defense"— that he suffered from periodic bouts of depression amounting to a major mental illness, and was therefore incapable of deliberation (one of the requirements for a first-degree murder conviction). In this condition, the defense argued, he had acted in "the heat of passion which fogs judgment"—in short, with diminished capacity.

'Diminished capacity' is a tried and true principle of criminal law and probably would not have ruffled popular feelings as much had it not been given an unnecessary twist in White's case. Newspaper and TV reports had erroneously interpreted certain defense testimony to mean that White's diminished capacity was attributable to his immoderate consumption of Twinkies and other sugar-laden junk food. "Dan White gobbled Twinkies," so read an entry, "which blasted sugar through his arteries and drove him into a murderous frenzy." But in fact, the cream-filled confections were mentioned at the trial only in passing, while junk food in

77

general was an insignificant part of the arguments. A defense therapist characterized by critics as "a throwaway witness…with a throwaway line" had testified that "the conversion of the previously health-conscious White to a diet of Twinkies and other junk foods was *evidence of his depression.*" Unfortunately, media passed this off as expert opinion proving that White's addiction to such food was the *cause* rather than a *symptom* or *effect* of his troubled state of mind.

As a result, says one observer, the 'Twinkie defense' "appears in law dictionaries, in sociology textbooks, in college exams and in more than 2,800 references on Google" with only a few being aware that it is pure bunk.

2. Reruns of an American Tragedy

Myth! Lincoln's son Robert unwittingly witnessed the assassination of three American presidents.

Lincoln's son Robert saw three assassinated US presidents before each succumbed to the bullet. However, it is not true that the young Lincoln personally saw any of the assassinations. He was not present during the actual shooting, appearing on the scene only after it had happened and when the victim was already dying.

From Appomattox, where, as a captain on General Grant's staff, he witnessed Lee's surrender, Robert proceeded to Washington for a visit on April 14, 1865. Lincoln was shot that night, and Robert rushed to his bedside, staying until the President expired the next morning.

Robert, a member of the cabinet in 1881, was on his way to the Washington railroad station to meet Garfield when the President was shot. Upon arriving, he saw Garfield being attended by a doctor. The injured President took Robert's hand as if to assure him that he was all right, but he was dead in three months.

Robert was president of the Pullman Company when he decided to take his family to Buffalo, New York, to meet President McKinley in 1901. No sooner had the Lincolns arrived than they heard the news that the President had been shot. Robert was able to see McKinley once before he died a week later.

3. Cry of the Wolf

Myth! John Wilkes Booth shouted, "Sic semper tyrannis!," after shooting President Lincoln.

Booth shot Lincoln and stabbed an officer who had tried to grab him. He then leaped out of the presidential box, caught his boot spur in the folds of an American flag, and broke his left leg upon landing on the stage below. According to some historians, he shouted what sounded like the patriotic words *Sic semper tyrannis* at some point in the violent proceedings.

The Ford Theater audience seemed divided on what they heard Booth exclaim. While the favorite was *Sic semper tyrannis!* (Latin for "Thus be it ever to tyrants!"), a few thought it was "The South is avenged!" Others insisted it was "Revenge for the South!" These utterances are sometimes mentioned together in the same account as though Booth shouted all of them that night. There is also the question whether Booth yelled the words when he jumped from the box, or after landing on the stage and before making his exit.

History's bias for *Sic semper tyrannis!* as Booth's battle cry is apparently due to certain aspects of the assassin's life. Booth, a Shakespearean actor like his equally famous brother Edwin, loved to play Brutus, another assassin. He would occasionally interject the phrase when, as Brutus, he plunged the dagger into Caesar's breast. It is said Booth, an ardent admirer of the South, liked the phrase because it was the official motto of Virginia, the capital state of the Confederacy.

4. The Name on the Bullet

Myth! Chicago Mayor Anton Cermak, hit by bullets intended for FDR, managed to say, "Better me than you, Mr. President," before he died.

79

The near-assassination of FDR at the hands of a thirty-two-year old gunman is one of the most inaccurately described events in the life of the 32nd US president.

The assailant was one Joseph Zingara, not Zangara. When it happened on February 15, 1933, FDR, though already elected, had not yet assumed office as president. The attack did not take place in Chicago, and FDR was not delivering a speech at the time. The incident occurred hundreds of miles away, at the Bay Front Park in Miami, Florida, where FDR had just given a speech. FDR could not have been on a grandstand or at a podium when fired upon, since he had delivered his speech standing in his car and with a microphone in hand. According to official reports, he was posing for photographers when the shots were heard.

There were five, not six, pistol shots coming one after the other, and only one, not two, hit Mayor Anton Cermak of Chicago. Cermak was not "coming up to greet FDR" (in other versions, he was sitting next to FDR or had flung himself in front of the President-elect) when the shots were fired; he was standing on the running board of the car waiting for an opportunity to talk to FDR. It is not true that Cermak said, "Better me than you, Mr. President," and died on the spot. A newspaperman made up the quote, not knowing that Cermak never said a word before he was taken to a hospital, where he died a few weeks later from complications.

5. End of a Long Story

Myth! Dr. Carl Weiss was guilty beyond reasonable doubt of the murder of Louisiana politician Huey P. Long.

US Senator Huey P. Long, the dictatorial 'Kingfish' of Louisiana, was gunned down outside the governor's office in the state capitol one September day in 1935. A 29-year old physician named Carl Weiss had reportedly sneaked up to Long, pressed a .32-caliber automatic pistol in his ribs, and fired once. Weiss had no clear motive, although he was the son-in-law of a Long opponent, a judge who was to be gerrymandered out of his position under a bill the Senator was pushing.

80

According to neutral observers, almost all of the witnesses to the shooting were Long's bodyguards and intense partisans who might themselves have killed the Kingfish. Within seconds after Weiss supposedly fired, everyone near Long had responded with a barrage of close-range shots from pistols and machine guns that hit Weiss 61 times and pockmarked the marble rotunda.

Some indications that Weiss might have been a fall guy include the fact that the bullets passed through Weiss' shirtsleeves, suggesting that he was holding his arms up defensively. Also, a .32 caliber bullet that did not come from Weiss' gun was found at the scene of the crime. No one could actually prove Weiss had carried a gun into the Capitol. Since Long was a controversial if not hateful figure, many did not discount the idea of a conspiracy, especially since the Senator himself expressed fears before his death that one was about to get him. Unfortunately, the killing of Weiss discouraged investigation of the murder, while the conspiracy theory has been dismissed as just another of Long's ploys while he was alive to gain more power.

6. A Short Film about Killing

Myth! Abraham Zapruder's film is the only graphic legacy of the Kennedy assassination.

Abraham Zapruder's 15-second 8-millimeter documentary is the starkest yet the most ambiguous of the evidence presented before the Warren Commission. The controversial nature of the film and the murky scenario in which it was taken may have contributed to the impression that it was the only one made of that historic event in Dallas on November 22, 1963.

The impression is wrong, of course. There are two other known films of the assassination and the Commission passed upon both. One—taken by onlooker Charles Bronson—tends to be forgotten even though it stimulated as much controversy as the Zapruder reel. The significance of the Bronson film is in its early frames, which provide a glimpse of the sixth floor windows of the Texas School Book Depository building—and some apparent activities there—immediately before the shooting

The second footage was made by another bystander, Orville Nix, and shows the grassy knoll area in Dealey Plaza at the time of the assassination. Popularly titled "the most trampled patch of greenery in America," and a favored conversation piece for conspiracy theorists, this is the place that several witnesses said harbored strange shadows and produced sounds of gunfire while Kennedy was being murdered. Like the Bronson film, however, Nix's production was unenhanced by telephoto magnification, and was too brief and peripheral to have the dramatic impact of the Zapruder masterpiece.

7. The Unlucky Stars of India

Myth! Indira's son Rajiv was the third member of the illustrious Gandhi clan to be assassinated.

Assassins killed all the Gandhis who had been outstanding figures in the political and social development of India. A Hindu killed Mohandas Karamchand Mahatma, the leader of India's drive for independence from Britain, on his way to conduct a prayer and pacification service in New Delhi. The Sikh bodyguards of Indira, India's ironhanded Prime Minister for 18 years, shot her to death in October 1984. A suspected Tamil terrorist bombed Indira's son Rajiv, a former Prime Minister, in May 1991 during an election campaign.

Of the three, the best known was Mohandas Gandhi, who cried out the name of God with his dying breath to remind friend and foe alike that he was also a holy man. And well should he be. For Mohandas was the only genuine Gandhi, whose direct descendants, numbering 47 in five nations in 1976, do not count Indira and Rajiv among them. The clan has done everything "from selling life insurance to working in space engineering," but—with the exception of Mohandas—not one has ever become politically involved. Indira acquired the Gandhi name from her deceased husband Feroze Gandhi, who was no relation to Mohandas, and won her elections primarily on the strength of her being the daughter of Jawaharlal Nehru, India's revered first prime minister. No real Gandhi, Mohandas and Feroze included, had a hand in shaping the Gandhi political dynasty, although its founder, Nehru, started out as a Mohandas protégé and owed much of his political education to that patriarch.

Indians continue to revere Mohandas Gandhi, a self-proclaimed Hindu, as a saint, and to call him Mahatma (Sanskrit for "great soul"). They see his advocacy of nonviolence, or *ahimsa* (Sanskrit for "noninjury"), as the expression of a way of life implicit in the Hindu religion. Yet Mahatma was a political, not a religious, advocate, with no professional affinity for or bias against any religion. Those who felt he didn't pay enough attention to Hinduism as it stood four squares against the inroads of Mohammedanism may have caused his assassination. In an interview conducted by *Time* magazine on February 21, 2000, Gopal Godse, the brother of the man who killed Mahatma, claimed the last words officially attributed to the great pacifist were actually not uttered. "You see," Godse said, "an automatic pistol was used. It had a magazine for nine bullets but there were actually seven at that time. And once the trigger was pulled, within a second, all the seven bullets had passed. When these bullets pass through crucial points like the heart, consciousness is finished. You have no strength." According to Godse, "the government knew that he (Gandhi) was an enemy of Hindus, but they wanted to show that he was a staunch Hindu. So their first act was to put 'Hey Ram' (Oh God) into Gandhi's dead mouth."

8. A Medieval Murder Mystery

Myth! To secure the English crown, Richard III had the Princes in the Tower secretly killed.

Most historians and writers in the traditional mold picture Richard III as having a hunched back and a withered hand. Others believe the attribution should not be taken literally but only as a metaphor, his real deformity being moral rather than physical. The king, they say, was a scheming monarch who, to fulfill his ambitions, murdered no less than his brother the Duke of Clarence, as well as Henry VI and his son Prince Edward.   He is also accused of ordering one John Tyrell to kill his two young nephews, the Prince of Wales and the Duke of York, in the Tower of London to protect his crown.

Still, there are those who think Richard III is almost surely innocent of the murder of Henry VI and his son, while in the case of the Princes in the Tower, some have posed the question why there was no contemporary accusation of Richard for the crime, and why the boys' mother remained cordial with Richard to the very end. Highly motivated members have formed various Richard III societies for the sole purpose of clearing the 'hunchback king' of any involvement in the death of the heirs, and of proving that Richard was the victim of a terrible intrigue created by his usurper Henry Tudor (Henry VII). The king's most articulate defender, Josephine Tey, in her book *The Daughter of Time,* argues through her series detective, Alan Grant of Scotland Yard, that Richard III had absolutely nothing to gain from the assassination and Henry VII everything. Tey believes Henry was more likely to have ordered the killing himself after defeating Richard at Bosworth, then shifted the blame on Richard to discredit the House of York and consolidate power in the victorious Tudors.

9. Death on the Dot

Myth! **Display clocks are set at 8:18 as the hour Lincoln died or was shot.**

Americans have this persistent notion that display clocks are set at 8:18 because that was the hour Abraham Lincoln died or was shot. Lincoln was actually shot shortly after 10:00 p.m. and died at 7:30 the next morning. In the English version, Lincoln is replaced by Guy Fawkes, one of a cabal that attempted to assassinate the king by blowing up Parliament. Some say the king's guards caught Fawkes at 8:18 a.m., others that the attempt was set precisely for that time of day.

The display has of late changed to 10:10 (or its reverse, 1:50), to accord with the universal way watches and clocks are shown in ads. In a survey conducted by William Pound (*Biggest Secrets*), only 13 of 100 timepieces in ads showed a different time, and of this, many were digital readouts. Pound says the reason is much more practical than the thought that 10:10 is nearer to the time Lincoln was shot. Like 8:18, 10:10 is a symmetrical arrangement that is not only pleasing to the eye but leaves the most room for advertising the brand printed on the face. Relative to the vertical axis, they both make a sort of equiangular tripod that strikes most people as more attractive than, say, 9:15, and one that frames the manufacturer's name and logo nicely. The practice is believed to be a marketing or advertising convention, though an informal one, dating back to the 1920s. It has been noted that the arrangement appears in issues of *Time* magazine during that decade, but was missing in the illustrations in a *Sears Roebuck* catalog from 15 years earlier.

10. Leading Death by the Nose

Myth! Cyrano de Bergerac was assassinated in fiction as well as in real life.

The real-life Cyrano de Bergerac was a French poet and novelist whose best works combined political satire and science-fantasy, inspiring such writers as Jules Verne. A notorious freethinker in a Catholic age, he was—according to one of the more popular fallacies about him—converted to Catholicism on his deathbed. Edmond Rostand's famous play, in which Cyrano is portrayed as a gallant and brilliant but shy and ugly lover, is the best known of the many romantic legends about this colorful character.

Rostand's comparison with the real Cyrano is authentic in some respects. There is a parallel between the two characters in terms of their military experience, their being wounded in one encounter, their literary and philosophical prowess, and their scientific theories mingled with fantasy and satire about the moon and the sun. Rostand was not being whimsical when he made his character fight a duel and at the same time compose what is probably the best literary paean to a part of the human anatomy. The real Cyrano is said to have fought 1,000 duels over insults concerning his enormous nose, and existing engravings of the man attest to the prominence of this feature of his physiognomy.

Rostand deviates from real life in one important respect. Enemies assassinated the fictional Cyrano, making his wounding look accidental. Other sources consider the episode as pure literary trimming: Cyrano in the flesh was barely 36 when he was hit on the head by a falling beam during a visit to a friend's house. As this did not kill him immediately, biographers are prompted to surmise that he died later either as a result of a street fight or from an infection caused by syphilis, for which his brother had him confined in a lunatic asylum. How he could have gotten syphilis remains a mystery, since Cyrano, despite his reputed romantic tendencies, was a suspected homosexual.

11. Hands of Fate

Myth! **The 1914 assassination of Archduke Franz Ferdinand, leading to World War I, could not have been prevented.**

The popular belief is that World War I was inevitable because the event that precipitated it—the assassination of Archduke Franz Ferdinand on June 28, 1914—was itself unavoidable. It is argued that even if the young student nationalist Gavrilo Princip had not been there, the heir to the Austro-Hungarian throne would have been martyred by one of five other assassins deployed in Sarajevo that day.

As details of the incident showed, of the six lurking in the crowds and waiting for the Archduke to pass by, four backed out, another threw a bomb that missed, and the last one—Princip— couldn't get a chance to fire his revolver.

The close call with the bomb on their way to the town hall that morning forced the royal couple to cancel a trip to a museum, and to drive straight back on the wide Appel Quay boulevard in their open limousine, a guard posted on the running board to protect the Archduke. However, the new route wasn't passed on to all the drivers, and by mistake, the lead car turned right into Franz Josef Street, with Ferdinand's driver following. Told to turn back, the driver stopped and began to back up—straight into the arms of the providential Princip, who was standing right on the corner of the intersection. Princip stepped into the street, fired his revolver twice, and brought about what many believe was foreordained destiny but was actually an accident of history.

12. Addressing the State of the President

Myth! U.S. Surgeon General Joseph K. Barnes attended the wounded Lincoln and Garfield as a function of his office.

The belief then as now is that the US Surgeon General must attend to matters of presidential health as a function of his office. This may have fostered the idea that Dr. Joseph K. Barnes, who attended both Lincoln and Garfield when they were assassinated in 1865 and 1881, respectively, was the US Surgeon General called specifically to his job on those occasions.

Barnes is described as being this officer in most historical accounts, implying that he was, for at least 16 years, the top man of the Public Health Service. Barnes was indeed a surgeon general, but he was surgeon general of the US Army, a position entirely different from the one in the federal government's civilian corps. Presumably, like the chief medical officers of the other branches of the US Armed Forces, Barnes was available on call to the President as Commander-in-Chief, although this did not make him, officially or otherwise, a designated physician to the White House. Similarly, the US Surgeon General as the top health officer in the federal system heads an agency that ministers to the public health, and is not a staff physician to a government official of any rank.

Incidentally, 'surgeon general' as used in both the military and the civil service is akin to 'attorney general' but not to 'adjutant general', since it is not a military title. It is likely, however, that the surgeon general of the various branches of the Armed Forces and of the Defense Department is also a general in the military, with the two titles being held separately.

13. With a Friend like Harry

Myth! Henry II had no hand in the assassination of Archbishop Thomas à Becket of Canterbury.

Henry II of England and the man he appointed Archbishop of Canterbury, Thomas Becket, had been an amoral twosome in the early years, but after his appointment, Becket repented his profligate ways and started taking his vows seriously. He excommunicated Henry's wicked nobles, angering Henry and leading to a complete severance of relations.

In 1170, after a seven-year voluntary exile in France, Becket returned to England but spurned Henry's attempts at reconciliation. Incensed, the king asked his most loyal knights who among them would rid him of "this troublesome priest," and four responded by visiting Canterbury to seek an audience with the Archbishop. Refusing to heed their desire that he quit England, Becket was slashed as he stood in front of the altar of St. Benedict in the Cathedral.

The Church absolved Henry in 1174 when he affirmed that the act was without his consent and knowledge. But many are curious why, for all his innocence, he still had to go through the rites of penance to regain his standing with the Church. Quite obviously, the killers had presumed they would be acting on his authority, and Henry himself must have known that murder by his knights would be the logical consequence if the Archbishop remained obstinate. Historians contend that Henry was at least guilty of murder by induction: by expressing a strong desire to force Becket out of his see, this put pressure on his loyal knights to fulfill that desire by the only means at their disposal,.

Incidentally, Thomas Becket is also commonly known as Thomas à Becket, although, as historian John Strype points out in a 1694 writing, this form was an oft-repeated error that arose only after the Reformation, possibly in imitation of Thomas à Kempis.

14. For King and Country

Myth! **Martin Luther King died in Jesse Jackson's arms.**

The day after King was assassinated in Memphis, Tennessee, the Rev. Jesse Jackson, wearing a bloodstained shirt, announced before media that he was the last to cradle the victim's head in his arms before he died.

Twenty years later, New York Mayor Ed Koch, who supported Tennessee senator Albert Gore against Jackson in the 1988 Democratic presidential primary campaign, alleged during an interview on an ABC TV news program that Jackson had greatly exaggerated his role. Although Jackson no longer insists he cradled King's head, and just says he "reached out" for him, the Afro-American clergyman was able to use the story to project himself politically and become a US senator, with ambitions to be the first black president of the United States.

In fairness to Jackson, the official account of the assassination puts him at the scene with King when it happened. King, who was on the balcony talking with Jackson and a mutual friend, musician Ben Branch, in the parking lot, was straightening up to leave when the bullet struck him in the right side of the jaw, entering his neck and severing his spinal cord. Jackson most probably rushed up to be by King's side, but, as Koch said, the business of cradling King's head in his arms and staining himself with his blood was an embellishment designed to make political hay out of the tragedy.

---

15. The Mighty Queen

Myth! **Russia's Catherine I grabbed power by having her husband Peter III murdered.**

The rumor is that to gain the Russian crown, Catherine had her husband Czar Peter III assassinated with the help of her lover Grigory Orlov.

In truth, Catherine had herself declared empress of Russia with the approval of the guard, the senate and the church, and without touching a hair on Peter's head. Peter, who was at his residence, formally abdicated the next day and was taken to the village of Ropsha under the custody of Aleksey, brother of Grigory. He was killed there, apparently in a brawl but suspiciously on orders of some conspirators without Catherine's consent or knowledge.

The real circumstances may be irrelevant, however, in light of the fact that Peter was not legally the czar at the time of his death. He had succeeded the empress Elizabeth without being officially

89

enthroned, so that when Catherine deposed him in 1762, he was only the *de facto* occupant of the throne and had been so for only six months. Nobody seems to know why, but thirty-five years later Catherine agreed to have Peter crowned czar and had his coffin opened for the purpose.

Incidentally, this 'scarlet' lady, though second only to Peter the Great as the greatest Russian monarch, was not really Russian, and neither was her husband Peter. She came to Russia as Sophie Frederike Auguste of Anhalt-Zerbst, daughter of a poor German princeling, to marry Peter in 1744. Peter was born to the German duke of Holstein-Gottorp and was raised in Germany, where he had been living when proclaimed heir to the Russian throne by her aunt, the reigning Tsarina Elizabeth.

16. Somos Diferentes

Myth! 1979 was the year the Sandinistas assassinated President Somoza and assumed power in Nicaragua.

It was George Bush's impression—and there are many who still share it—that the Sandinistas grabbed power in Nicaragua in 1979 by assassinating President Anastasio Somoza. Bush's foreign affairs advisers may not have known it either, or else they would have told him that it was a young Nicaraguan poet and composer who had killed Somoza in 1956 after twenty years of dictatorial rule, with the Sandinistas having no part in the assassination. Bush no doubt made the faux pas because he had mistaken Somoza for his two sons, neither of whom was assassinated, but who had continued his regime until the Sandinistas drove out the last of them in 1979.

Augusto Sandino was a guerrilla leader who started to wage war against the US-backed government of Nicaragua earlier in this century. But after making peace with his country's new president, he was ambushed and killed by the henchmen of Anastasio Somoza Garcia, the powerful leader of the US-trained National Guard. Somoza illegally seized the presidency three years later, and when he was assassinated in 1956, his son Luis Somoza Debayle took over.

Meanwhile, Sandino became a martyr in the war against 'Yankee Imperialism', and his supporters, calling themselves the Sandinistas, never gave up. In 1979, ironically with the US State Department playing a significant role, they overthrew Somoza's other son, Anastasio Somoza Debayle, as the last in the family dynasty that held Nicaragua in a vise for decades.

17. Caught in Charlotte's Web

Myth! The French revolutionary Jean-Paul Marat was murdered for purely political reasons.

Jean-Paul Marat headed the Jacobins, the fiercely anti-royalist faction of the French Revolution that launched the Reign of Terror. Considered the most radical and ruthless figure emerging from that cataclysm of history, the 50-year-old Marat was killed on July 13, 1793, while soaking in his bathtub to alleviate the agony of a festering skin infection. His assassin was a 25-year-old conservative named Charlotte Corday, who had gone up to Marat's apartment ostensibly to show him a list of conspirators to be executed. While showing Marat the list, Corday suddenly pulled a six-inch kitchen knife from her dress and stabbed him in the left side of the chest.

Corday, who was executed four days later, said she did it to avenge friends who had been killed on Marat's order. But the unspectacular act made her victim a French national hero despite the bloodiness and extremism of his acts and beliefs during the Revolution and despite the little-known fact that he was not French at all. Marat was born in Boudry, Switzerland, on May 24, 1743, and educated in London in the early 1770s to become a successful physician. He wrote his early philosophical and political tracts in English, and begun to write French only after returning to France in 1777.

18. Fall Guy

Myth! Guy Fawkes' memory is forever condemned for his leading the cabal that tried to assassinate King James I and his chief ministers.

Some western countries might desist for some political reason from condemning their villains and outlaws, but none surely would have the impudence to memorialize them for their deeds. Or would they? In the United States, John Dillinger has a monument in Nashville, Tennessee, and Jesse James is honored by a museum in Stanton, Missouri. This is not at all a late-breaking phenomenon, for in the Old World, we have England, which to this day perpetuates the memory of a failed assassin—Guy Fawkes—with bonfires and fireworks once a year.

To be sure, Guy Fawkes Day is an inapt name for the November 5 holiday, since the honoree's sole claim to fame is a minor role in the infamous plot to kill King James I and his chief ministers in 1605 by blowing up Parliament while they were in conference. The principal actors in that undertaking were Roger Catesby, who masterminded the plot, and Francis Tresham, who gave it away. Fawkes was a mere technician enlisted from abroad by the group and had not even been told of the precise details of the bombing. Unfortunately, he was the first to be apprehended while acting suspiciously in the basement of the Parliament building when it was being rigged for the job.

VII

Abraham And John

On US Presidential Assassinations

"A man may die, nations may rise and fall,
but an idea lives on."

•

John F. Kennedy

1. A Parallax View

Myth! Both Lincoln and Kennedy were deeply committed to civil rights for black Americans.

Perhaps the most impressive of the Lincoln-Kennedy connections in Dr. Matrix' list (Martin Gardner, *The Magic Numbers of Dr. Matrix*) is the deep commitment both had to civil rights for black Americans. Unfortunately, this is the one 'truth' in the presidential dossiers that cannot be etched in stone. Kennedy may have been a civil rightist in heart and mind, but Lincoln seems to have been so only in appearance. According to Lincoln's biographers, this president disliked slavery but refused to adopt abolitionism as a principle, letting down many of the radicals that supported him by allowing the execution of the abolitionist John Brown. While he was opposed to the extension of slavery, he was even more opposed to reducing it on the ground that it would endanger the Union. His myth says he waged the Civil War on the moral issue of slavery, when in fact he waged it on the political issue of federalism. Although he is known as the Great Emancipator, his Emancipation Proclamation didn't end slavery; it was a ploy that applied only to the states that had rebelled and where the president didn't have any authority. He gave the Proclamation a humanitarian look when it was actually for a military-political purpose, calling it 'a fit and necessary war measure, for suppressing rebellion'.

About Kennedy, on the other hand, a former adviser, Theodore C. Sorensen, says: "In 1963 he was deeply and fervently committed to the cause of human rights as a moral necessity inconsistent with his political instincts" (*Kennedy*, 1966). Well and good, except that, in making his not too impartial evaluation, Sorensen chose to ignore a 'civil rights' bone in Kennedy's closet. When he was a senator and just before becoming president, Kennedy voted for the final passage of the Civil Rights Act of 1957, subject to the 'Jury Trial Amendment' that he had earlier supported. As any political writer this side of Capitol Hill will affirm, the Amendment practically rendered the whole exercise nugatory because it made convictions for violations under the Act difficult if not impossible to obtain.

2. Escape Sequence

Myth! John Wilkes Booth fled to a warehouse after shooting Lincoln in a theater; Harvey Lee Oswald fled to a theater after shooting Kennedy from a warehouse.

Booth shot Lincoln while the President was watching the play 'Our American Cousin' in Ford's Theater in Washington, DC. The assassin then fled south to Virginia and took refuge in a warehouse used for storing tobacco. It was there that Booth, cornered by pursuing federal troopers, met his own death. The Kennedy assassination supposedly provides a parallel, with the sequence of events reversed. Oswald shot Kennedy from a warehouse—the Texas School Book Depository—while the President's motorcade was passing around Dealey Plaza. After killing a police officer, Oswald went into a movie theater, where pursuing lawmen captured him.

As Dr. Matrix implies, there is indeed an obvious coincidence in the flow of events of the two assassinations, altered only by the fact that the beginning and ending points in one are switched in the other. The comparison nevertheless fails because of a flaw in the notion that Booth fled to a warehouse, when in fact it was a tobacco-curing barn located on a farm near Port Royal, Virginia. On the other hand, Oswald fired the fatal shot at Kennedy from a book depository, which is, strictly speaking, not a warehouse either.

In a generic sense, a barn and a depository are as much warehouses as they are large buildings intended for storage or shelter. At times, they are like most other structures in that they may be devoted to general uses or to uses not germane to their design (e.g., as a concert place or a town hall). But technically, there is enough difference between a barn and a depository to warrant their separate and specific categorization. One is for an agricultural purpose, which is to contain livestock and farm products, whereas the other is a facility commonly found in the commercial/ business sector for keeping and securing money, merchandise, commodities and small fungible items.

In short, Dr. Matrix would be standing on firmer ground if he had used the word 'building' for both 'depository' and

95

'warehouse', but that would have meant a lower level of synchronicity.

---

3. Time Triplets

Myth! **Kennedy and Lincoln were the only presidents to have a former southern Democratic senator named Johnson as vice president.**

Dr. Matrix makes much of the following uncanny similarities in the circumstances of Lincoln and Kennedy, not realizing that the two shared these similarities as well with other American presidents:

1. Vice presidents named Johnson who were southern Democrats and former U.S. senators succeeded both Lincoln and Kennedy. Not many people know that President Martin Van Buren's vice president (1837-1841) was also a southern Democrat and former U.S. senator named Richard Johnson. Richard aces out Andrew (Lincoln's VP) and Lyndon (Kennedy's VP) with his reputation for allegedly killing the great Indian leader Tecumseh and for staying away from his job most of the time, which gives him the distinction, according to the scuttlebutt, of being 'the most effective VP the US ever had'.

2. Both Lincoln and Kennedy lost a son while living in the White House. A third president, Calvin Coolidge, had a 16-year-old son residing with him in the White House who died of a bacterial infection from a blister on the toe after playing tennis.

3. Both John Wilkes Booth and Lee Harvey Oswald were Southerners who held extremist views. The killers of Garfield and McKinley were political terrorists in their own rights, and were probably more extremist than Booth ever was. Booth might have been unfairly condemned for entertaining a view about separatism at a time when this was the legitimate view of half the population of the United States. Besides, Booth was a Southerner only by accident of the Mason-Dixon Line; he hailed from Maryland, a border state that fought with the South but belonged geographically to the North.

4. Four Scores and Twenty Years Ago

Myth! It is strangely coincidental that certain corresponding events in the Lincoln and Kennedy presidencies were exactly a century apart.

Numerologists see some mystical significance in what is apparently a coincidence—certain pairs of events related to the assassinations of Lincoln and Kennedy occurring exactly 100 years apart. The scientifically inclined are, however, unimpressed. For one, there are actually only two such pairs, and not three as was originally thought. The first is the year the two presidents were elected, Lincoln in 1860 and Kennedy in 1960, and the other is the year their successors were born, 1808 for Andrew Johnson and 1908 for Lyndon B. Johnson. The claim that Booth was born 100 years before Oswald misses by a year; Booth was born in 1838 and Oswald in 1939. According to Martin Gardner, the error arose when Booth's birth date was listed as 1839 in Funk and Wagnall's *New Standard Dictionary of the English Language* (1945 ed.) and Chamber's *Biographical Dictionary* (1962 ed.).

As significant as all these may sound, the 100-year difference between the Lincoln and Kennedy occurrences is really more casual than phenomenal. It is not any more surprising than, say, the 20-year gap separating Garfield's election and assassination from those of McKinley. Since the Lincoln and Kennedy administrations were exactly a century apart, it is not beyond normal to expect some of the corresponding events under those administrations to be separated from each other by that same number of years.

5. Four from the Cold Files

Myth! Lincoln and Kennedy were both assassinated on a Friday in the presence of their wives.

The following 'coincidences' in Dr. Matrix' list are not as synchronistic as they appear to be:

• Unlike Garfield and McKinley, Lincoln and Kennedy were assassinated on a Friday in the presence of their wives. Catholics will probably haggle over this point and insist that Lincoln died on a Good Friday whereas JFK died on an ordinary Friday. They and others might also say that the presence of the wife at a high-profile assassination is not really unusual, since most government officials, and especially heads of state, are expected to be seen with their spouses in public places or while heeding the call of duty. What makes the parallel truly uneven is that Lincoln was shot on a Thursday and died on a Friday, while Kennedy was shot and died on a Friday. Dr. Matrix is careful to use the word 'assassinated' in lieu of 'shot', but 'died' would have been more like it. An assassination occurs at the time the act of aggression causing the death is committed and not at the moment the victim dies. The distinction becomes evident when, as in the cases of Presidents Lincoln and Garfield, there is a hiatus between the shooting and the resulting death.

• Lincoln was killed in Ford's Theater, while Kennedy met his death in a Lincoln convertible made by Ford Motor Company. Not to quibble again, but wouldn't it be neater if the Lincoln assassination site were called the Kennedy Theater or Kennedy's car were a standard Ford?

• Both Booth and Oswald were murdered before they could be brought to trial. This is correct, although it has been noted that if Booth had lived, a military commission, probably the same one that tried his co-conspirators, would have tried him. Oswald, on the other hand, would have been brought before the state courts, as in the Garfield and McKinley cases. Assassinating a US president was made a federal offense under a law passed only after the death of JFK.

6. Dear Secretary

Myth! Lincoln's secretary was named Kennedy, and Kennedy's secretary was named Lincoln.

Another supposed coincidence involving Lincoln and Kennedy has to do with the names of their private secretaries. Writers who thrive in trivia 'oddities' have helped promote the belief that

Lincoln's secretary was named Kennedy, based on nothing more than that Kennedy's own private secretary was named Evelyn Lincoln. In fact, Lincoln's private secretary was a man named John Nicolay, and the real coincidence, albeit flimsy, is that, while Evelyn's last name is the same as Abe's, Nicolay's first name is the same as Kennedy's.

In furtherance of the parallel, it is alleged that both secretaries warned their respective bosses not to attend the fatal event. There is hardly anything to prove that this did not happen, but in Kennedy's case at least, it is doubtful that a staff member would have dared ask the president, on the basis of a mere foreboding, to change a decision that he had already made jointly with his political advisers. McKinley's secretary, George B. Cortelyou, had a similar intuition about the misfortune that would befall his president in Buffalo. But instead of telling the President about it, he quietly tried by himself—and failed—to cancel the public reception that McKinley would later attend to shake the hands of, among others, his own assassin.

7. Bullet in the Head

Myth! Kennedy's backward thrust when he was hit proves he was not shot from behind, as Lincoln was.

Dr. Matrix states that a bullet that entered the head from behind killed both Lincoln and Kennedy. The popular belief is that, in the case of Kennedy, this circumstance was contradicted by a short sequence in the Zapruder film showing Kennedy being thrust violently back against the rear seat of the limousine at the moment the bullet hit. According to critics of the Warren Commission, it is a 'manifest impossibility' for this reaction to have been in consequence of the shot being fired from above and behind the President. Those who viewed the film couldn't understand the silence of the Warren Commission, as well as its lawyers, investigators and witnesses, "in regard to this visible evidence clearly implicating at least two riflemen in the crime."

Subsequent to the Warren Commission, another government body—the Rockefeller Commission on the CIA—convened a panel of experts to review the film and other evidence. Its objective was to inquire why the President appeared to move backwards in response to the fatal hit. Some of the panel members were convinced that the unusual movement was due to a 'neuro-muscular reaction' from Kennedy. In 1948 the US Army had filmed studies of the impact of bullets on a hundred goat's heads, demonstrating that a neuromuscular reaction could cause a backward motion even with a shot from behind. Others saw an occurrence of the so-called 'jet recoil effect', by which fragments of bone fly forward so fast that an 'energy transfer mechanism' pulls the rest of the head backward. The panel unanimously affirmed the Warren Commission's conclusion that Kennedy's rearwards motion was caused by a single shot from the rear.

Some of the critics may have been assuaged, but others say that explaining away clear visual proof with a mere theory, as the Rockefeller Commission did, seems like an attempt to justify an already predetermined official position. For this group, the full details of how Kennedy's assassination was carried out would probably be known only at some 'appropriate' time—if that time ever comes.

8. The Mirror has two Faces

Myth! Kennedy and Lincoln are the only American presidents whose assassinations are linked by coincidences.

Considering the weaknesses in the Lincoln-Kennedy dichotomy, some writers deem more impressive the parallels found in the lives—and deaths—of the other two assassinated presidents, Garfield and McKinley. Author Barbara Holland even makes the facetious suggestion that the two were really the same President, since "they were both Republicans from Ohio, both had been senators and congressmen, both died in September from gunshot and doctors, and both had eight letters in their last names." In addition to Miss Holland's list, Garfield and McKinley were elected presidents in a binary year ending in zero and assassinated in a binary year ending in 1. Immigrants who held extremist views, one religious and the other political, killed both. The two assassins were brought to state courts for trial, during which it became obvious that they were mad—an extenuating

100

condition that ordinarily should have prevented their execution. In each case, two shots were fired, with only one shot finding its mark. Both presidents could have been saved following medical procedures in effect today.

After all the foregoing, the only coincidence that seems to matter in the case of Kennedy and Lincoln is the one most everybody is aware of, which is that both were assassinated while holding the office of US President in the prime of their lives. But, alas, even this coincidence wilts into insignificance in the face of the fact that Presidents Garfield and McKinley also died in their primes (Kennedy and Garfield died in their forties, Lincoln and McKinley in their fifties). Indeed, many more US presidents might have exited via an inglorious route at their peaks had there been no Clint Eastwood types in the Secret Service to intervene. Now if you ask an enterprising New Orleans DA and an Oscar-awarded Hollywood director-producer which of the Lincoln-Kennedy coincidences is worthy of attention, they might say it was something the politically correct Dr. Matrix deliberately failed to mention, *viz.*, Lincoln and Kennedy were the only American presidents assassinated under the shadow of a suspected conspiracy

VIII

P As In Pirate

On Pirates of the Golden Age

"Damnation seize my soul if I give you
quarters, or take any from you."

•

Blackbeard

1. Say 'Arr', not 'Arrrgh'

Myth! **Pirates had a distinctive way of speaking.**

Pipe, peg leg, patch, parrot, pierced ear, plank, and pieces of eight—could there possibly be one more 'p' to bless or curse the pirate's stereotypical image? Some enthusiasts say there is, *patois*, which refers collectively to the words, phrases, interjections, idiom, grammar and usage commonly used by, and peculiar to, a disparate group such as pirates. Movies and classic literature would suggest that pirates of the Golden Age had an odd way of talking, rolling their 'r's and their eyes while dishing out original yet colorful expressions. One notable example is the meaningless 'arrr', a growl emitted by the talented Robert Newton, the actor who defined the role of Long John Silver in the 1950 film adaptation of *Treasure Island*. Newton must have been emulating Lionel Barrymore, who was the first to mouth the expression while playing Billy Bones in the 1934 version of the film. Actor Wallace Beery, the original Long John, didn't bother to say 'arrr', and rightly so, since the sound is never spelled out in Stevenson's book. Newton also utters the phrases 'blow me down' and 'shiver my timbers' intermittently in the movie, but in the book Long John occasionally speaks only the latter. Other words that Hollywood scriptwriters have traditionally assigned to pirates, including 'mate', 'avast' and 'swabs', as well as expressions like 'pieces of eight', 'top of the morning', 'aye, aye' and 'a bottle of rum', are spoken only sparsely in Stevenson's adventure novels and mostly by seafaring characters who are not pirates at all.

The obvious conclusion is that there is no such thing as pirate lingo, only sailor language enhanced or corrupted by regional slang and their accompanying accents. This may account for why 'arrr' befits Newton, a Briton from Dorset, England (where many English pirates supposedly hailed from), but not Beery, who was American. This may also be the reason Hollywood never adapted Newton's linguistic style to pirate movies that starred non-English actors like Errol Flynn, Tyrone Power and Douglas Fairbanks Sr. As one Internet source aptly observes, any so-called pirate speech "was most likely underclass British sailor with extra curse words, augmented with a polyglot slang of French, Italian, Spanish, and Dutch picked up around the trade routes."

If there was no patois for British pirates, the more reason there was no patois that bound all pirates from the Caribbean to the Spanish Main. The multi-national character of piracy militated against the idea of a universal lingo for the pirate profession, meaning that French, Dutch and Spanish pirates could not have said 'me hearties' or 'aye, aye, cap'n' except in their own respective languages. The only time one might hear, say, a French pirate speaking idiomatic English would be in a Hollywood movie of the likes of *The Buccaneer* (1958), in which France's infamous Jean Lafitte, *sans* interpreter, discusses a common strategy with Andrew Jackson for the defense of New Orleans against the British.

2. They Smoked and Chewed Tobacco at the Same Time?

Myth! **Many of the pirates of the Golden Age were pipe smokers.**

Our idea of a typical pirate captain comes from Robert Louis Stevenson's classic adventure story *Treasure Island* (1883). The protagonist in question is the colorful but mysterious ship's cook named Long John Silver. We learn from the book that this character's distinguishing features include a peg leg, a pipe and a parrot. Some illustrations would add a fourth 'p', a patch, which is wrong—neither of Long John's eyes is shielded in any manner.

In *Treasure Island*, Long John goes for the pipe while the others in his scurvy lot prefer the pleasure of chewing tobacco—implying that Stevenson added the pipe merely as a glamour fixture to Long John's image. The other pipe smokers mentioned in the novel are the supporting cast of Dr. Livesey and Captain Smollet, but they are not pirates.

Pleasantly surprised that Depp's character Jack Sparrow does not smoke, an anti-tobacco propagandist tells us why she believes that, unlike Sparrow, pirates of the golden age were heavy into pipe smoking. "You would expect to see them smoking," she says, "because pirates are dirty and gross, and because of the time period." The lady's indictment, clearly a *non sequitur*, assumes that tobacco, particularly when smoked from a pipe, is a cause or effect of human dereliction. She hints as well that most of the general male population of the 16th, 17th and 18th centuries, in the areas where piracy flourished, were addicted to pipe smoking—a view that's hardly supported by the evidence. We can be sure tobacco has been prominently used in the West ever since its introduction from the Americas to Europe in the 15th century; however, there is no way we can determine the relative incidence of pipe smoking among various identifiable groups, such as pirates, in any era. On the contrary, the available historical records would indicate that (a) pipe smoking was only one of the ways tobacco was used before cigars and cigarettes became the vogue in the 19th century, and (b) the habit was more popular with the upper than with the lower classes to which pirates presumably belonged.

3. Didja Hear About the Parrot...?

Myth! **The parrot was the favorite pet of Golden age pirates.**

The popular mind relies too easily on the images created by *Treasure Island* when it concludes, among other things, that the favorite pet of Golden Age pirates was the parrot. Long John does have a parrot, which, it is claimed, he named Captain Flint after a real pirate, although the existence of such a person has never been established. Other than this fictional stereotype, there is no evidence that real-life pirates kept pets, much less parrots, on board their ships.

No doubt some animals, such as cats and dogs, were deployed on board to rid the ship's premises of vermin, while other animals, like pigs and chickens, were allowed to roam freely on deck before being slaughtered for food. Pets may have been brought along occasionally, such as on long journeys, but it was most unlikely that a seafarer would keep a parrot when he could have a more useful animal like a dog. To paraphrase an observation, a dog doesn't usually make a mess on one's shoulder, and is not liable to be consumed during hard times at sea.

It was more likely that parrots were seen as exotic animals and, therefore, acquired as 'booty' to be sold or traded ashore. The parrot's bright plumage, its social behavior and its affinity for tricks and mimicry made it especially attractive for owning by royals, courtiers and social climbers as a status symbol.

4. Ocean Viewing in 2D

Myth! The eye patch was a typical pirate appurtenance during the Golden Age.

A typical pirate of the Golden Age was no more prone to wearing an eye patch than any other person of that era who saw a need to protect a defective eye against the light or against infection or even derision. The list Wikipedia has compiled of real and fictional celebrities from all ages who have worn an eye patch only proves that this item has never been unique or common to any distinct group and is as old as when the reason for its use first arose. A researcher notes not surprisingly that there is no known pirate featured in the list, and that he did not see any eye patch in a host of period pictures of pirates he looked at in the course of his own investigation.

The starting point of the myth that the eye patch was a standard part of pirate makeup is obviously the assumption that a pirate's eye often got wounded during his predatory jaunts. How often this happened—or, more precisely, how often pirates resorted to the eye patch for this reason—would probably not be enough to influence the modern image of that outlaw breed, but leave it to Hollywood and writers of period novels to change the trend in order to serve their own ends. Logically, the incidence of eye losses among soldiers who fight in wartime should be higher, yet we don't see many of these veterans wearing eye patches like we do the pirates that cavort on the big and small screens.

Incidentally, the popular TV program *MythBusters* has tested and deemed 'plausible' the idea that pirates used eye patches for a less obvious reason, i.e., to have the uncovered eye adjusted to the light of the top deck of their ship and the covered eye to the darkness when suddenly going below deck. According to Wikipedia, the "strong sunlight while above deck on an oceangoing vessel could require minutes of adjustment to the dim lighting below deck. With virtually no light sources below deck, pirates would have to rely heavily upon their eyes to adjust. In the critical moments of modifying the rigging, navigating, and especially during battle, those minutes were too precious. A simple switch of the patch from one eye to the other saved time and was more convenient than being temporarily blinded when going between decks."

Apparently, the historical basis for the foregoing is the practice, long predating pirates, of maritime navigators looking directly into the sun at high noon with the use of one of their key tools, the cross staff; to prevent or alleviate any potential eye damage, they resorted to the eye patch as a crude but neat solution. This may have been the reason some sailors, navigators and even airline pilots, as late as the 20th century, wore eye patches while on duty, but it's hardly a credible one for pirates, who would have found it both risky and inconvenient in critical or battle situations to use eye patches just to be able to find their way in a ship's hold. A pirate worth his salt would no doubt opt for his full visual capacity at all times, particularly when he has to scan the high seas and estimate the defensive strength of an attractive source of booty.

5. Depp Ears

Myth! Pierced ears were a distinctive trait of Golden Age pirates.

Ah, but are those earrings we see on Johnny Depp, or are his ears just shaped that way?

Some literature supports the view that real pirates did have a common 'p' feature—pierced ears. According to Toby Gibson (cited in David Feldman's *How Do Astronauts Scratch an Itch?* [1996]), movie pirates wear earrings to make them look suave and exotic. Real pirates did too, but their reason was not as evident. Says Gibson: "It was believed that piercing the ears with such precious metals as silver and gold improved one's eyesight. This was the main reason pirates performed such a ritual. It must also be noted that most other seafaring men also indulged in this practice." Movie posters often display both eye patch and earrings on the same individual, as if to say that a half-blinded pirate would grasp at anything to improve the remaining sight in his good eye. Under other circumstances, it's hard to understand why anyone would believe that a useless and inert piece of metal dangling from his ear could possibly benefit his eyesight.

6. Mapping their Future

Myth! **Most pirates of the Golden Age buried their loot for later retrieval.**

Again, thanks to Robert Louis Stevenson's *Treasure Island*, another myth—that of pirates burying their treasure in desert islands—has become widely accepted as fact. Historically, however, pirates distributed the loot among them and sold their shares at the earliest opportunity to brokers or buyers who thrived on the trade. Many were unable to amass wealth because, more often than not, the adventure turned into a fiasco and they went home with nothing.

The idea of pirates burying their plunder might have been inspired by the true story of Captain Kidd, who was rumored to have hidden some booty on Gardiner's Island in Long Island Sound when he heard he was going to be arrested on his return to New York from the high seas. Actually, the authorities recovered practically all of the treasure that Kidd had come by from his limited adventures. None of these had been buried, although the entire amount, which was forfeited to the state, was small compared to the legitimate fortune in Manhattan real estate that Kidd had built before turning pirate.

Since Kidd's days, the legend of pirate treasure has persisted despite little evidence to support the tales. The most sought after by fortune hunters is believed to consist of Spanish dollar coins looted from Spanish merchant vessels, each coin stamped with the figure 8 to indicate it was worth 8 *reales*. Thus, the term 'pieces of eight' has become a pop-culture fictionalization of the historical Spanish dollar, integrating into pirate myth as soon as Long John Silver's parrot Captain Flint squawked "pieces of eight, pieces of eight" in Stevenson's book and later in the movies. The coin was legal tender in the United States until 1857, causing numismatists to speculate that the typographical sign for the US dollar was a variation of the 8 engraved on its face. Wikipedia reports that, through widespread use in Europe, the Americas and the Far East, pieces of eight became the first world currency by the late 18th century and the basis of many existing currencies today, such as the Canadian dollar, the United States dollar and the Chinese yuan, as well as the pesos of Latin America and the Philippines.

7. Where'd he Get those One-legged Johns?

Myth! Pirates of the Golden Age were liable to lose a leg or an arm from swashbuckling.

People tend to forget many of the finer details of the stories they heard in their childhood, especially details that are sometimes presented differently in the media. This may be why a critic claiming to be an aficionado of the pirate genre made a serious lapse once by likening Long John Silver to Douglas Fairbanks, Sr., the silent screen swashbuckler known for his special ability to move on two good and agile legs. Or why an illustrator for an old edition of *Treasure Island* drew Long John walking the deck nimbly as if he were indeed Douglas Fairbanks, Sr. A straight read of Stevenson's classic or a full screening of its film adaptations would have shown both worthies that Long John has his left leg cut to the hip, and he uses a wooden peg for a prosthetic and a crutch to help it along.

This doesn't mean that in the old days, many real-life pirates had the same type of infirmity, and that a ship's cook was always prepared to have an emergency amputation performed on a leg injured during fighting. A historical account mentions an unnamed pirate who was fierce-looking, heavily whiskered, and with a wooden leg and a belt stuffed with pistols. He gained attention when he saved Captain James Macrae of the Cassandra, an East India man, from being killed on the spot by the pirate's mates after they had captured his ship. Though he was not a captain nor did he seem to be a ranking officer in the pirate crew, his appearance is, as far as is known, the only one of a real pirate having a peg leg and looking a bit like Long John.

A 'p' feature not unusual with fictional pirates is the 'Peter Pan hook', so named in allusion to the eponymic left hand displayed by the character Captain Hook in the popular children's classic *Peter Pan* by J.B. Barrie. However, as most real-life pirates were presumably right-handed, the right hand was more liable to be injured from sword fighting than the left. In contrast, Disney placed the hook on his villain's left hand because he "wanted Hook to be able to do things that are usually simpler to do with the right hand." Although in modern times the hook hand has assumed pop culture dimensions as a standard accessory for Halloween costumes, it was, like the peg leg, rarely seen on real pirates. The myth has no doubt arisen from the unwarranted belief that when a pirate lost a hand in battle, the first thing he did was to search for a useful and easy-to-construct substitute, like a metal hook, which would be 'handy' around the ship.

To be sure, pirates of the hardy type carried the scars of battle on the high seas. Still, it was rare for anyone with a major physical impairment, like having only one leg or one hand, to stay on as a fighting man, much less a captain.

8. Dead Man Walking

Myth! **Walking the plank was the pirates' most popular form of capital punishment.**

Finally, a 'p' to end all 'p's, and a pirate's career as well—the plank.

The famous artist *cum* author Howard Pyle cut an engraving in 1887 of a blindfolded captive standing on a narrow plank laid over the side of a pirate ship, the threat of the cutlass forcing him to walk the length of the board until his inevitable plunge into the sea. The work is believed to have inspired the popular belief that 'walking the plank' was the typical method of execution employed by pirates on the high seas during the 17th and early 18th centuries. The phrase itself has become a popular English metaphor for being forced out of an office or position.

It's what Hollywood since the inception of movies has imagined it to be, but experts think it's wrong. Pirates, they insist, were a down-to-earth lot who engaged in little ceremony, preferring to dispatch their victims in the most direct manner by heaving them overboard dead or alive. Where some protocol was to be observed because of the rank of the victim or the gravity of the crime, pirates resorted to marooning. This called for putting the offender ashore on some inhospitable and sometimes hostile desert islet, to be left there to die. The place selected for the prisoner was far from the romantic haven awash with vegetation that Robert Louis Stevenson depicted in his novel. Marooning, though nonviolent, was intended to be a torturous death sentence. The convicted man was usually left with a pistol "so that he might take his own life, thus ending his misery in this world but condemning his Christian soul to hell for all eternity."

One historian says he knows of "only one report of a sailor being made to walk the plank; on the ship of Derdrake, a Danish pirate, around 1700." However, not being documented, even this report is of doubtful authenticity. Another account, equally suspect, is of Bartholomew Roberts terminating his captives by this method. David Feldman says that Patrick Pringle, the most prestigious historian to write extensively about pirates, could not find a single instance of walking the plank during the Golden Age. The practice may have been mentioned once or twice in sea journals, but it did not concern pirates.

9. Flagging Concerns

Myth! The skull and crossbones were the usual symbols on a pirate flag.

If the movies are to be believed, the typical pirate flag, called the Jolly Roger, is a white skull and crossbones on a black background. The quaint name is said to have originated from the Malayan title Ali Rajah, or 'King of the Sea'. The Ali Rajahs of the 17th century roamed the South China Sea in native watercraft, attacking all forms of shipping—and even coastal villages—in pursuit of booty. Sea pirates that still thrive in this part of Asia (one of the few places in the world for this kind of activity today) have little in common with their ancestors in both hemispheres. One thing is certain: a modern-day pirate worth his salt chooses high-tech gizmos over slogans, flags and symbols, especially where stealth and surprise are required to ensure success against a heavily armed or secured vessel.

Contrary to popular myth, the skull and crossbones was not a standard pirate's emblem. Notable pirates like James Plantain flew this classic configuration, but its use was not universal. No single pirate flag stood out in the 17th and 18th centuries. Solid red or black flags were as popular as the graphic ones, which showed skulls and bones as well as skeletons, swords, devils, wineglasses and hourglasses.

The reason for thinking that the skull and crossbones was the favorite pirate flag arose from a mistake. Austria, which had no navy of its own, was notorious for issuing so-called Letters of Marque in return for a split of pirate booty. The Letters were a set of documents serving as Austria's official authority for privateers to fly the Austrian flag while plundering ships hostile to that country. The flag's imperial black spread eagle with two heads against a yellow background resembled a skull and cross-bones from a distance.

10. The Gin tasted Rummy

Myth! **Rum was the favorite drink of pirates.**

Most pirates were notorious drinkers. After looting a ship, they would often hide out on desert islands or disembark at friendly ports, seeking to entertain themselves by singing, dancing and staging mock trials as a way of exalting their deeds. During all this time, they would be drinking their favorite concoctions, getting boozed up and becoming totally oblivious of their surroundings. Disneyland's caricature of pirates slumped in every conceivable position after filling themselves to the gills with heady stuff may not be too far from the truth.

The popular belief that rum was the favorite drink of pirates when carousing probably stems from the famous ditty that ends with the refrain, "Yo-ho-ho, and a bottle of rum." But it is likely the word 'rum' is used here, as in much of pirate literature, to mean any kind of liquor. If pirates had any special liking for rum, this was probably dictated less by taste than by circumstance. Being sugar-cane-based, rum was ubiquitous in those days and was easily produced by natives in the Caribbean. This general availability of the brew notwithstanding, pirates preferred brandy, which was the classier drink and was considered a prized item of plunder from merchant ships that plied the Atlantic route.

11. Hook and Blood in the Movies

Myth! **Pirate attacks on the high seas are depicted accurately in most Hollywood movies.**

When pirate flicks were in vogue, the most exciting action scene that fed the viewer's imagination was of a huge pirate ship cannonading and pulling up alongside another ship, and then disgorging swarms of cutthroats that swung across on ropes and unmercifully slashed their way directly to the hold where the loot was kept. The same films would oftentimes soften the violence by providing romantic interludes for the principal characters, usually the pirate captain and the daughter of a noble or wealthy family traveling on the ravaged ship. Hollywood trivialized the image further by employing incredible stunts, glamorous actors and light-hearted plots that border on satire.

Experts say that in real life, pirate ships were not as large as those seen on the screen, but were small, swift vessels that could be relied on for hit-and-run attacks. Moreover, most ship captains owned their cargoes, which were usually fully insured. Rather than risk their lives protecting them, they preferred to surrender the minute they were approached by a pirate ship. As merchants, they regarded piracy as simply one of the costs of doing business.

Hollywood's idea of pirates becoming romantically inclined on the high seas is also unrealistic in light of the unwritten provision in the golden days that barred women from pirate ships. Conceivably, there were female pirates who could be seduced by their shipmates, guests or captives, but this was not known to happen except in heavily fantasized movies such as the 1952 *Against All Flags*, in which Maureen O'Hara played a lady buccaneer who falls in love with a government operative portrayed by (who else?) Errol Flynn. In history, the romantic incidents in the life of Anne Bonny, daughter of a plantation owner who married a small-time pirate and subsequently ran off with a pirate captain, had already transpired before she herself turned pirate disguised as a man. Finally, except for the usual chance encounters

113

with slaves, prostitutes and other female lowlifes, there were few opportunities for pirates to get involved in serious on-shore relationships considering their highly transient status.

12. Sir Harry Meets Billy the Kidd

Myth! Captain Kidd and Henry Morgan were typical English pirates.

One would have thought William Kidd was English, but he was actually Scottish and he was not a pirate strictly speaking. This son of a Presbyterian minister was a respectable ship owner from New York who became a privateer only because he was asked by the English authorities to engage in that task as an agent of the Crown.

Hired by the King to hunt pirate ships and French vessels down, he was forced by circumstances to attack two private ships, once when he ran out of provisions and another to prevent a mutiny by his crew. He killed his gunner by walloping him on the head with a bucket, but the gunner had been rebellious, and the killing, the only one Kidd could be linked to, looked more like an accident. His men eventually joined another pirate ship, and when Kidd was asked to cooperate, he sailed home instead.

Accused of pirating by the East India Company, he was railroaded through a trial in which his defense—that the ships he had attacked had French safe-conduct passes—was suppressed by the prosecution. After conviction by the very same politicians who had pressured him into accepting his royal commission as a privateer, Kidd was hanged from the gibbet while five of the men convicted with him were reprieved. Many believe Kidd was the victim of political machination and did not deserve his fate.

Henry Morgan, a Kidd contemporary but not an associate, was a Welshman who came to the West Indies in 1655 as an ensign in the English army, and soon afterward took command of a privateer vessel, looting his merry way through Spanish cities in America. He and his cohorts termed themselves buccaneers, which meant they limited their prey to vessels belonging to the enemy of their country. Morgan in particular insisted that all their depredations— no matter how piratical—be directed only against the Spaniards, then at war with England. After mending his ways, Morgan was knighted and appointed lieutenant governor of Jamaica.

In 1684 John Esquemeling, one of Morgan's former crew members, published the book *Buccaneers of America*, giving a colorful account of their adventures. Morgan sued the publishers, winning damages and apologies with the argument that he was not a pirate but a government agent.

13. Ain't he a Jolly Rogue?

Myth! The pirate term 'Jolly Roger' comes from the Malayan word Ali Rajah, or 'King of the Sea'.

About the middle of the eighteenth century, the pirate flag became known to the English as a Jolly Roger despite no one being able to give a cogent historical reason. Its supposed link to the Malayan title Ali Rajah, or 'King of the Sea', which the natives uttered in awe of the pirates that used to ply the South China Sea and the East Indies, has no basis except the apparent similarity in sound of the two phrases. An equally speculative source is *joli rouge* (pretty red), a wry French description of the bloody banner flown by early privateers and regular navies. When hoisted before battle, it meant no quarter would be expected or accepted—in other words, a fight to the death.

The British themselves may not know that 'Old Roger' was once a familiar English word for the devil, whose face or figure decorated many a pirate flag. This could be why people started to call a flag that showed a grinning devil or skull a 'Jolly Roger'. One historian, offering an etymological possibility, says 'Roger' was then pronounced with a hard 'g', and among members of the underworld, the name had long been applied to a beggar or rogue. Jolly meant 'carefree', and the two combined in Jolly Roger could have been a reference to carefree rogues seeking booty, such as what pirates were thought to be. Assigning as it does an appropriate indigenous origin to a quaintly English term, this last theory ranks as the most plausible.

14. When beached Sharks Lose their Teeth

Myth! The typical pirate was authoritative, totalitarian and completely ruthless on land and sea.

Surprisingly, many pirates led ordinary private lives, particularly while sojourning on land after an adventure, with some even becoming patrons of coastal towns and cities. And on the high seas, ethical rules often guided their conduct. Thus, prisoners were allowed to join the pirates or sail off on their own ships. In return, authorities imposed light penalties, granting reprieves to some and returning confiscated booty to others.

Pirates, who disliked overbearing authority and class distinctions, elected their captain mainly for his leadership and naval knowledge rather than his dueling superiority. They could depose him at will. Once elected, he became a figure of authority only in the heat of battle, leading by command and example.

In most situations, pirates were extremely democratic, with major decisions taken by a show of hands. At times, the captain's authority was subordinated to that of others who were deemed to know better. The quartermaster, for instance, determined the sharing and disposition of the booty, while pirate courts were preferred to the captain's mediation in the settlement of disputes. Pirates often operated under a document that had some similarity to a constitution. It defined the powers of the captain, the sharing of booty, the penalties to be meted acts, and the amount of rewards or payment for injuries.

15. Those Yankee Buccaneers

Myth! The US was one of the earliest to outlaw piracy on the high seas.

Many today would be surprised to know that the United States at one time did not only tolerate a form of piracy but actually legalized it. In its Constitution of 1787, a specific provision authorized Congress to issue 'letters of marque and reprisal', allowing a private person to attack and capture merchant ships belonging to an enemy country. This was a time when international convention recognized the rights of nations to issue such letters guaranteeing that a privateer shall not technically be charged with piracy while attacking the targets named in his commission. Robert Morris, the first American millionaire, partly became wealthy from privateering, and George Washington, the first US president, owned part of at least one privateer ship. American and British privateers were heavily involved in the Revolutionary War and the War of 1812, attacking enemy vessels according to their official missions but looting them for private gain. The USA was not one of the initial signatories of the 1856 Declaration of Paris, which outlawed privateering, and would agree to abide by its terms only during the American Civil War, when the Confederates commissioned privateers from many nations.

A privateer would be considered a pirate if captured by the country whose vessels it attacked. Spanish authorities, for instance, were known to execute foreign privateers with their letters of marque hung around their necks to emphasize Spain's rejection of such defenses. Privateers like Thomas Tew of Rhode Island often skirted the edges of piracy, exceeding the bounds of their letters of marque by attacking nations with which their country was at peace, and thus made themselves liable to conviction for piracy. The Spaniards considered the most famous privateer of any nationality, the Englishman Sir Francis Drake, a pirate because of his indiscriminate plundering of Spanish ships and New World forts even in peacetime.

IX

Salem's Blot

On the Witches of Salem

"Ah! destructive Ignorance, what shall be done
to chase thee out of the World!"

•

Cotton Mather

1. The Town that Cast a Spell

Myth! The infamous witch trials of 1692-93 were held entirely in Salem, Massachusetts.

The main attraction of modern Salem as a tourist town is its past—one remembered mostly for the deadly witch-hunt it pursued with neighboring jurisdictions between February 1692 and May 1693 under lawful pretenses. A series of hearings before local magistrates was followed by county court trials seeking to prosecute people accused of witchcraft in Essex, Suffolk, and Middlesex Counties of colonial Massachusetts.

Despite being generally known as the Salem witch trials, the low-level hearings were held in a variety of towns across the province, including, along with Salem Town, Salem Village, Ipswich and Andover. The event took its name from the sessions conducted by the Court of Oyer and Terminer in 1692 in Salem Town, culminating in the conviction of all the twenty-six persons who were charged before it. Other sessions were those of the Superior Court of Judicature in 1693, of which only one was in Salem Town and the rest were in Ipswich, Boston, and Charlestown; these produced a mere three convictions out of the thirty-one who were tried.

Although Salem Town and Salem Village were geographically and politically united at the time, their residents were at odds because of the existence of two factions in the Village, one wanting to separate from the Town and the other to remain with it. In 1752, Salem Village finally split from Salem Town and changed its name to Danvers. This left Salem Town as the only one of the several communities involved carrying the name—and the stigma—of the Salem witch trials until modern times. Ironically, the rash of 'afflictions' that befell the supposed victims of the witchcraft occurred mainly in Salem Village, and of the twenty 'witches' executed by the court, ten were from the Village and none was from Salem Town. The rest were residents of Amesbury, Ipswich, Topsfield, Andover and Marblehead, with one, a retired minister, drifting into the scene from as far away as Wells, Maine. Also, of the four accused 'witches' who died in prison while awaiting trial, one was from Salem Village and none was from Salem Town.

Salem Village, later Danvers, should have borne the full brunt of the scandal but for the redeeming factor of one of its residents, John Proctor, blowing the whistle on the witch-hunt and inspiring the leading heroic character in Arthur Miller's *The Crucible*. Proctor hailed originally from Ipswich and afterwards settled in Salem Village, among a community that would send him in the end to the same dreadful fate as the others. As it happened, the onus fell on Salem Town, ironically the only town that could have avoided responsibility were it not the venue for some of the hearings and the site of Gallows Hill, where all the convicted 'witches' were hanged. Although Salem Town's ignominy has turned into a boon over the years thanks to its enterprising elders, sympathizers insist it should never have been blamed for this unwanted moment in American history.

2. Necks on the Line and Lives at Stake

Myth! Salem was the first to hang a 'witch' in colonial America, while England had the most number of 'witch' killings in the Old World.

The image of Salem, Massachusetts, as Witch City is encouraged by officials and elders to promote tourism, but contrary to what that image may imply, Salem was not the first to hang a 'witch' in America. An old woman in Boston had been hanged in 1688, four years before the first execution in Salem. Between that date and 1692, there were 200 more incidents involving 'witches' in New England, ending in the deaths of more than 25 victims. Neither was Salem the end of the witchcraft hysteria. Andover in Massachusetts and some towns in Maine had their share of witch hunting before America wrote finis to the whole sordid affair.

Because of the Puritans' noted aversion to witches, the popular belief is that England as the seat of Cromwellian Puritanism put the most number of witches to death. In reality, English witches were executed not for their witchcraft *per se* but for using the 'black arts' to cause harm to King or country. Unless the act committed qualified as treason, death would not be meted to a condemned person just for being a witch. There were many more executions in either Germany or France, where the typical killing was by fire and the motivation was religious rather than political. In a 13-year period in the German city of Bamberg alone, 900 alleged witches were burned in the mid-17th century, earning that region the title of 'shrine of horror' in all of Europe. Another 5,000 were killed in the French province of Alsace, along the Rhine border of Germany. While most of the witch-hunt had a religious or supernatural flavor, a few cases were pursued for profit or gain, as when the accuser expected to come into the property of the condemned. At times also, inquisitions launched by the Roman Catholic and Protestant churches were ostensibly to seek out witches and sorcerers, but the real purpose was to aid the state in weeding out political enemies.

3. According to 'Wiccapedia'

Myth! The Salem witch trials were inspired by the on-going persecution of witches in Europe in the 17th century.

It is often suggested that the Puritan loathing for witches was inspired by the experience of the Christian Church in Europe in medieval times. Using its strong influence during this troubled period, the Church had succeeded in convincing the masses that witchcraft was a potentially harmful force and that witches should be put to death.

Critics debunk this view, saying that, had the Salem elders only bothered to keep an eye on European history, they would have thought twice before embarking on their infamous witch-hunt. They would have realized that, in earlier times, the Christian fathers of the Old World were in total denial as far as witchcraft was concerned. In the pre-medieval era, the Church as much as European society generally ignored the existence of witches, often to the point of declaring that belief in these beings was a sin. St. Augustine of Hippo, who proclaimed in the early 5th century that witches were not supernatural beings and not worth bothering with, was affirmed by Saint Boniface in the 8th century, and the idea was eventually accepted into Canon law.

When, later, the Church decided to unleash the witch-hunts, it was not because witchcraft was causing any perceived material harm, but because it was believed to be professing spiritual doctrines opposed to Church teachings. Beginning in the 13th century, heresies emerged proclaiming the supernatural qualities of Satan and his minions, and these pressed Church defenders such as Pope Innocents III and VIII and St. Thomas Aquinas into reversing their official position on witchcraft and witches. On the pretext of supporting the Church, rulers took similar action to ferret out the political enemies of the state. Foremost of the witch-hunting despots was the paranoid King James of Scotland, who, true to the Biblical mandate (in the version he sponsored), "suffered no witch to live" for nearly a decade; his burning of witches in the North Berwick area was the culmination of the largest witch-hunt in British history. But there were also enlightened rulers, such as King Coloman of Hungary, who would seek an end to witch-hunting at least in their areas of influence by reiterating that witches do not exist.

What is most important, however, is that the persecution of witches in Europe had already abated by the time of the Salem occurrence. The number of trials began to drop sharply in the late 1640s, and by 1648, Holland, original homeland of some of the Puritans, was a tolerant society that had done away with punishments for witchcraft. In the 1680s, the Enlightenment began to bring with it empirical reason, skepticism, and humanitarianism; the movement contributed to the end of witch-hunts throughout Europe and generally helped to defeat the superstitions of the previous age. Ten years before the Salem trials, Temperance Lloyd, a senile woman from Bideford, became the last witch ever to be executed in England.

Even after Salem, institutions and individuals, including members of the Church hierarchy, have not stopped condemning witchcraft either as a form of Satanism or as inextricably linked with it. Horror fanciers continue to spread the belief that witches conduct devilish rituals ranging from sex orgies in the woods to animal worship or sacrifice. Rumors persist that practices are sometimes taken to the extreme, e.g., innocent people are hexed, malevolent spirits are invoked, or impossible feats are attempted. Witches are caricatured as 'wicked old women with wrinkled skin and pointy hats, clothed in black or purple, with warts on their noses and sometimes long claw-like fingernails'. These 'creatures of the night' are seen concocting potions in large cauldrons, and heard cackling as they ride through the air on broomsticks accompanied by black cats. The stereotype images of witches generated, on the one hand, by imaginative confessions and reports of close encounters, and on the other, by fairy tales (Grimm's *Hansel and Gretel*), young people's fiction (*Harry Potter*), classic literature (*Shakespeare*) and Hollywood fantasy fare (*Bedknobs and Broomsticks, The Wizard of Oz, The Craft, The Blair Witch Project*), have all become part of pop culture. Whether they ought to be a credible part is, of course, another matter. As both the Enlightenment and the aftermath of the Salem trials have demonstrated, there is no empirical evidence to even imply that alleged witches cause real harm to persons other than possibly the practitioners themselves.

Wiccans (modern witches) concede "there are Satanic Witches out there, since Witchcraft can work with many different theological systems, and Satanism can be considered a Pagan religion." But they are apparently a very small minority and probably harmless. On the whole, witches are normal and law-abiding. They "are scientists, lawyers, mechanics, and waitresses. (They're) on the PTA, take the kids to soccer, and shop at the same grocery stores and malls. (They're) sitting next to you on the bus or the plane, browsing next to you in the bookstores. (They're) different in many ways, but they're still a part of society."

4. Toil and Trouble

Myth! All the 'witches' that died in Salem were duly tried, convicted and executed.

Over 150 people were arrested and imprisoned, with even more accused whom the authorities did not formally pursue. The two courts convicted twenty-nine people of the capital felony of witchcraft. Nineteen of those convicted were executed as 'witches', while four more awaiting trial passed away in prison. Thus, a total of 23 individuals died at Salem in 1692, although not all were strictly 'witches'—at least five were males and should be called 'warlocks' or 'wizards' instead.

In addition to the 23, one—the husband of a convicted 'witch'—was also killed even though he was not himself tried and convicted. An octogenarian named Giles Corey, he was crushed to death under a pile of stones for refusing to plead either yes or no to the charge against him (in the movie but not in the play, Corey was killed for refusing to name a witness). His obstinacy has often been explained as a tactic to prevent the authorities from depriving his heirs of his property, which, under the law, would have been sold at auction had he confessed or been found guilty—and he would surely have been convicted even if he had denied the charge. However, some historians doubt this was Corey's real reason, as there had been occasions when the possessions of persons accused but not convicted were confiscated before a trial, as in the case of Corey's neighbor John Proctor and some wealthy Englishmen of Salem Town. They hypothesize that Giles acted not out of concern for his heirs, who were well off, but in accordance with his character, which preferred quiet disobedience to positive resistance. This stubborn and defiant old man knew he was to be convicted anyway, and so decided on martyrdom as the best means of calling attention to the unfairness of the system that was gearing up to condemn him.

It is frequently missed in most accounts that two animals were pronounced guilty and hanged with the 19 human 'witches'. These were dogs believed to be of the same devilish ilk as the others, although it is not clear if they were killed as witches or only as accomplices. Regardless, this brings to 26 the total number of deaths that occurred in connection with the witch trials in Salem.

---

5. Hanging Jury

Myth! The Salem witch trials were eventually voided for lack of due process.

There is no definite indication that the Salem witch trials were ever impugned for lack of due process. It is true that on October 17, 1711, an Order of Compensation signed by Governor J. Dudley reversed the attainders of 22 of the 31 convicted in Salem, with damages awarded to the heirs. This was an executive pardon, however, and did not reflect on the integrity of the convictions. Moreover, seven women inexplicably never received its benefits. Some believe a 1957 resolution of the General Court of Massachusetts corrected the defect, but a closer reading reveals it merely absolved the descendants of 'disgrace or cause of distress'. This implied that the conviction, though manifestly unjust, was in compliance with due process as then understood.

Due process in those days was defined to a large degree by the Puritan ministry, represented by its stalwart Increase Mather, the president of Harvard University in 1692. Playing an influential role in determining the conduct of the Salem witch trials, Increase published treatises that urged moderation in the use and credence of 'spectral evidence', in the same breath defending the judges and trials that used them. A critic says his refusal to repudiate completely the lack of due process in Salem was likely because of his longtime friendship and religious affinity with the judges involved. Increase attended only one of the trials, that of George Burroughs, Jr., a fellow Puritan minister and Harvard co-graduate, and he seems to have fully agreed with the result. His son Cotton Mather, another prominent Puritan minister, insisted on proceeding with the hanging of Burroughs even after the latter had recited the Lord's Prayer faultlessly before the scaffold. Burrough's accomplishment was a sign to the townsfolk that he was no witch, but Cotton reminded them that the accused was duly convicted in a court of law. It didn't seem to cause the Mathers any concern that many of the depositions against Burroughs were obtained only after his trial and execution in order to help bolster the verdict.

6. Congressional Witch List

Myth! Arthur Miller's 'The Crucible' does not depart in any major way from the true incidents at Salem.

Some critics believe Arthur Miller wrote the play *The Crucible* to address the moral and political issues arising from Senator McCarthy and the House Un-American Activities Committee's crusade against supposed communist sympathizers. Others say the play was 'self-contained', i.e., it had no objective other than to portray the events surrounding the Salem witch trials. Miller probably had both in mind, admitting as much in his 'Why I Wrote the Crucible: An Artist's Answer to Politics'.

His real purpose notwithstanding, Miller used an exceedingly free hand to fictionalize the Salem incident, an Internet source listing as many as 22 variances between the play and the actual happening. A major discrepancy is the affair between John Proctor and the minister's teenage niece Abigail Williams, which could not have happened because, in real life, Williams was probably about eleven at the time of the accusations while Proctor was over sixty. Another is the slave woman Tituba, who is made black in the movie Miller scripted when she was actually of American Indian descent.

The Hollywood movie goes astray when it suggests that the hysteria died down due to the martyrdom of John Proctor, who, by refusing to allow the publication of his false confession, inspired more and more people to refuse to save themselves by giving false confessions. In fact, the Proctor incident encouraged the opposite reaction, as it became more apparent that only a confession could save the remaining accused from the noose. What ended the trials was the belated intervention of Governor William Phips, who came forward at last to pardon the defendants and impose control on the local authorities.

Despite various theories on what could have caused the 'afflictions' in Salem (e.g., ergotism, encephalitis lethargica and menorrhagia), no scientific explanation has been credible enough to pass the scrutiny of medical and history scholars. It is evident, however, that non-physiological reasons, such as politics, family squabbles, religion, economics and the imaginations and fears of people, contributed to an even greater degree to the tragedy.

7. The Broom is out of the Closet

Myth! **The traditional witches' tools for the practice of the black art are bell, book and candle.**

Any lesson to be learned from the unfortunate events at Salem seems to have passed us by because we feel the same negative way about witches. Popular media have not helped any; some movies, like *The Wizard of Oz* (1939) and *Bell, Book and Candle* (1958), tell us that witches can be good, but others, notably *Rosemary's Baby* (1968) and *The Witches* (1990), confirm the worst of our

126

childhood fears about these sinister beings. Today, witchcraft is considered a form of black art regardless of whether its members are called white or black.

People don't realize, of course, that in the original sense of 'black art', witches hardly count as real practitioners. According to Rawson, black art is a product of folk etymology that has nothing to do with color, night or evil. It was taken directly from the Old French *nigromancie*, which was in turn taken from the Medieval Latin *nigromantia*. These sources are corruptions of the Greco-Latin *necromantia*, compounded from the Greek *nekrós*, dead body, and *manteía*, divination. Black art originally referred to necromancers, who foretold the future by examining corpses.

The movie *Bell, Book and Candle* corrected a misconception about white witches, but with a title suggesting that a bell, a book and a candle are the tools of a witch's trade, it created another. The triplet 'bell, book and candle' is the popular phrase for ceremonial excommunication in the Roman Catholic Church, and has nothing to do with the black arts. After pronouncing sentence the officiating cleric closes the book from which it is read, quenches the candle by throwing it to the ground (to create darkness for the soul of the excommunicated person), and tolls the bell as for one who has died.

8. Burning Issue

Myth! Some of those convicted at the Salem witch trials were burned at the stake.

The 'witches' of Salem were not burned at the stake despite the traditional image of a witch being destroyed in this manner. Those condemned were sent to the gallows, which was the proper method of execution prescribed for capital cases in the American colonies. Burning was considered a heinous penalty and was never allowed anywhere in New England.

The Puritans were erroneously thought to have brought the idea of witch burning from England. Despite the common belief, a witch was never dispatched by this method in that country. But in most other places in Europe, notably Germany, France and Scotland, the fiery stake was the most common form of capital punishment for sorcery because it was believed to be the best or only way of ensuring that the witches did not return.

Wars
&
Revolutions

I

An Affair To Remember

On the Battle of the Alamo

"Throughout the day no time for memorandums now.
Go ahead! Liberty and independence forever."

•

Davy Crockett

1. Counterfeit Heroes

Myth! The Alamo was defended to the last by men who were willing to die for a principle.

That the Alamo was defended to the last man eulogizes the San Antonio event but has little regard for the facts. According to some historians, five (others say seven) Americans, including Davy Crockett, were taken prisoner, tortured and executed. They would have been spared if only Mexican General Manuel Fernandez Castrillon had had his way. Unfortunately, General Antonio López de Santa Anna overruled Castrillon and had them killed. This was evidently in compliance with Santa Anna's own directive that US citizens and other "foreigners" found fighting in Texas be classified as pirates and, upon capture, executed immediately.

Others argue that the ones captured were only those who, like the seriously wounded, were in no condition to fight, and who would not have surrendered especially knowing there was no way of surviving under Santa Anna. Be this as it may, pragmatists decline to see any need to propagate the belief that the defenders of the Alamo fought to the last man. As one of them puts it: "The real story of the Alamo is good enough as is. The defenders had shown remarkable courage in fighting at all rather than surrendering right from the first." Idealists are not convinced. They say the story that the defenders went down fighting must be retold as often as necessary to avoid the innuendo that American heroism at the Alamo was less than voluntary. Unfortunately, the claims that the defenders remained only because they were expecting to be rescued by reinforcements, and that Travis was alone in insisting that the fortress be defended despite Houston's orders to abandon it, have proved to be more than just innuendo. Travis was prepared to risk his life and those of others to bring home a point, but later on, even this proud and impulsive man retracted his position by offering to surrender the fort to Santa Ana if every American life would be spared. The Mexican general turned him down, and the rest is, as they say, history.

2. Crossing the Line

Myth! **Commander Travis of the Alamo forces drew a line in the dirt and asked those unwilling to surrender to the enemy to step across it.**

Given an ultimatum to surrender by General Santa Ana, commander William Travis called all the men and stood before them. He drew a line in the dirt and asked those willing to fight for Texas independence to step across it. All except one did.

Unfortunately for hagiographers, the story is hearsay, lacks plausibility and was published too late. The anecdote appeared in an account published forty years after the fact by a man who claimed his parents had told him the story as it was related to them by one Louis 'Moses' Rose, a fifty-year-old decorated but illiterate French veteran in Napoleon's Army. Rose admitted to being the man who, if the anecdote is to be believed, decided to flee rather than cross the line.

Many doubt the veracity of Moses' account about Travis' actuations in the light of the American's own 'unheroic' background. Before going to Texas, Travis had lived in Alabama, where he killed a man who made advances on his wife. A short time later he left her pregnant and with a son and moved to Texas, swearing under oath in one place that he was a widower and in another that he was a simple bachelor. Not a few insist Moses' story should be given credit anyway as an admission against interest; by asserting that he had refused Travis' challenge and fled the garrison, Moses had in effect branded himself an unprincipled coward. This inference notwithstanding, Moses' claim has never been validated and he remains listed in some monuments as one of the Alamo heroes who died.

3. Cutler's Last Stand

Myth! **Jim Bowie, inventor of the bowie knife, was one of the freedom fighters that fought to the death at the Alamo.**

Certain details in Jim Bowie's life dress up the man as an authentic Texas hero. For example, it is reputed that, before dying at the Alamo for Texas independence, he killed many of the attackers with his famed bowie knife.

Bowie is popular as a freedom fighter and an inventor to boot, but the little known fact is he is neither. There are Hollywood films of him going down fighting at the Alamo, contradicting real-life accounts that he was butchered in his sickbed after the attacking Mexicans had captured the fort. It is said the cause he died for was Texas independence, but his background betrays his real purpose, which was to preserve the institution of slavery in what was then Mexican territory. He was not a Texan but a Kentuckian whose pro-slavery sentiments dated back to the days when he and his two brothers John and Rezin engaged actively in the slave trade in Louisiana in the 1820s, smuggling blacks into the country from the great pirate Jean Lafitte's stronghold on Galveston Island.

Jim has long been identified with the bowie, a strong hunting knife with a blade ten to fifteen inches long, double-edged and curving near the point. He may have lent his name to the weapon, but it was another Bowie—his brother Rezin Pleasant—who invented it in the early 1820s. More precisely, Rezin designed it, then had it fashioned by a blacksmith named Jesse Cliffe out of a blacksmith's rasp. Jim carried the blade all the time and made it famous beginning with the day in 1827 when a duel on a sandbar in Mississippi near Natchez ended in a general melee. Six of the seconds and spectators were killed and fifteen wounded in the confusion. The rumor was that Jim inflicted all the wounds single-handedly with his knife, but in fact, he killed only one, a Major Norris Wright. The knife attracted so much attention that Bowie sent it to a cutler in Philadelphia, who marketed copies under the Bowie name until it became standard equipment for the American frontiersman.

4. A Monumental Error

Myth! The Alamo defenders were fighting for the cause of Texas independence.

No matter what folk history may tell us, the Alamo defenders were not fighting for Texas independence. They were fighting for something less noble—the right to own and exploit slaves. Most of the Americans had come from the southern states, bringing their slaves along, to colonize Texas upon the invitation of the Mexican government. But on April 6, 1830, the same government passed a law outlawing slavery. When Santa Ana rose to power, he began to enforce the Mexican ban on slavery strictly, and the colonists rebelled. The cause of independence, along with opposition to customs regulations, the required use of Spanish and the absence of trial by jury, was offered as justification to give a moral and political backbone to the real goal—slavery.

Ironically, most of the 'Texans' who died fighting at the Alamo had never been in Texas before the first few weeks of 1836. Some had just arrived from the Southern states of Tennessee, Kentucky and the Carolinas, others from the Northern states of New York, Pennsylvania and Ohio. It is quite likely these out-of-towners had the same general purpose in coming to Texas as the more than thirty would-be settlers in their group that had immigrated from Europe, mainly Britain, Germany and Denmark. All of the newcomers were Caucasians, except for the few black menials and slaves they brought along. Of the very small group that could be considered old Texas hands, six were Texas-born Tejano Mexicans. Apparently, a good majority of the men who lived in Texas prior to the revolution against Mexico chose not to join the cause. Analysts say these indications are as good as any that independence from Mexico was not foremost in the minds of the Alamo defenders.

5. The End of the Affair

Myth! The highly organized Alamo defense inflicted heavy losses on the attackers before eventually succumbing to overwhelming forces.

As portrayed on the movie screen and in popular literature, the battle is about 183 intrepid Americans deployed in a fortress, methodically killing 1,500 of a 4,000-man Mexican army before they themselves are wiped out.

But a Mexican eyewitness account painted an entirely different picture. Santa Ana's troops, which were underpaid, ill fed and poorly trained, had been exhausted by a grueling march over the desert. Without waiting for his artillery, and losing the advantage of surprise, Santa Ana made a rash attack on the strategically valueless target, an old crumbling mission that offered no real threat. He had heard that the Americans were on the verge of surrendering, but he didn't want to win without some battlefield heroics first.

With a clumsy system of dual leadership that had the regulars answering to William Travis and the volunteers to Jim Bowie, the Americans turned out to be as disorganized in their defense as the Mexicans were in their assault. The Texans moreover had not bothered to store much food or ammunition, and did not have enough men to defend the place.

The assault was a nightmare. The Mexicans commenced firing while still out of range, and for lack of ladders scrambled over the walls on the backs of their fellows. Once the Mexicans were inside, the battle degenerated into a melee, with soldiers shooting at their comrades as often as at the enemy. American losses are variously given as 182, 188 and 253, including non-combatants, while the Mexicans lost more than 300—not 1,500 as is generally believed.

II

Splendid Little Wars

On America's Minor Wars

"If there is not the war, you don't get the
great general...if Lincoln had lived in a time of peace,
no one would have known his name."

•

Theodore Roosevelt

1. Woody and the Teddy Bear

Myth! Called the Rough Riders, the main US contingent in Cuba during the Spanish-American War made a full charge on horseback up San Juan Hill under the personal leadership of their commander Teddy Roosevelt.

It is not well known that Roosevelt's famous Rough Riders actually became foot soldiers for at least two months of the Spanish-American War. The US shipped the Rough Riders to Cuba, but there was only enough room on the boat for 560 men and no room at all for their 1,200 horses and pack mules. While the horses waited it out in Florida, the entire cavalry unit charged on foot up San Juan Hill. The panorama is captured realistically in Frederic Remington's *Charge of the Rough Riders at San Juan Hill* (1909), debunking the popular image—preserved in works of art kept in the Bettmann Archive—that everyone on the offensive was on horseback.

Furthering the myth is the impression that the Rough Riders formed the larger part of the American forces that landed in Cuba. In fact, they numbered just a few hundred men out of an army of more than sixteen thousand. Also, the term 'Rough Rider' was only a nickname; they were officially called the First Regiment of U.S. Cavalry Volunteers. 'Rough rider' was originally applied to a man who specialized in breaking horses to harness, i.e., a bronco buster, and had been known in print at least since the early eighteenth century and in Western lingo even before that. Roosevelt's regiment acquired the sobriquet primarily because its members were former broncobusters and cowboys many of whom rode with Buffalo Bill's Rough Riders in the fabulous Wild West Show that wowed Europe in the 1880s.

Most history books depict Teddy Roosevelt as the doughty leader of the action on San Juan Hill, but this is far from accurate. Roosevelt had participated in the earlier assault on Kettle Hill, and from this position he watched another group of Rough Riders going up San Juan Hill. Teddy was as proud and heroic as though he himself were part of the death-defying charge, but he was actually elsewhere when another figure—Col. Leonard Wood—led it.

In fact, Teddy Roosevelt was not the leader of the Rough

Riders at all, as he was only the second in command. He did organize the group only to see its command go to Wood, who, unlike Teddy, had military experience. This Army veteran was the real 'hero of San Juan Hill', despite the absence of his name in most popular accounts. After the Spanish surrender, he served as military governor of Cuba, suppressed the 1903 insurrection in the Philippines, and was army chief of staff from 1910 until World War I. He lost the 1920 Republican Party nomination for president to Harding.

2. Hearst Breaking News

Myth! When Frederic Remington reported from Cuba that he could not find any evidence of hostilities there, publisher William Randolph Hearst wired back, "Please remain. You furnish pictures. I'll furnish the war."

Wanting trouble in Cuba to promote US expansionist interests and his paper's circulation, Hearst—so the story goes—sent American artist Frederic Remington to gather evidence of clashes between the Spanish authorities and the native insurrectionists. When the artist reported that he could not find any, Hearst, not to be denied his war, wired back the famous reply.

This prime example of Hearst's fraudulent methods to get what he wanted has become the subject of biographies, popular histories, and at least one film parody. But with Hearst himself denying the story, there is no way to prove it ever happened. No record of Hearst's telegram exists, and it seems unthinkable that one like it could have passed the Spanish censors. Ralph Keyes *("Nice Guys Finish Seventh,"* 1993) traces the myth to journalist James Creelman's 1901 memoir of Hearst, which mentioned the incident without citing any source.

Analysts say the Spanish-American War was instigated less by the sensationalism of the Hearst press than by the long-standing antagonism of the US towards Spain due to the so-called Virginius affair. In 1873, or 25 years before the war erupted, the Spanish had seized the US ship Virginius at Santiago and summarily executed 53 of its crew and passengers, among them US and British citizens. The Spanish later paid an indemnity to the families of the executed Americans and Britons, but a promise to punish the Spanish officers responsible was never fulfilled.

3. Havana Interlude

Myth! **Resenting the presence of the USS Maine in Havana, the Spanish authorities exploded a submarine mine that sank the ship and killed 266 men.**

McKinley had sent the USS Maine to Havana Harbor ostensibly to protect American interests during the early stirrings of the Cuban Insurrection. Actually, America already had a wet eye on Havana as one of the few 'foreign' ports in the Americas that continued to pose a challenge to the Monroe Doctrine. And the USS Maine as one of the first warships built wholly by Americans could not have been a better choice for the task.

On February 15, 1898, after three weeks that the ship languished at the port, a mysterious explosion sank it and put both Spanish and American nerves on edge. A US Navy team joined the locals in the investigation, and their report, released on March 17, pinpointed the cause of the sinking as "the explosion of a submarine mine." However, despite the failure to obtain any evidence fixing the responsibility, newspaper sensationalism made the Spaniards the scapegoats. Six weeks later, roused by the famous cry 'Remember the Maine!', Congress declared a state of war between the United States and Spain.

At the time, there was no known torpedo or mine that could have triggered such a powerful explosion. A 1911 Board of Inspection Report confirmed that the coalbunkers located very near the ship's gunpowder magazines were the more likely culprits. This finding was based on a scientific inspection of the Maine after it had been dewatered and every bit of the wreckage accurately identified. The hull side and whole deck structures, when peeled back, made it obvious that the blast was from twenty thousand pounds of powder from the inside.

139

4. The Medium, not the Message

Myth! Lt. Andrew Rowan delivered President McKinley's famous message to Cuban rebel General Garcia in a pouch.

The 1936 film *A Message to Garcia* was based on an essay of the same title written by Elbert Hubbard and published in March 1899 in the monthly magazine *The Philistine*. The essay was widely reprinted and is said to hold the world's record for circulation and translation into foreign tongues. It related the story of one Lt. Andrew Summers Rowan who had heroically delivered a message in a sealed oilskin pouch from President McKinley to General Calixto Garcia Iñiguez, leader of the Cuban rebel forces against Spain, somewhere in the eastern mountain districts of the island.

Critics say Hubbard's piece, which was "written one evening after supper, in a single hour," is shot full of holes and fails as a documentary. Apparently, the message itself was not from McKinley nor was it committed to writing, being nothing more than a verbal order from Rowan's superior officer, Col. Arthur Wagner, to determine the strength of Garcia's forces and arrange their cooperation with American forces should a war break out with Spain. Also, the incident occurred before rather than during the war, hence it was not an unusual or particularly hazardous task. But as sensationalized by Hubbard's essay, it fired the imagination as keenly as if it had been a rip-roaring adventure.

There are those who believe the essay was not meant to tell a true story but only a parable to illustrate the writer's intent. This was to teach workers the meaning of perseverance, as well as to admonish them to obey authority and place devotion to duty above all else. Admittedly, the excuse didn't hold up well in the face of the claim that Lt. Rowan never really visited Cuba, and was nearly court-martialed for completely fabricating his adventures. Hubbard's story nevertheless boosted Rowan's stock, and he was commended by the President before a meeting of the Cabinet and later raised to the rank of lieutenant colonel. In 1922 he was awarded the Distinguished Service Cross by Congress for the 24-year-old heroic exploit that many insist never happened.

140

5. Big Booty, Small War

Myth! Winning the Spanish-American War turned the US into a major world power.

The Spanish-American War was "a splendid little war, begun with the highest motives, carried on with magnificent intelligence and spirit, favored by that fortune which loves the brave." This was US Ambassador to England John Hay's condescending message to Theodore Roosevelt, and it was diplomatic cajolery of the first order. *First*, the war may have been little, but it was not splendid. While US fatalities were reported at 5,462 men, the real cost was only 379, the rest dying not from the war but from disease.   There were more American battlefield casualties—at least 5,000—from the Filipino insurrection that ensued after Spain ceded the Philippines to the US at war's end.

Second, the war could not have had the highest motives, since it had no motive to begin with. It was the vile Hearst press that instigated the conflict, practically forcing Spain to jump the gun on the US and declare war first. The US retaliated by declaring war on Spain, backdating the declaration by three days to make the American side look more heroic.

Third, the 'magnificent intelligence' is simply not evident, for, as one historian puts it, "only the incredible ineptitude of the Spaniards and the phenomenal luck of the Americans kept the war from stretching into a struggle as long and as full of disasters as the Boer War became for the British."

Despite the claim that winning the Spanish-American War put the US on the world stage as a major power, it was actually Commodore Matthew Perry's opening up of Japan to commerce that did the trick.

6. UN-pacifying Korea

Myth! The 1950 Korean War involving the US and Korea was the first war in which the UN gave full and open support to a protagonist.

141

As incredible as it may seem, the United States has never gone to war against Korea despite the extensive military clashes that have occurred between these two countries in the past. For one, the Korean War that came five years after World War II was not fought by the US but by the United Nations, although the US provided most of the combatants for the UN side.

The only other confrontation between the US and Korea happened in 1871, but it lasted only a few days and was not reported by the American press until a month after the fighting was over. It was brought about by the Koreans' refusal to consider the proposal for bilateral trading that the US minister to China, Frederick Low, had presented. The diplomat was tactless enough to be accompanied on his mission by the 'Asiatic Squadron', a flotilla of five run-down boats under the command of Admiral John Rodgers and manned by 1,500 sailors and marines. When the mission failed, Rodgers led two of his ships up the Han River and exchanged fire with the Koreans, killing 350 of them while suffering 10 dead and 10 wounded. The American ships sailed on claiming victory, while the Koreans declared they had driven the Americans away.

Incidentally, the first war fought by the United Nations was not the 1950 Korean War, as most people might think, but World War II. To rally the Allies against the Axis, twenty-six countries calling themselves the Associated Powers and later the UN made the pledge in 1942 to continue their joint war efforts against the enemy and not to make peace separately. This purpose was firmed up at Dumbarton Oaks in Washington, DC, in 1944.

7. Wagging the Dog in Vietnam

Myth! The US Congress passed the Gulf of Tonkin Resolution authorizing President Lyndon Johnson to wage the Vietnam War in response to aggression by North Vietnam.

The Vietnam War cost 55,000 American dead, yet it was not even officially a war. There was no declaration of war by the US, and neither by North or South Vietnam. The Gulf of Tonkin Resolution, often cited as the legal authority for calling it a war, did not authorize the American President to commit combatants specifically to any war, but only to "take all measures" to repel attacks against US forces and to "prevent further aggression."

Vietnam apologists argue that the President by himself can legally prosecute an already existing war-like situation without the formality of a declaration of war. Still, when the Tonkin Resolution was passed, the only war-like situation in Vietnam was the one the President himself had created. Johnson had ordered an air strike consisting of more than sixty sorties against North Vietnam, purportedly in retaliation for what occurred previously in the Gulf. In that earlier incident, US jets sank one of three North Vietnamese patrol boats that came out to investigate the presence of a US warship—the USS *Maddox*—ten miles off the coast of North Vietnam. The case was one of American, not North Vietnamese, aggression, and LBJ would compound the lie further by falsely reporting a second attack on the *Maddox* to congressional leaders. For obvious reasons, Congress wasn't told that the Resolution they were signing had been prepared months before the Tonkin encounter happened.

8. Moses' Promised Land

Myth! Stephen Austin led the move for the US annexation of Texas after founding the first Anglo-American community in the territory.

Most Americans are taught that Stephen F. Austin (1793-1836) is called the Father of Texas because (1) he founded the first Anglo-American community in that territory, and (2) he spearheaded the move for the US annexation of Texas from Mexico. Some realize only later that both reasons are far from satisfactory and the honorific title may have gone to the wrong Austin. It was Moses Austin, Stephen's father, who nearly a generation earlier secured permission from the Spanish government to colonize 300 families on a grant of 200,000 acres. Stephen is given the credit only because he obtained approval of the grant from Mexico as soon as it turned independent in 1821. It is true that the son set up several more colonies and by 1832 had contributed 8,000 inhabitants to Texas, but there were other impresarios who, with similar grants, brought the territory's Anglo-American population to about 20,000.

Stephen Austin was actually opposed to US annexation, arguing that without the resources to maintain Texas independence, it was better off as a Mexican state. His intention was not to pass Texas from one colonizer to another, but as his motto attested, to "redeem Texas from the wilderness, show fidelity and gratitude to his adopted country, and keep inflexible truth to the interests and just rights of the settlers." After being imprisoned for more than a year in Mexico City for encouragement of insurrection, Austin changed his mind and joined Sam Houston in forming a provisional government for an independent Texas in 1835-1836. But he still did not advocate US statehood, and Texas would join the Union only ten years later.

9. Dancing to the Bourbon St. Beat

Myth! The War of 1812 erupted when Britain passed the hated Orders in Council, and ended at the Battle of New Orleans with the US as clear winner.

The Orders in Council authorized the blocking of all French ports and required that neutral vessels first call on British ports and pay duties. But President Madison signed the declaration of war on June 18, 1812, without realizing that the day before, Britain had already repealed the controversial measure. Lacking any rapid means of communication, such as the telegraph, there was no way the news could reach the US on time, and so the two armies in North America proceeded to carry out the conflict as planned.

The war ended the same way it had began—with a costly *faux pas*. Jackson's performance was overwhelming—more than 2,000 British, including their commander, Edward Pakenham, died, while the Americans lost only eight. The battle became a symbol of American might and resolve, and catapulted Jackson to national prominence and eventually the US Presidency. What is not generally known is that the battle was fought in peacetime—after the War of 1812 had already ended—and was totally unnecessary. Yielding to pressure from their war-weary constituents to put a

144

stop to what was apparently a silly conflict, negotiators on both sides had signed the treaty of Ghent officially ending the hostilities on December 24, 1814. This was fifteen days before Jackson's intrepid crew met their British adversaries at New Orleans. News of the agreement, which was conveyed by overseas mail, did not reach the US—and Jackson—until more than a month after the encounter (Jackson's superiors in Washington came to know about both the battle and the treaty even later!). This promoted the erroneous belief that it was Jackson's victory that convinced the British to sign the treaty.

Despite the popular contention that the US won the War of 1812, it was actually inconclusive. At the end, the US recovered previously lost territory but was unable to invade Canada, and the British remained in full control of the sea. Several circumstances that had nothing to do with the war contributed to the illusion of victory for the Americans. First was the success at the Battle of New Orleans, which, as noted, was achieved after the war had already ended; second was the cessation of British impressments and paper blockades, which came about only with the end of the Napoleonic Wars; and third was the pacification of the Indians, which was due mainly to the death of the great Indian chief Tecumseh.

10. How to Beat a Black Jack

Myth! The senseless British attack on Washington, DC, in 1812 was the last flagrant invasion of the US mainland by a foreign power.

It is said that the only good thing to come out of the War of 1812 was the feeling of unity that an unnecessary British depredation—the burning of Washington, DC—stimulated in Americans. British soldiers rampaged through the capital and razed government buildings, including the Capitol, the Library of Congress and the White House. Coincidentally, many of what the British destroyed were symbols of the freedom the Americans had previously won from their former colonial masters.

But in their indignation, Americans tended to overlook the fact that the British simply did what they had to do, which was burn the US capitol in retaliation for the American attack on a British stronghold in Canada. The destruction of several government buildings, including a parliament, occurred near Lake Ontario at York (now Toronto), the capital of Upper Canada, at the end of April 1813, more than a year before the burning of Washington in August 1814. Some historians on the US side believe the British action was unjustified because the Americans had acted without the knowledge and consent of their superiors, whereas the British officers were not only aware of the burning of Washington but ordered it. The more neutral ones argue that both depredations were acts of war, and one cannot be placed on a higher moral plane than the other.

Americans may be disappointed to learn that the British sortie into Washington, DC, in 1814 was not the last invasion of the US mainland by a foreign army. On March 9, 1916, the Mexican Francisco 'Pancho' Villa, angered by the US alliance with a Mexican revolutionary faction other than his own, led a guerilla force across the border and attacked the 13th US Cavalry in Columbus, New Mexico. During the raid, Villa's men killed 18 Americans, burned down several buildings, and stole a quantity of weapons. He lost 50 of his troops in the ensuing pursuit by the US Army. President Wilson ordered John 'Black Jack' Pershing to cross the Mexican border and capture Villa, but the so-called 'Punitive Expedition' was a dismal failure.

Many saw Villa as a mere outlaw and his American foray an ordinary act of banditry, while a few doubted that Villa was present during the raid. But to the people of Chihuahua, Mexico's largest state, Villa was a folk hero and a major arm of the Mexican revolutionary movement. In fact, the U.S. government had previously recognized Villa's legitimacy, and it was his repudiation later on by the same authorities in favor of his rival, Venustian Carranza, that made Villa decide to retaliate. Analysts have long established that Villa's act of pitting 1,550 followers (part of a total of 40,000 in his whole army) against a contingent of the US Army was political rather than criminal.

The most recent military action against the US mainland by a hostile power was the Japanese bombing of Oregon in World War II. Critics say this should have set the record for being the last invasion of America by a foreign army were it not for the fact that only one enemy pilot carried out the entire adventure.

146

III

Last Man Standing

On Custer's Last Stand

"There are not enough Indians in the world
to defeat the Seventh Cavalry."

•

George Custer

1. All the Brothers were Valiant

Myth! On the day he died, Custer was a general who had won the Medal of Honor twice.

George Custer was not a general at the time he made his famous last stand against the Indians. It is true that he had once been a brigadier general, the nation's youngest at twenty-three; his promotion was at the instance of Major General Alfred Pleasanton, and not the result of a paperwork error as suggested in the 1941 film *They Died With Their Boots On*. He was elevated to major general later during the Civil War, but once the conflict had ended, Civil War officers lost their prewar volunteer ranks in an army reorganization, and Custer was relegated to captain. On the day of the battle at Little Bighorn, he was a lieutenant colonel in the 7th Cavalry under Brigadier General Alfred H. Terry.

Custer's Hollywood glamour has been tarnished somewhat by certain details of his military life, one of which is that he finished last in the 1861 graduating class of 35 students at West Point. The film itself reveals that Custer had the "lowest marks and the highest demerits of any cadet who ever attended the academy, including Ulysses S. Grant." The demeaning of Grant, who graduated 21st out of 39 cadets in the Class of 1843 is obviously false, but the remark about Custer is wholly accurate. Moreover, contrary to the hype that he had been a fast rising star in the US Army due to his derring-do, Custer had recurring disciplinary problems. When he was lieutenant colonel, he was assigned to Kansas to take part in General Winfield S. Hancock's expedition to awe hostile Plains Indians with the military strength of the US Army. Custer disobeyed orders to wait for supplies to be loaded at Ft. Harker, and went instead to Ft. Riley to visit his wife Elizabeth. He was court-martialed in 1867 at Ft. Leavenworth and suspended for one year without pay.

Custer was so disliked by his superiors that not one would recommend him for any decoration while he was alive. He did receive honorary (brevet) promotions, as was customary for officers during the war. But the Custer listed in the records as the highest decorated soldier of the Civil War, being the only two-time recipient of the Medal of Honor during his lifetime, is Tom, one of George's two brothers who were killed with him at the

Little Bighorn. Wikipedia notes that the worthier Tom was never portrayed in the definitive *They Died With Their Boots On* despite having served under George for nearly the entire time period depicted in the film.

2. Dress right, Dress!

Myth! At the time of the attack, Custer wore his blonde hair long and was neatly dressed in military uniform, complete with hat and scabbard.

The famous 1878 Steinegger painting of Custer's Last Stand, reprinted in *The American Heritage History of the Indian Wars*, shows him wearing a clean, neat, and perfectly buttoned uniform, a scabbard on his side and his hat well brushed and perfectly angled. Custer himself is clean-shaven and sporting a neatly trimmed mustache, standing cool and in control while fighting ferocious Indians.

Reason dictates that this is totally unrealistic. Custer, who had been riding for three hard days through dusty frontier territory, was actually sweaty, grimy and tired. Not having shaved in five weeks, his face was covered with a full beard, and he had on plain functional buckskins and a tattered flannel shirt. Neither he nor any of his men brandished a saber since all the swords had been left behind.

Custer, who is said to have worn long blonde hair as part of his maverick image as an Indian fighter (he was called 'Yellowhair' or 'Long Hair' even by Indians who hadn't seen him in person), is most often portrayed in this manner in paintings of the battle. But Custer must have cut his hair short before the fatal day because, as the Hunkpapa Chief Crow King later commented: "We did not know him, dead or alive. When the fight was over, (we) gave orders to look for the long-haired chiefs among the dead, but no chiefs with long hair could be found." Custer's wife Elizabeth identified a lock of auburn hair found in his battlefield grave, but the bones seemed to be those of an unknown enlisted man.

3. The Bold and the Vainglorious

Myth! **Custer attacked the hostile Indian encampment at the Little Bighorn on the orders of his superiors.**

Custer's Last Stand assumes a heroic luster when regarded in the light of the report that he was ordered by his superiors to fight an unwinnable battle against tremendous odds. But the real story is that he went into battle against orders and the advice of his own men, and it was his characteristic imprudence, not unfavorable numbers, that led to the debacle.

In command of a regiment that he later split for a projected three-pronged attack, Custer arrived near the Little Bighorn on the night of June 24, 1876. His immediate superior General Alfred Terry was to join him with the main column in two days, but Custer was determined to wipe out the Indians' hidden encampment by himself. Without waiting for Terry, he initiated the attack the next morning.

The village at the Little Bighorn (or the Greasy Grass River, as the Indians called it) included families from the Sioux and Cheyenne tribes, who were encamped in defiance of a US government order to return to a reservation. They were less than hostile, however, and had adopted a policy to fight only when necessary. Of the 8,000 in the encampment, about 2,000 were fighters and the rest were old men, women and children. The odds of 3 Indians to 1 trooper were actually more favorable to Custer than what he had faced in many previous Indian battles. But threatened by annihilation on their home grounds, the Indians fought harder than ever, in large part accounting for the rout.

4. The Chairman did not Sit

Myth! **Sitting Bull was the fighting chief who presided over Custer's defeat.**

Under Sitting Bull, the Sioux were abiding by the permanent terms of a treaty that placed them on a reservation in the Black

Hills of South Dakota. After the discovery of gold in the region, the U.S. government rescinded the treaty and attempted to relocate the tribe to another reservation. When Sitting Bull refused to move, the US Army sent a force against the camp to compel the transfer. Thousands of Sioux then joined Sitting Bull at the Little Bighorn, igniting the conflict that culminated in Custer's tragic end.

Contrary to the myth surrounding this episode in American history, Sitting Bull was not present during the battle and had nothing to do with Custer's defeat. He was not a fighting chief, and Sitting Bull, like most well known Native American names, was not even his real name but a coinage of the white man. To the Indians, he was Tatanka Yotanka, a chief of the Hunkpapa Sioux and a medicine man who ministered to the whole encampment. During the battle, the warrior chiefs who fought Custer were Gall, Crow King and Crazy Horse. Sitting Bull, true to his reputation as a great invoker of the spirits, was up in the mountains 'making some medicine'.

The skull of Sitting Bull is one of the artifacts rumored to be stored in the Smithsonian's vaults. Curators at the Institution have been denying this for years, stating that the chief is buried whole at Fort Yates, North Dakota.

---

5. Comanche with Bloody Knife

Myth! Everyone and his horse on Custer's side perished in the Battle of the Little Bighorn.

The widely held belief that the Indians left no survivors at the Battle of the Little Bighorn is based on standard history texts expressing the view that Custer and his entire force of more than 600 men were slain. It appears not even the horses were spared, as the beleaguered soldiers in their desperation slaughtered the animals still standing after the initial clashes and used them as shields.

But comes Robert Ripley of *Believe It Or Not* fame, stating that two on Custer's side emerged from the holocaust unscathed. One was Comanche, a horse that had belonged to Captain Myles Keogh and for years after the battle served as the mascot of the US

Army's 7th Cavalry, appearing riderless in parades. The other was Custer's half-breed scout Bloody Knife (or Curley in other writings), who had warned him before the battle that an attack on the Indian encampment would mean certain death. However, it is not clear if Bloody Knife escaped before the battle started, or was captured and later freed by the Indian braves.

Ironically, while Ripley debunked the myth that Custer and his men were annihilated, he created the no less fallacious bit that there were only two survivors. Official statistics of the battle reveal that, of the 600 men of the US Seventh Cavalry Regiment that engaged the combined Indian force at Little Big Horn, only less than half were killed. Just before the battle, Custer had spun off from his column two groups of about 390 men, deploying them under separate commands, and of these some 300 survived. What probably accounts for the belief that the whole regiment was totally decimated is the fact that Custer and the 210 men that remained with him all died.

6. Suicide brings on Many Changes

Myth! Custer's body was spared from mutilation because of the high respect the Indians had for this brave leader.

The bodies of Custer's soldiers were stripped and mutilated in the belief that the soul of a mutilated body would be forced to walk the earth for all eternity and could not ascend to heaven. But Custer's own was spared of the indignity—except for his ears, which were pierced allegedly so he could hear better in the next world the Indians' complaints that the white man was breaking his word. Although Indian tradition prohibited the dishonoring of a slain enemy leader by mutilating his remains, this couldn't have been the reason in Custer's case since he was not personally known to any of the braves. Some say Custer's body was protected by an Indian mistress with whom he had had a child, and whose relatives had continued to regard him as a member of the family even after the child's untimely death. This presupposes, however, that his lover discovered Custer's corpse in the battlefield before the braves had a chance to tamper with it. Other theories even more far-fetched have been advanced, e.g., since Custer had been wearing buckskins instead of a blue uniform, the Indians thought he was not a soldier and so, thinking he was an innocent, left him alone. Or, his hair was cut too short for battle that not enough was left to allow for a very good scalping.

The only other marks of violence on the corpse were a neat bullet wound in the left temple and one in the left side. This has led some historians to suspect that the general, seeing the futility of the situation, saved his final bullet for himself, aware that an Indian would never touch, let alone mutilate, the body of a suicide. However, for the Indians to recognize that Custer was indeed a suicide, some forensic knowledge on their part would have been required. This they evidently lacked, considering that they still mutilated the corpses of other soldiers who, according to later findings, had killed themselves to avoid torture.

7. His last Grand Stand

Myth! **Custer was among the last to die on what is now Custer Hill.**

Archeological evidence and eyewitness accounts obtained at Little Big Horn point to a scenario substantially different from what is described in most history books.

First, Custer's men were not only outnumbered by the Indian force by more than three to one, they were also outgunned by a factor of almost four to one. Even without the guns the Indians took from the slain soldiers and added to their armory, the weaponry used against Custer was superior in both number and quality. The Cavalry's main weapon was the single-shot Springfield rifle, a poor comparison to more than half of their enemy's arms consisting of Winchester and Henry repeating rifles. It is alleged that many of the soldiers' carbines had jammed, but assuming they had not, the Indians could still fire five to six shots for every one that the Cavalry could manage.

Second, the tactics Custer followed based on the standard US Army manual did not work and actually backfired. Worse, the men, who were not fit and healthy to begin with, were exhausted by the ride and lacked sleep; they became easily confused in the heat of battle, and, overwhelmed by their enemy's number, many abandoned their weapons and fled in panic.

Third, there is no evidence that Custer was the last to die in battle. Knowing his penchant for quick action—the better words are 'rash' and 'impatient'—and the early disintegration of his group, it's more likely he was one of the first to fall.

Lastly, the final moments of the battle took place in a small area: just two little hillocks, Custer Hill and Calhoun Hill, and a gully. But the common perception—that the last fighting was on Custer Hill—is simply not so. Custer's initial deployment of soldiers on Custer Hill was in fact successful, but the subsequent Indian counterattack broke their cohesion and they fled down into a deep ravine area, where presumably the last man standing of Custer's men surrendered to his fate.

IV

The World In Flames

On World War I

"Bear yourselves as Huns of Attila."

•

Kaiser Wilhelm I

1. Words of War

Myth! What President Wilson described as "the war to end all wars" was named World War I once it became clear a second world war was coming.

It was known in the beginning as the Great War, since there was no way of knowing at the time that it would be the first of the global conflicts to be denominated 'world wars'. However, even before World War II became imminent, a British army officer, Col. C.A. Court Repington, changed the name to 'World War I' in his diary for September 1918 to avoid confusion with the Napoleonic War, which was also called the Great War. On that date, the conflict was still raging, and Hitler would not begin rattling the Nazi saber throughout Europe until almost two decades later. Repington saw no sense in calling it 'The European War' after non-European nations, such as Japan and Australia, joined the fray.

Not convinced that this latest in endemic violence would be 'the war to end all wars', Repington added the number 'I' in anticipation of future wars no less extensive and devastating. In 1920, he published his writing, calling it *The First World War, 1914-1918*. The name stuck, despite the claim of historian Thomas Bailey that the word 'first' is a mistake—by his reckoning, there have already been nine world wars, with World War I as the eighth.

There is no record of President Wilson inventing the phrase 'the war to end all wars'. He did say the war was "the most terrible of all wars" in a speech to a joint session of the US Congress on April 2, 1917, just four days before America voted to participate with the Allied Powers. The British Prime Minister David Lloyd George was closer to the point when he announced the terms of the Armistice to the House of Commons in this wise: "I hope we may say that thus, this fateful morning, came to an end all wars." Even more significant was a remark he once made—"This war, like the next war, is a war to end war"—but no one seems to know if he had World War I in mind when he said it.

H. G. Wells, pulling the plug on both Wilson and George, wrote: "I launched the phrase 'The War to End War'—and that was not the least of my crimes." Wells was referring to the book *The*

War That Will End War, which he had published on the eve of the great conflict. The sci-fi notable made his admission only in 1934, but the evidence of his 1914 book leaves no doubt that it is the earliest known source for the phrase.

2. Tripped by a Wire

Myth! The sinking of the Lusitania heightened anti-German feelings among Americans and ultimately triggered the US' entry into World War I.

Experts say that while America's moralists were put on edge by what happened on May 7, 1915, this was not sufficient to upset prevailing pacifist feelings. For one, the ship was not American but British, and for another, only 128 out of a total death toll of 1,198 were Americans. President Wilson could do nothing better to alleviate his conscience than send a note of protest to the Germans, and it would be another two years before America would take Germany to task and involve itself in the great conflict.

A later incident perhaps more aggravating than the Lusitania debacle was Germany's announcement in February 1917 that it would sink every vessel, military or not, approaching Great Britain, Ireland and various Mediterranean ports. Within two months, Wilson would address Congress, calling for America's participation in the war and proclaiming: "The world must be made safe for democracy." But by this time, America had already made up its mind to intervene in the conflict and prevent a German victory against its British ally. What triggered a turn-around in the national sentiment—something neither Wilson nor Germany's naval actions could do—was the so-called Zimmerman telegram, which the German Foreign Secretary Arthur Zimmermann sent on January 16, 1917 to his ambassador in Washington, DC. It said that in the event the US was drawn into the war and Germany should win it, Mexico as an ally would be rewarded with the 'lost' territories of Texas, New Mexico and Arizona. British intelligence intercepted and deciphered the secret message, and President Wilson released it to the press the following day.

157

3. Hell on High Water

Myth! The Germans struck the unarmed Lusitania without warning.

Serious historians have long discarded the view that the Lusitania was ambushed in favor of the German position that the ill-fated ship was sufficiently warned. On the very day the Lusitania sailed from New York, the German government took space on the front page of the New York World and in several American newspapers, to give notice that they had mounted a blockade of the British Isles, and any vessel (without specifically mentioning the Lusitania) attempting to run it would find itself the target of submarine attack. Ironically, the notice was placed right next to Cunard's announcement of the imminent departure of the Lusitania. It is said that another privately placed ad giving warning to those sailing on the Lusitania was received by fifty newspapers just a week before the ship's departure from New York, but only one, the Des Moines Register, printed it.

Contrary to legend, the German commander of the U-20 was not lying in wait for the passenger liner. As a British inquiry proved, it was the Lusitania's captain who was at fault for ignoring instructions and steering the ship into the path of the German submarine. It appeared British authorities were even aware of the presence of the submarine as it prowled along the southern Irish coast, and of the Lusitania approaching, but chose not do anything about it.

Official investigation further revealed that the Lusitania was not quite the innocent passenger liner Allied propaganda made her out to be. A second huge explosion occurring after the Lusitania was hit could only have been caused when the torpedo ignited the fuel in the coalbunkers and set off the vessel's cargo. This cargo, as was later determined, consisted of 1,248 cases of shrapnel shells, 1,639 copper ingots, 76 cases of brass rods, and 4,927 boxes of .303 caliber cartridges (1000 rounds per box) weighing over 10 tons. All in all, there were 24 pages of manifest of which only one page was used for "clearance to sail," and three manifests were false while a fourth found in the papers of Woodrow Wilson verified that the cargo was contraband. The sixty-seven Canadians

158

aboard were in fact soldiers who mixed with the civilian passengers to avoid detection.

A writer discovered records in the Cunard archives showing that the liner was secretly outfitted with twelve six-inch guns in September 1914, confirming that the Lusitania had been built with the intention of equipping her as an armed merchant cruiser in wartime.

4. Never second Gas the Enemy

Myth! The worst killers of World War I include chemical weapons, which were first applied in war at Ypres in 1915 when the Germans used mustard gas against the Allies.

The first time the Germans used poison gas against the Allies in Word War I was on January 3, 1915, in the Battle of Bolimov on the Eastern Front. The Second Battle of Ypres on April 22-25, 1915 was only the first time the Germans used the gas on the Western Front. Contrary to popular belief, chlorine gas, not mustard gas, was used; the latter, though also called Yperite from the name of the city, would not be applied until the autumn of 1917 near Ypres.

The long history of chemical warfare actually began with Alexander the Great, whose army threw lime at enemy soldiers to distract them with burning and itching. The Barbary pirates burned opiates to create a lethal gas, and the Spanish in the seventeenth century used smoke bombs filled with blood. The mustard gas the Germans used in World War I was an oily, volatile substance that is not really a gas but an atomized liquid. Although it has nothing to do with mustard, it has the color and smell of one, which is what accounts for its name. The liquid, $(ClCH2CH2)2S$, is corrosive to the skin and mucous membranes and causes severe, sometimes fatal, respiratory damage.

The belief that chemicals were some of the worst killers in World War I stems from the fact that not many people are able to differentiate between chemical and germ warfare. It is also not readily known that germs more than chemicals, bullets and bayonets combined were the biggest single killer of soldiers in the war. In spite of that conflict's popular image of combat involving trench warfare, poison gases and pitched battles, more U.S. soldiers were killed as the direct result of disease than died in action on the battlefield. Of the nearly 113,000 Americans who fought and lost their lives in the war, more than half, or almost 63,000, died from disease. This is actually nothing to be surprised about. Until the end of World War I, disease-related deaths outnumbered battle deaths in every war throughout history.

5. Those Rampaging Huns

Myth! The Germans committed one of the most horrible atrocities against civilians in World War I by cutting off the hands of helpless Belgian children.

Schindler's List (1993) and *The Pianist* (2002) are two of the most memorable movies that dramatize the Nazis' ravishment of the Jews during World War II. Hollywood has been kinder to the Germans of World War I, as witness the classic pacifist film *All Quiet on the Western Front* (1930). Yet we keep hearing of the indescribable horrors committed by Kaiser Bill's military in every country in which they had a presence. Media has long reached the conclusion that many of these atrocities were simply made up as part of Allied propaganda. The real atrocity, according to one historian, was an unsubstantiated British government report (the Bryce Report) blaming the Germans for the wanton slaughter and mutilation of foreign civilians and the plunder of their homes. The Report gave undue credence to the rumor, which had a most disturbing effect on the fighting attitudes of Allied soldiers, that the Huns cut off the hands of hundreds of Belgian babies.

After the first lurid incidents were reported by the Paris correspondent for the London Times on August 27, 1914, the mutilated babies grew in number over the next few months and gradually moved from France to Belgium. As the story gathered momentum, Allied propaganda photographs were manufactured showing groups of the handless children. A few reporters made efforts to get at the truth during the war, but their findings tending to disprove the brutal acts were largely ignored.

After the war, more people came forward to refute the mutilation stories. One of them was Italian Prime Minister Nitti,

160

who wrote that his government, in cooperation with the British, had looked into the truth of the reports of handless Belgian children, but found that "every case investigated proved to be a myth."

6. The Archduke of Hazards

Myth! The assassination of Archduke Francis Ferdinand of Austria in Sarajevo was the principal cause of World War I.

On 28 June 1914, Archduke Franz Ferdinand of Austria, heir to the Austro-Hungarian throne, and his wife, Sophie, Duchess of Hohenberg, were shot dead in Sarajevo by Gavrilo Princip, one of a group of six Bosnian Serb assassins coordinated by Danilo Ilíc. It would have been a trivial political event—par for the course in that jittery age—had not Princip and his co-conspirators admitted to being supporters of the separatist movement that wanted Bosnia, then under the protection of Austria, brought under the control of Serbia. Austria-Hungary declared war on Serbia after failing to obtain satisfaction for the assassination, while Germany, siding with Austria-Hungary, declared war on Russia when the latter mobilized in support of Serbia. France and Britain declared war on Germany, all within the same week, and three months later Turkey joined the Germans and the Austrians in an alliance known as the Central Powers.

Historians who take a broader view don't see how a minor political murder in a remote corner of Europe could have brought about World War I. The assassination may have been a catalyst, they argue, but the deeper, more potent reason for the belligerency was the keen competition for economic dominance and colonial supremacy that had created an unbearable tension in the relations of the Great Powers in 1914. Media had already been reporting months before the assassination that countries all over Europe were rearming and war seemed "more and more likely." When Serbia was attacked despite its meeting virtually all of Austria's demands, any remaining doubt that the war would have occurred even without the assassination was removed.

161

7. Angels in the Battlefield

Myth! At the Battle of Mons the hard-pressed British corps sensed a host of angelic cavalry wielding swords of burnished gold and protecting them from the Germans.

Billed as the only British military involvement in history with supernatural undertones, the Battle of Mons, which pitted the German First Army against the 3rd and 4th Divisions of the Old Contemptibles under the command of General Dorrien-Smith, was first reported by Arthur Machen, a Welsh journalist on the London Evening News. The media described the 'miracle' as "the Spirit of St. George, clad in white and leading a host of angels to hold back the German advance." But Machen would later confess that that part of the episode involving the heavenly vanguards had been plucked out of thin air. He had simply intended his account to be a somewhat purple and extended metaphor using St. George to symbolize the British spirit, but others in the business misunderstood and it had got out of hand.

British losses were heavy, but since there was no down-to-earth explanation for those who survived against the odds, one could only stick to the claim that the troops had indeed been saved by a miracle. Machen's public confession did no good to dampen the belief persisting to this day that the mystical appearance was a real occurrence.

8. Immortal Sergeant

Myth! Sergeant Alvin York was a conscientious objector when he performed the singular act of valor for which he was honored in World War I.

The popular lore varnished many times over does not accurately describe what Sgt. York did to merit his larger-than-life persona. Though an unusually skilled sharpshooter, York did not accomplish his acclaimed feat—i.e., the capture of 132 Germans in one sweep—all by himself, but was aided by others just as heroic as he was. On October 8, 1918, a group of six American soldiers that included York encountered Germans in the Argonne Forest. York shot 20 of them in quick succession, and the other Germans, thinking they were outnumbered, abandoned their positions and surrendered. To fool the enemy, the Americans marched the 92 prisoners ahead of them toward the American lines. Whenever they came to a German machine-gun nest, the gunners assumed that a large army battalion was behind prodding the group of prisoners. When York and his men reached the American lines, they had captured 132 prisoners and put 35 machine-gun nests out of action.

When he performed his acts of valor, York was still a corporal, although he was no longer the conscientious objector people thought he was. He had tried twice to be excused from service because of his religion, only to be rejected. But after a two-day meditation in the mountains, his belief changed and he became a dedicated trooper instead.

York should not be confused with Pfc. Desmond Doss, a GI from Virginia, who, like York, was one of the highest awarded in any war, yet unlike him was a steadfast conscientious objector during the entire period of his service in World War II. Barred by his faith from carrying a weapon, this Seventh Day Adventist waded into battle as a courageous medic, getting wounded twice while tending to his compatriots under heavy enemy fire.

9. Peace with no Beginning, War without End

Myth! All the major combatants, including the US, signed the Treaty of Versailles, which contained the terms of Germany's surrender and formally ended World War I.

No agreement or treaty, not even that of Versailles, evidenced the German surrender in World War I for the simple reason that Germany never surrendered. As a practical matter, the war ended when hostilities formally ceased with an armistice—in fact, a series of armistices—entered into freely by the combatants in 1918. To those who consider war as a legal or diplomatic state of affairs, it ended only when the cease-fire was capped by the signing of several treaties the following year. However, the termination was made ambiguous by the number of treaties affecting some combatants, and by a lack of treaty for others. The Paris Peace Conference of 1919 inaugurated the international settlement and gave rise to the Treaty of Versailles with Germany, the Treaty of Saint-Germain with Austria, and the Treaty of Neuilly with Bulgaria.

That the war had as many terminal dates as there were treaties is exemplified by tiny Andorra, for whom the belligerency was not deemed over until her signing in 1958. For the US, which was the only major combatant not to sign any treaty, World War I may never have ended at all. President Wilson brought back the Treaty of Versailles from the Versailles Peace Conference in 1919, but ran smack against "the little group of willful men" in the US Senate who wanted some alterations. The Chief Executive refused to make any concessions to the revisionists, and because of the stalemate, the treaty never became binding on the Americans.

10. Pyrrhic Defeat

Myth! The Allies wrought tremendous material and financial ruin on Germany in World War I.

Most people are surprised to learn that the First World War did not ravage Germany at all, as no German territory was ever under foreign occupation and no battle so much as touched German soil during the entire period of the conflict. In fact, it was the Germans who were in control of Allied territory, and not the other way around, at the time the Armistice was called.

When hostilities ended in November 1918, the German army on the western front was still within Belgium and France. On the eastern front, the same army was well entrenched in a part of Finland all the way to the Don. Besides occupying the Ukraine and portions of the Crimea, the Imperial Reich in its dying moments owned all of the territories exacted from the Soviet Union under the Treaty of Brest-Litovsk.

According to economist John Kenneth Galbraith (cited by Shenkman), the allegation that Germany became bankrupt after World War I is not true either. Some of the country's resources may have been destroyed and much of its population decimated,

164

but it came out better situated than France. The German economy was adequate to support the remaining population, and could even have met the payment of reparations without much difficulty by accepting a lower standard of living.

Not a few historians agree with Galbraith, despite Hitler's own belief that Germany's greatest difficulties could be traced to the financial burden imposed by the Versailles Treaty. Shenkman points out that the payments Germany made to the Allies, which reached $32 billion, were more than offset by the loans the Allies, mainly through their private citizens, made to the Germans. The main stress on Germany's finances was from the conduct of the war itself, for which Germany spent $100 billion. The reparations under the Versailles Treaty were in fact less exacting than the concessions in both territory and money that the Germans had obtained from Russia under the Treaty of Brest-Litovsk when the new Bolshevik government sued for peace the previous year.

11. Hour of the Dove

Myth! The term 'the eleventh hour' arose from the signing of the Armistice at the 'eleventh hour of the eleventh day of the eleventh month' of the year 1918.

The coincidence would have been striking were it not for the fact that the Armistice was signed at the fifth hour to take effect at the eleventh hour. Some critics have suggested that the Armistice, though legally agreed to earlier, was deferred to the eleventh hour in order to avail of the mystical significance of the number eleven. Others have dismissed the idea as too horrifying, since it would have meant that thousands of soldiers were sacrificed for another six hours of war just for the sake of numerological symmetry.

The belief that the term 'the eleventh hour', meaning the latest possible moment, originated from this peculiarity of World War I is another fallacy. While it can be said literally and figuratively that the Armistice did not take effect until 'the eleventh hour', the genesis of the phrase presages World War I and all other wars in the present millennium. The earliest known source of the words is Jesus, who, in Matthew 20:9, relates the Parable of the Laborers in the Vineyard, saying, "Now when they of the eleventh hour came, they received each a denarius."

It is noteworthy that Americans celebrated the signing of the Armistice four days before it actually happened. On November 7, 1918, offices and factories across the country were closed as people started pouring into the streets in numbers. New York City hosted one of the largest ticker-tape parades in its history, and in other places, private thanksgiving parties were held in homes, clubs and centers. A message from Paris had announced the signing, which was conveyed in Brest to Roy Howard, president of United Press, and Howard in turn wired the news to the United States. The rejoicing didn't stop until the next day, November 8, when the wire services turned it into a surreal exercise by sheepishly admitting that a mistake had been committed and that the war was still in progress. Hostilities finally ended on November 11, the day the Armistice was actually signed, but Americans were no longer as ecstatic about honoring the event, having gone through a heady celebration four days earlier. Observers noted that even Wilson's dramatic pronouncement before Congress that day—"The war thus comes to an end"—had to endure a few moments' pause before finally being acknowledged by both the floor and the galleries.

12. Last Action Hero

Myth! **Pvt. Henry Gunther of the US Army was the last Allied soldier to die in World War I.**

Pvt. Gunther was killed at 11:01 AM on November 11, 1918 as his battalion was advancing upon Metz near the German border. For being recognized by General Pershing as the last Allied soldier to die in World War I, Gunther was posthumously awarded the Distinguished Service Cross. Critics say this might be stretching things somewhat, since it was already one minute past the Armistice when Gunther met his fate. According to them, the last soldier of any nationality to be killed in the war was Pvt. G.E. Ellison of the 5th Royal Irish Lancers. Ellison was shot to death five seconds before the clock struck the hour of eleven that November morning.

General Pershing may have merely wanted to cite Gunther as the last American to die in the war. Even then, many find the choice between Gunther and Ellison irrelevant in the face of the fact that the Armistice merely suspended hostilities on a broad front and was not the real cut-off point for World War I. If there was any formality that ended the conflict legally, it was the Treaty of Versailles, and on the premise that many more died after the Armistice but before the Treaty, neither Ellison nor Gunther was the last casualty of the war.

V

Red Curtain Down

On Communism and the Russian Revolution

"The death of one man is a tragedy.
The death of millions is a statistic."

•

Joseph Stalin

1. The 'N' is for *Nyet*

Myth! **Lenin was known to his closest associates as Nikolai.**

He was born Vladimir Ilyich Ulyanov, son of a schoolmaster named Ilya Nikolaevich Ulyanov, but to admirers and detractors alike he is known simply as Lenin. The initial 'N.' is obviously to dress up his icon, since it does not stand for 'Nikolai' (or 'Nicolae' or 'Nikolay'); contrary to the legend, this was not a first name given him to honor his father, whose middle name, Nikolaevich, means 'son of Nikolai'. In European and particularly Russian writing, 'N.' (possibly for the Russian *nyet*) is a conventional symbol for anonymity, thus a hint that Lenin is a pseudonym, one of about 75 that he used. These include Petrov, K. Tulin, Ilin, William Frey, Meyer, Karpov, Starik, Jacob Richter, Ivanov, I, L, and S.T.A., Lenin with or without the 'N.' being his most common. His full name in many reference works, such as V. I. (or Vladimir Ilyich) Lenin, V. I. Ulyanov-Lenin, or any other variant, combines his name at birth with his pseudonym and is, for that reason, inaccurate.

One story, apparently originating with the writer Walter Duranty, is that Lenin adopted the name in honor of striking workers at the Lena gold fields. The strike must have prompted immediate Communist action, for in an apparent display of concern for the proletariat, the Soviets acquired the private company that owned the site—Lena Goldfields Limited—for three million pounds in 1934. There can be no truth in the story, however, since Lenin was in use as a pseudonym long before the strike took place. It may be that Lenin, as sometimes speculated, is a kind of anagram or perhaps variant of llyin, from Ilyich, the man's middle name.

Incidentally, Joseph Stalin is also a pseudonym. This ruthless Bolshevik who eventually became the powerful leader of the Soviet Union was born Iosif Vissarionivich Dzhugashvili. As Dzhugashvili he went through three significant changes of profession: first, as a seminarian in the Georgian Orthodox Church, from which he was expelled for missing his final exams; second, as a bank robber, ostensibly for the purpose of raising funds for the Bolshevik revolutionary cause (but continuing with this activity after resigning from the party over its ban on bank robberies); and, finally, as a journalist, in which capacity he founded Pravda. Shortly thereafter, he adopted the name 'Stalin' as an alias and pen name in his published works. Unlike Lenin, Stalin was not from Russia, as is generally supposed, but from the southern province of Georgia. 'Stalin' is Russian, however, a derivation of the word for 'steel' and a fitting label for this Communist man of steel.

2. Mayday or May Day?

Myth! **Russia proclaimed the Communist holiday called May Day to honor the common worker.**

May Day is associated in the popular mind with a Communist red-letter day that was supposedly launched in Russia to honor its workers. Historically, May Day was an ancient festival celebrating spring and courtship rites, and had nothing to do with labor or laborers; in socialist countries today, it has lost this cultural and religious significance in favor of the political and the military.

Some suspect a connection between the May Day celebration and the distress signal Mayday, but there is actually none. The latter derives from the French *m'aider*, meaning 'come help me', and is used to signal a life-threatening emergency by police forces, pilots, firefighters, transportation agencies, and similar other public or private organizations.

What is surprising to most is that May Day as the celebration of worker solidarity around the world did not originate in the Soviet revolution but in the struggle for the eight-hour workday movement in the United States. The holiday, if it means anything at all, commemorates the 1886 Haymarket Riot in Chicago. The Federation of Organized Trade and Labor Unions in the US, the forerunner of the AFL-CIO, had set May 1, 1886, as the date of effectivity of the eight hour work day, as opposed to the nine- and ten-hour days then prevalent. On the day in question, a general strike went off peacefully in Chicago, but on May 4, at a workers' demonstration in Haymarket Square, someone threw a bomb into a crowd of policemen, killing seven. In the ensuing melee the cops killed two workers, and four radicals were later hanged for their roles on the basis of flimsy evidence.

The Haymarket affair established the importance of May Day as a rallying point for radicals, socialists, communists and liberals everywhere. In Paris in 1889 the Second International, a federation of socialist organizations, called for demonstrations of labor solidarity on May 1, 1890, and May Day has been observed one way or another ever since—although not, ironically, in the US.

3. The Guns of November

Myth! The Russian Revolution started in the month of October.

'The Ten Days That Shook the World' is an imaginative though not imprecise reference to the time it took the Bolsheviks to overthrow Kerensky's provisional government in 1917. All of those ten days are heralded as having occurred in October, which is why the phrase "October Revolution" has become a popular Communist shibboleth and why October itself ranks among the highest in Soviet iconology. Filmmaker Sergei Eisenstein pays homage to the event with his small epic titled *October* (1928), and a favorite cult heroine in contemporary Soviet comics is a leather sex goddess of the underground named Oktobriana.

Oddly, however, the Soviets had never celebrated the Revolution in the month of October until 1990. The reason is an idiosyncrasy of the calendar rather than of politics and is traceable to one of the first acts of the new Bolshevik government. Along with nationalizing the banks and setting up revolutionary tribunals, the victorious regime abolished the Old Style dating system, which the czarist government had maintained in force even after Pope Gregory XIII instituted the New Style, or Gregorian, calendar in the sixteenth century. To align the Soviet Union with the rest of the modern world, the Bolsheviks adopted the New Style and moved all dates thirteen days forward, so that October 25, the date of the Revolution under the Old Style, was now November 7 under the New. Apparently, the shift to the new system revised the official date of the historic event but had little effect on popular thinking.

171

Incidentally, the Oktoberfest regularly held in Germany is a non-political celebration that started in Munich in 1810 and has nothing to do with the communization of East Germany in 1949.

4. Some Parts are Stronger than the Whole

Myth! **The Russian abbreviation CCCP stands for Central Committee of the Communist Party.**

Most people in the non-Communist world think CCCP is the abbreviated name of the Communist Party. Actually, it is the Russian abbreviation for what is rendered in English as USSR, or Union of Soviet Socialist Republics. Russian script, which is based on the Cyrillic alphabet, does not contain the English letters S and R, and instead uses the equivalent for these letters in Russian, which are C and P. When romanized, the Russian name of the federation is Soyuz Sovetskykh Sotsialisticheskikh Respublik. Written in the Russian alphabet, which is quite dissimilar to English, the first letters of each word form the abbreviation CCCP.

The USSR was established in December 1922 with the union of the Russian SFSR (proclaimed after the Russian Revolution of 1917) and various other soviet republics, including Belarus and the Ukraine. After a strife-torn beginning, marked by internal power struggles and disastrous economic plans, it became a major industrial and manufacturing nation, with influence far beyond its borders. In 1991 a number of constituent republics, including Estonia, Latvia, and Lithuania, gained their independence, and the USSR was officially dissolved on December 31 of that year.

One who is asked if the Soviet Union was considerably weakened by its break-up need not be a political expert to say that it was. In fact, the Soviet Union, being a federation, has ceased to exist, and in its place are fifteen independent and competing republics that share the tremendous political and economic power it used to have. What is not readily seen is that, while power of every type was dispersed, Russia—by far the largest republic—has been more than proportionately strengthened. It now has most of the resources, including 51% of the population, 60% of industrial production, and 76% of the territory. It may also have ended up

172

with all the nuclear weapons. Thus, the misconception lingers that the breakup had only a minimal effect on the power balance in the region because Russia and the Soviet Union were practically one and the same.

The belief that the Soviet Union was not a republic, whereas Great Britain is, happens to be wrong on both counts. People tend to confuse republic with democracy, which is a system by which government is made responsible to the will of the people or, at least, their elected representatives. On the other hand, a republic is any form of government, whether or not dictatorial, that has no hereditary ruler or monarch. Thus, the United States is both a democracy and a republic, the Soviet Union is a republic but not a democracy, and England, one of the world's oldest democracies, is not a republic.

---

5. Ice Palace

Myth! 'The Storming of the Winter Palace' is an accurate portrayal of an event in Soviet history, when the Bolshevik peasant army attacked the Tsarist retreat in Petrograd.

The portrayal on canvas and in other types of media of the so-called 'Storming of the Winter Palace' is typically how artists envision the action that led to the capture of this royal residence in what is now St. Petersburg and the ultimate demise of the Romanov regime.

In reality, the keeper of the Winter Palace on this occasion was no longer the Tsar but Alexander Kerensky, the non-Bolshevik revolutionary leader, who had taken over the premises after they were abandoned by the regime. There was no storming by peasants nor any last ditch shoot-out between the Bolsheviks and Kerensky's minions, which consisted of a handful of cadets and a women's battalion. The Bolsheviks had sent an ultimatum by messenger to the palace, and Kerensky, on receiving the message with only about five minutes of the allotted time left, agreed to give up and told his people to leave.

Ironically, before Kerensky's acceptance of the terms of the ultimatum could be brought back by the same messenger, the impatient revolutionaries signaled the guns of the cruiser Aurora and those of the Fortress of Peter and Paul to open fire on the palace. Both ship and fort did, but incredibly, blanks were used, as these were the only ammunition available. The Bolsheviks then marched on the Winter Palace, engaged in some sporadic gunplay around the grounds, and quite successfully killed six, all from their own side, in the confusion. As one report concluded, "Kerensky simply wandered out of his office, got into his car, and drove away leaving the Bolsheviks hopelessly lost in the labyrinth of the palace's 1,000-odd rooms."

In James Trager's *The People's Chronology* (1996), the Winter Palace is described as having 1,050 rooms with 117 staircases, 1,786 windows, and a 290-square foot map of Russia set in emeralds, rubies and semiprecious stones. The invaders were so awed by the magnificence that they eventually left the palace unmolested.

6. Red is Beautiful

Myth! The most famous of Russia's plazas is named Red Square to symbolize communism.

Despite, or maybe because of, its having witnessed so many executions, demonstrations, riots, parades, and speeches during its colorful past, Moscow's Red Square made it to UNESCO's World Heritage List in 1990. Many are of the mind that the history of the square is intertwined, if not contemporaneous, with that of communism, and this is because, unlike white, red is politically significant to the Russians, particularly the Communists, as demonstrated by the Red Flag motif and the slogan "East is Red." The word 'square' is an accurate description for this 73,000 sq. m. open area adjoining, on one side the Kremlin, the former royal citadel and currently the official residence of the President of Russia, and on the other a historic merchant quarter known as *Kitay-gorod*. The site dates back to the late 15th century, just after the Kremlin walls were completed, and since then has endured as the central square of Moscow and of all Russia.

Contrary to popular thinking, however, Red Square was not named deliberately to relate it to Russian ideology. The famous site shares neither its history nor its etymology with anything communistic; the word 'red' was attached in the later 17th century, long before the advent of communism, with no purpose in mind other than to replace the square's older name *Pozhar*. While some say the new tag may have been derived from the color of the bricks or of several of the structures in the area, the more credible view is that at the time of its adoption, the Russian word *krasnaya*, for 'red', also stood for 'beautiful'. According to *The Straight Dope*, there is no coincidence involved: "To the pre-12th-century savages who settled in what is now Great Russia (around the Volga, between White Russia and the Ural Mountains), redness and beauty were one; red was a kind of superlative ideal. Modern Russian retains the idea of red being beautiful." The earlier Saint Basil's Cathedral (actually, the Cathedral of the Intercession of the Virgin) was originally nicknamed the Red Cathedral not because of its color but because of its beauty, and this was exactly the same concept the Russians had when they named Red Square. Today, the word for 'red' is *krasnaia* (or some reasonable phonetic equivalent), and for 'beautiful', *kracivaya*.

Even as a symbol of revolution, red predated communism by as much as sixty years. The red banner emerged in 1792 during the French revolution and later during the revolt of June 5-6, 1832, in Paris. Symbolizing the blood spilled by the people after the Paris Commune of 1871, it became the banner of the proletarian revolution and was flown for the first time in Russia in 1861. It was formally adopted as the Soviet flag in 1918.

7. Jack in the Wall

Myth! The Communist John Reed is the only American buried in the Kremlin Wall.

Warren Beauty won an Oscar for his portrayal of John Reed in the movie *Reds*. Reed, the American journalist who wrote "Ten Days That Shook the World," describing the Russian Revolution, is widely believed to be the only American buried in the Kremlin wall. In fact, William 'Big Bill' Haywood, the labor leader who founded the radical Industrial Workers of the World (IWW), was also interred there after he fled to Russia to avoid imprisonment

175

for sedition in the US. However, Reed is the only American Communist buried in the Kremlin Wall, since Haywood, despite his conviction in the US, never became a Communist, only a Socialist.

Reed is also often mistaken as the US journalist who, after seeing Russia, said: "I have seen the future, and it works." The real commentator was Lincoln Steffens, a Communist sympathizer who paid a visit to the newly formed Soviet Union as part of the William C. Bullitt diplomatic mission of 1919. He returned to America with this optimistic view, which he expressed in his autobiography somewhat differently, thus: "I have been over into the future, and it works." Steffens is famous—or notorious—for having written the first muckraking article, *Shame of the Cities*, a series published in McClure's at the turn of the century.

8. How to Sight a Kremlin

Myth! Kremlin is the name of one of the most architecturally distinctive structures in Moscow.

Media—and constant repetition in travel and tourist books—have fostered the belief that there is only one Kremlin in Russia and that this is a specific building located in Moscow. Pictured as a massive multi-towered structure called 'The Kremlin', it is said to contain the residence of the Russian (formerly Soviet) head of state and the offices of the most exalted members of his government. The term has thus become a metronym for the entire government of the Soviet Union (until 1991), including its general secretaries, premiers, presidents, ministers, and commissars. In much the same way, 'The White House' has been made to refer to the executive branch of the US government, although in its case, the treatment is better justified because the White House is one of a kind whereas there is at least one kremlin in almost every major Russian city. The Kremlin in Moscow is the largest and best known, but the Suzdal Kremlin (a UNESCO World Heritage Site) and the Kolomna Kremlin are equally notable. The capital cities of Pskov, Novgorod, Smolensk, Mostov, Yaroslavl, Vladimir, and Nizhni Novgorod were all built around old kremlins, which are walled, triangular fortresses, or citadels, containing a bewildering

176

array of complex buildings including cathedrals, palaces for princes and bishops, governmental offices, and munitions stores.

Kremlin is actually a Russian generic term for a citadel, fortress or large walled space, a throwback to medieval times, when there were not only outer walls around many major cities but also inner walls protecting an area at the center from invaders. As in Moscow, the word does not refer to any specific structure but to the whole complex contained in the fortification. Though the kremlins were built as fortresses with moats, ramparts, towers, and battlements, their principal use was not so much for military purposes as for civic government.

The Moscow Kremlin dates back to the 2nd century BC, and originates from a Vyatich fortified structure, or 'grad', on Borovitsky Hill. Located at the heart of the city overlooking the Moskva River, Saint Basil's Cathedral and the Alexander Garden, it includes four palaces, four cathedrals, tombs, government buildings and the enclosing Kremlin Wall with Kremlin towers. Cathedral Square, and not Red Square as is commonly believed, is smack in the center in an area encompassing about ninety acres. Considering that Russia has never been bereft of great architects, it is surprising to know that the Moscow Kremlin, initially built of wood but later converted to brick, was largely the work of Italians. This includes its centerpiece, the Grand Palace, which was designed by baroque architect Rastrelli.

9. Colorable Differences

Myth! Anticommunist Russians and those loyal to the Tsarist cause are called White Russians.

Inhabitants of the former Soviet Union who supported the loyalist cause during the Russian Revolution are sometimes called White Russians. Obviously, this is to differentiate them from the Reds. The popular view finds support in movies like *Anastasia* (1956), which portrays White Russians taking refuge in France in their pursuit of the anti-Communist line.

In fact, the term 'White Russian' has absolutely nothing to do with political ideology. White Russia is a geographical division, one of the Russias comprising the western provinces that border on Poland and the Baltic states. It was a constituent republic of the USSR from 1922 until 1991, when it became an independent country of 9,942,000 called Belarus, or Byelorussia, with Minsk as the capital. Most of the Byelorussians were opposed to the Reds during the revolution, but this is a mere coincidence and is not the reason for the nomenclature 'White Russian'.

The real reason has never been determined, although there are two possibilities. The first has relevance to the color of the skin of the Caucasian inhabitants of the region, in contrast with that of the Mongolians in eastern Russia. By extension, the term 'Black Russia' is sometimes applied to any part of the country inhabited by colored people, without regard to the fact that Black Russia is really central and southern Russia and named for the black soil. The second and more plausible explanation is that Belarus was once Byelorussia, which was coined in reference to the traditional costume of the region consisting of white smock, shoes, trousers and homespun coat (*byely* is Russian for white).

10. To Each his Own

Myth! Karl Marx is the most famous proponent of the principle of equal pay for everybody.

In popular thinking, the pairing of Russia with Communism seems inescapable, but in fact, the congruence is flawed. For one, the belief that Communism was conceptualized and founded by Russian revolutionaries who fought for the working class is false.
The first proponent, Plato, was Greek, and the founders of the modern doctrine, Karl Marx and Friedrich Engels, were both German. Marx was Jewish to boot, and France, England, and Germany were the targets of his reform more than Russia was.

Both Marx and Engels, collaborators in the writing of the Communist Manifesto, acted differently from what they preached. Marx was a hypocrite, a spendthrift and a freeloader who never took a job. He was prejudiced against real working-class people, as well as against females and blacks. Engels was no oppressed proletarian either; far from it, he was an outright capitalist, for many years a highly paid executive in the sort of factory he so savagely criticized in his works. In the 1850s, he moved to

178

Manchester, England, where he lived a markedly comfortable life, with memberships in the stock exchange and exclusive clubs, and entertained lavishly—all the while supporting Marx with frequent checks and maintaining their collaboration.

Marx popularized the slogan, "From each according to his abilities, to each according to his needs," though not in the Communist Manifesto or *Das Kapital* but as part of the concluding statement in his *Critique of the Gotha Program*. In this latter work, Marx asserted that every person should contribute to society to the best of his ability and consume from society in proportion to his needs regardless of how much he has contributed. In his view, such an arrangement is perfectly possible in a developed communist society where enough goods and services are produced, or are expected to be produced, to satisfy everyone's needs. Although Marx is popularly thought of as its originator, the slogan was quite common to the socialist movement and was first used by Louis Blanc in 1840, in "The organization of work," as a revision of a quote by the utopian socialist Henri de Saint Simon. According to Wikipedia, an even earlier origin would be the New Testament, particularly Acts 4:32-35, in which the Apostles' lifestyle is described as communal, i.e., with no individual possession, and "distribution was made unto every man according as he had need."

Despite Marx's efforts, the layman's assumption of Communism—that under the system, everybody gets, or is supposed to get, the same income—departs significantly from the slogan's intent. This popular view of the Communist credo is encapsulated in yet another slogan—"equal pay for everybody"—and its most famous proponent was not Marx but George Bernard Shaw, who mentioned it in his *The Intelligent Woman's Guide to Socialism and Capitalism* (1928). Shaw was no Marxist, nor did he enunciate the principle to describe Marxism; in fact, he remarks in the same book that Marxism "is not only useless but disastrous as a guide to the practice of government." "Equal pay for everybody" was a summation of Shaw's beliefs as an ardent socialist and Fabian, among which were: (1) men and women are entitled to equal political rights, (2) there is a pressing need to alleviate abuses of the working class, and (3) government must control land and resources to ensure that they are reasonably allocated. Unlike Marx, however, Shaw could only envisage his reform as something gradual and induced by peaceful means rather than by outright revolution.

VI

Europa Europa

On the Atlantic War

"I might have had trouble saving France in
1946 - I didn't have television then."

•

Charles de Gaulle

1. Blitzkrieg—This is no Drill!

Myth! World War II started officially when Germany invaded Poland on August 25, 1939.

To track the true dimensions of that great war, one would have to go back six days earlier, when Hitler ordered a first strike on Poland in pursuit of his original plan. The 16 combat units the Führer had asked for were already deployed and ready for battle when the attack was called off at the last minute. Late-breaking political developments, including Mussolini's sudden vow not to assist Germany in any Polish venture, convinced Hitler that the time was not ripe for an invasion. Also, on August 25, less than 24 hours before Hitler's troops were scheduled to break across the Polish frontier, the Anglo-Polish treaty was signed transforming Britain's unilateral guarantee of Poland into a pact of mutual assistance.

The Nazi combat teams were radioed and summoned home, but none could be reached. On August 26, Lt. Albert Herzner's men managed to exchange some shots with the Polish and capture the strategic Janlunkuv Pass in Poland along with the railway station at Mosty and some Polish prisoners. When Herzner telephoned central headquarters after the encounter, he was told that the plans had been scuttled and that he should release his prisoners and come home.

Incredibly, the Polish let the incident pass without notice and were taken by surprise when the Nazis invaded again on September 1st.

2. Nothing to Fear But...

Myth! FDR rejected the Munich Agreement as a viable means of avoiding World War II.

Actually, FDR supported the Munich Agreement more strongly than the British did, and, as Shenkman writes, he even "tried to take credit for it." He mentions a number of overt acts that showed FDR's support for appeasement from the time Hitler took power.

First, in 1933, he told his roving envoy Norman Davis that "political appeasement" was needed to provide for lasting peace. Then, in 1935 he asked an old business crony, Samuel Fuller, to find out what the Germans wanted in exchange for peace. Later in the same year, he told the German ambassador to the United States that Hitler was the right man to lead Germany.

In 1937 he sent Sumner Welles to Europe to see if Britain would agree to the return of Germany's African colonies. The next year he fired William Dodd, the United States ambassador to Germany, after Dodd made some speeches attacking the Nazi Party. Finally, he showed his entire hand by announcing his support for the Munich Agreement itself.

To make matters worse, he did all these even though he was not compelled to appease Hitler the way the British were. A war in Europe was hardly his concern, since, as he himself had said a number of times, he was expected by most Americans to keep the US neutral.

3. Know thine Enemy

Myth! Adhering strictly to the Allied-Axis dichotomy of World War II, Italy, Romania and Finland sided with Germany, while Thailand stood by the US and Great Britain.

Actually, the dichotomy was flawed and these kept many people from knowing for sure who was declaring war on whom. For example, Fascist Italy, after declaring war on England in 1940, made a formal declaration of war against Nazi Germany on June 14, 1945. This was two years after Italy had surrendered to the Allies in September 1943. Romania, an Axis satellite, declared war on the US on December 12, 1941, but after Fascist dictator Antonescu was overthrown on August 23, 1944, Romanians briefly fought German troops without declaring war on Germany. Finland was a minor Axis power until early 1945, when it switched sides against Germany. Thailand declared war on the US on January 25, 1942, but the US refused to counter with its own declaration of war on Thailand. The US believed that Japan, by returning many French-occupied territories to Thailand, had pressured that country to support it.

The demarcation between the Pacific and the European segments of the war was blurred as well when the Soviet Union declared war on Japan and invaded Manchuria on August 8, 1945, a week before the Sons of Nippon surrendered to the Allies. This was history in reverse for the Japanese, who, as members of the Allies, declared war on Germany during the last few moments of World War I.

4. Escape Artistry

Myth! The rescue operation at Dunkirk, ably assisted by an armada of private vessels from England, was so well managed Hitler could not have prevented it.

Most accounts of the massive escape operation by the Allies at Dunkirk do not mention that Hitler could have prevented the escape but chose not to for private reasons. By not ordering his tanks to press on to Dunkirk, he allowed the British to mount Operation Dynamo and salvage what threatened to be a disaster. Although the retreat was a clear debacle for the British army— even Churchill had to confess in private that it was "the greatest British military defeat for many centuries"—it came to be regarded almost as a heroic victory.

In the weeks leading up to the retreat, the French had demanded that the British put up a fight but the British military had refused. It took a direct order from Churchill to Lord Gort, the commander of the British army on the coast, to get him to fight. British reluctance and weakness of strategy combined to produce no less than disastrous results. Some officers abandoned their positions to catch the earliest boats out, while British sailors had to resort to armed threats to keep the troops from storming the ships. Upon returning to England, the troops were so demoralized that "they threw their rifles and equipment out of railroad carriage windows."

The British refused at first to allow French forces to leave with them. The French were officially asked to join their British allies only two days after the withdrawal began. The great majority of troops were evacuated in Royal Navy ships, with only eight percent going on the legendary armada of 861 small boats that volunteers sailed across the Channel from England to participate in the rescue operations.

5. The Story of G.I. Joe

Myth! The branch of the US Armed Forces most instrumental in winning World War II for the Allies was the infantry.

War movies dramatizing the travails of the foot soldier as he slogged his way through Europe in 1944 effectively ascribe the victory of the Allies to the aggressiveness of US ground troops. The reason obviously is that movies, as opposed to documentaries, are generally character-oriented and more likely to portray the heroics of the infantry than of any other branch of the armed forces. The truth, according to S. L. A. Marshall's 1947 study *Men Against Fire*, is that only about 25 per-cent of the American soldiers fired their rifles in the European theater of war, and often not more than 15 percent at any given time. This was confirmed by E. A. Reitan, professor of history at Illinois State University, who pointed out that the purpose of infantry is to advance on the enemy and occupy friendly and enemy territory regardless of whether rifles are fired or not.

The infantry action at D-Day was impressive, but on succeeding days, the Allied offensive was mostly heavy saturation bombing and offensive tank tactics. Historians say the misleading role of ground troops in Europe stems from too much media attention paid to D-Day, and too little to the nearly three months of fighting required after D-Day to push the Germans out of France

6. Running on Empty

Myth! The US implemented gas rationing during World War II as a means of conserving fuel.

185

The fact is that there was no need for conserving gas at all. At the beginning of the war, the Allies had control of about 85 percent of the world's oil production and the US had one of the largest stocks of the fuel.

But there was one thing the Allies lacked: rubber. The US had only a one-year supply of rubber in reserve, which was considered inadequate to meet the huge anticipated military demand for the war. After its incursion into Indochina, Japan had control of about 97 percent of the world's natural rubber supply. When the US imposed an embargo on oil against Japan, the latter reciprocated with an embargo on rubber.

With the Japanese controlling the highly endemic resource, the need to conserve rubber tires arose. As rationing tires alone would not have the immediate effect of reducing driving and tire wear, US authorities decided that the better way of cutting down on the use of rubber tires was by restricting the gas supply of motor vehicles. Thus, along with the setting of speed limits at 35 MPH, gas rationing was imposed, to take effect for the duration of the war or until a synthetic rubber product could be developed. Implementation by the federal Office of Price Administration began on a nationwide basis on December I, 1942, and ended with the war on August 15, 1945.

7. The Longest Day

Myth! The Allies' combined effort to liberate France, called D-Day, was launched as scheduled on June 6, 1944.

Contrary to most people's understanding, D-day the Sixth of June, the greatest military operation of all time, was not an end in itself. It was only preparatory to the Allied move, beginning in 1944, to liberate Europe and ultimately defeat the Nazis. Its purpose was to gain a foothold in the European mainland from which to launch successive Allied efforts to carry the war to the heartland of Germany.

For all its meticulous planning, D-Day was delayed by twenty-four hours and nearly didn't materialize. It should have been D-Day the Fifth of June, since this was the day originally set for the exercise, but the Allies decided against proceeding in highly inclement weather. It was agreed to postpone the invasion for the next day, which then became D-Day the Sixth of June. Any further delay would have put off the attack for another two weeks in order to get the favorable early morning tides again at Normandy. Afraid that this might give Hitler sufficient time to be warned and to redeploy his troops, Eisenhower gave the signal to proceed on the sixth.

It is worthwhile noting that 'D-day' was not coined specifically for the day Normandy was to be invaded. The word had been in use even before World War II and meant 'deadline day', not in reference to a specific event but generally to any day on which some action of important magnitude was set. One of its earliest applications goes back to World War I, when the D in D-day stood for nothing more than 'day' as the H in H-hour was for 'hour'. Based on either etymology, Normandy Day is not just D-day but D-day the Sixth of June.

8. Things that Go 'Blam' in the Night

Myth! **Europe of World War II was the most bombed continent in any war.**

However fearful that war theater has been made to appear in the history books, it's not Europe that's backed up by the figures as the most bombed continent in any conflict. Rather, it was Asia during the Vietnam War. North Vietnam alone suffered twice that of everyone combined in World War II. The United States dropped 7 million tons of bombs, along with Agent Orange and other chemical defoliants, on an area about the size of Massachusetts. This overwhelms the 3 or 4 million the Allies and the Axis dumped on Europe and Asia during all of World War II.

Between May 1964 and February 26, 1973, Laos took some 2 1/2 million tons of bombs of all kinds, most of them dropped along the North to South Ho Chi Minh Trail supply route to South Vietnam. As with Coventry, which was pummeled by Nazi bombs for 10 hours, the objective was purely psychological and nothing in the targets was really worth destroying.

187

9. Bull in a China Shop

Myth! The most criticized in moral terms of all the bombings conducted in World War II were the Allies' nuclear attacks on Hiroshima and Nagasaki.

The bombings of Hiroshima and Nagasaki, which brought harmful effects on more than one generation of Japanese, were criticized by Allies and Axis alike for humanitarian reasons. So was the American-led fire attack on Tokyo on March 9, 1945. But the air raid that elicited the most recriminations was yet another of the Allies' misconceived efforts—the conventional bombing of Dresden.

The German city was the target of a combined American and British bombing attack through most of the night of February 13-14, 1945. It was and still is considered the most controversial example of aerial overkill, as tons of explosive and incendiary bombs were rained on the city of nearly a million. The Germans officially reported the deaths of 400,000 people, mostly civilians (the British pared this down to 250,000), as the greatest firestorm ever known destroyed nearly the entire city. There were 200,000 refugees and some Allied prisoners-of-war in the city when it happened.

Dresden was a cultural center, a "Florence on the Elbe," as it was then known. Although it was believed to be a key German communication point for the eastern front, it seemed more likely that the attacks were indiscriminate area bombing and "not proportionate for the commensurate military gains."

10. Blitz Spirit and Heinz Sight

Myth! Hitler invented the word 'blitzkrieg', but it was Nazi General Heinz Guderian who originated the concept for adoption as a military strategy.

The word 'blitzkrieg', referring to a maneuver that called for coordinated massive air attacks and lightning-fast rapid advances, was not coined by Hitler or any of his strategists and was not known to them before 1939. Karl-Heinz Frieser, in his book *Blitzkrieg Legende*, points out that the pre-war use of the term was rare, and that it practically never entered official terminology throughout the war. Rather, it was invented by Western newspapermen to convey to their readers something of the speed and destructiveness of German ground-air operations in the three-week campaign against the ill-equipped and outnumbered Polish army. It was first popularized in the English-speaking world by Time magazine describing the 1939 German invasion of Poland in its issue of September 25, 1939. The term was later widened to refer generically to the strategy of a fast, coordinated and unrelenting mode of attack, including that employed in American football and in the game of chess.

For the concept itself, although credit is usually given to Tank General Heinz Guderian, one of Nazi Germany's greatest military tacticians, the fact is he did not devise it and neither did Hitler or any of his other officers. Guderian is remembered, first, for writing the military treatise 'Achtung - Panzer! In 1936-37', explaining the potential of the tank and aircraft in modern warfare, and, second, for creating the panzer force that would become the core of the German Army's power and unleash the fighting style known as blitzkrieg. Guderian most likely lifted the idea of blitzkrieg from the writings of a contemporary Englishman, B. H. Liddell Hart, a military historian and philosopher who had developed what he called the 'expanding torrent'—finding the enemy's path of least resistance or weakest point and striking repeatedly through it. Liddell Hart's inspiration was Genghis Khan and the thirteenth-century Mongols, who called their theory 'tulughma', and in modern times General William Tecumseh Sherman, who had resorted to the method in his 1864 march to the sea during the Civil War. Notwithstanding the recognition given to Genghis Khan and Sherman in Liddell Hart's writings, Hitler, who was a closet Anglophile, liked the idea because he thought it was originally English.

To the Germans, blitzkrieg was not a strategy in the true military sense but a necessity dictated by economic conditions. The German economy initially couldn't support sustained warfare, so the military had to resort to lightning-quick strikes to achieve prompt results. The Germans took advantage of the intervening lulls to restore depleted stocks in time for the next attack.

Guderian proposed blitzkrieg to Hitler in 1939 to subdue France quickly, as the Nazis could not afford too long a war on two fronts, one with Britain and the other with Russia. The German general staff, initially opposed to Guderian's proposal, yielded to Hitler, and in May 1940, Nazi tanks broke into France and swept through the French defenses using strictly blitzkrieg timing.

11. Panzers on a Short Leash

Myth! The Nazis used blitzkrieg to full advantage and made it account for many of Germany's victories in World War II.

Blitzkrieg was probably not the real reason for the unprecedented Nazi victories at the onset of World War II. Military analysts say there were more important factors, such as the unpreparedness and the inadequate equipment of the country under blitz, as in the case of Poland, Czechoslovakia and the Low Countries. The effective use of other arms, such as artillery and aerial firepower, was equally important to the success of German (and later, Allied) operations. In other cases, blitzkrieg simply didn't work. Leningrad did not fall despite an entire Panzer Group being assigned to take it, nor did Moscow. "In 1942 panzer formations overstretched at Stalingrad and in the Caucasus, and what successes did take place—such as Manstein at Kharkov or Krivoi Rog—were of local significance only." In Russia on the whole, where the campaigns became unduly long because of terrain and temperament, the seemingly imprudent application of blitzkrieg eventually led to German defeat.

In later years, German production could no longer keep pace with blitzkrieg's accelerated degree of sustainability. The strategy had the inherent danger of the attacking force overextending its supply lines, and in the case of Germany it took its toll when new tanks and vehicles could not be provided fast enough and old ones were short of fuel and ammunition. Although production of Luftwaffe fighter aircraft continued, they would be unable to fly because fuel was diverted to panzer divisions. And even this palliative would prove inadequate for Germany's erstwhile vanguards, the Tiger tanks; of those lost against the United States Army, nearly half were abandoned for lack of fuel.

Blitzkrieg attained its hype in only one instance: France. Unlike Poland, France could not have been any more prepared for war, what with the Maginot Line defending its north-east frontier with Germany and armaments that surpassed those of Hitler's army in number and quality. The Line, flawed as it was in hindsight, fully reflected the state of alertness of the French at the start of World War II. It was just unfortunate that Hitler changed his plans at the last minute and decided to attack through Holland and Belgium, as the Germans did in World War I, completely bypassing the fortifications. Nevertheless, this happenstance was not the real reason the German tank divisions overran France in six weeks. The French had more tanks, while 90 per cent of the German tanks were obsolete training models. France also had plenty of planes, including the squadrons contributed by Britain, and as of August 1939, France had more than twice Germany's strength at sea. But faced with the awesomeness of blitzkrieg power as projected by media, the French lost the will to fight. They would realize too late that, without the hype, blitzkrieg power was based less on equipment or strategy than on simple tactics. In the small matter of refueling tanks, for instance, tankers slowly refueled French tanks while the Germans accomplished faster results using handier 'jerricans'.

12. A Puzzle Wrapped in an Enigma

Myth! Churchill could not provide the RAF protection that Coventry needed based on intelligence reports because it would reveal that the British had cracked the Nazi code Ultra.

This, in a nutshell, has been the story behind the tragedy of Coventry, but a number of considerations tend to becloud it. *First*, against the claim that Churchill and his advisers were forewarned by "at least forty-eight, possibly sixty, hours," the earliest Churchill could have learned of the Coventry plan was four or five hours before the impending attack. *Second*, the information that Coventry was the bombing target did not come directly from Ultra

191

but from signals intercepted by the RAF on the very date of the raid from a navigation beacon that the Germans had set up to guide the Luftwaffe to their destination.

Third, allegations to the contrary notwithstanding, the British did their utmost to protect Coventry even without knowing that the Nazi incursion would be in the nature of an annihilation raid. A plan to jam the German beams and mislead the bombers would have been the best countermeasure under the circumstances, but it failed when the interceptors gave the wrong frequency to the jammers. Finally, much of the desolation that resulted must be attributed to the inefficiency of civilian facilities, such as civil defense and fire-fighting reinforcements, which arrived at or near Coventry only after the raid was over.

13. Suppress that Bulge!

Myth! 'Bulge' in reference to the last German offensive of World War II stands for the Belgium-Luxembourg area where the battle was fought.

The Battle of the Bulge raged from December 1944 to January 1945, with the Germans under General Karl von Rundstedt launching a mighty but desperate counterattack against the Allied line in Belgium-Luxembourg. While the term may suggest that the Bulge was where the battle was fought, in fact it does not refer to any place but to the shape of the German formation that resulted from the offensive. As the northern and southern armies ran into stiff opposition after early successes, the units in the middle plunged forward with almost alarming speed. This action created a large salient, or dent, about 60 miles deep into the Allied line, the shape of which resembled a bulge.

Weak at the sides, the bulge was most vulnerable to Allied attack, and in January 1945 the Allies advanced and straightened it, putting an end to the last German offensive of the war. Despite 100,000 dead and wounded, military experts saw it as a German tactical victory that stalled the Allied crossing of the Rhine and— until March 7, 1945—the invasion of the Fatherland itself.

The Battle of the Bulge is what the conflict is popularly called, but officially it is named the Battle of Ardennes II for that section of Belgium where the fighting occurred. The Battle of Ardennes I saw Germany fighting in the same place in World War I against France.

---

14. Too Late the Hero

Myth! Inarticulate as he was, Dwight D. Eisenhower was one of the most bemedaled generals of World War II.

Political opponents complained they couldn't reach Eisenhower, and vice-versa, because of his 'eisenhowerese', referring to the 'fuzzy locutions and opaque syntax' that came out of his fudging and hedging at the presidential podium. Supporters have insisted, however, that 'eisenhowerese' was a deliberate tactic to avoid those sticky situations in which politicians often find themselves. Indeed, Eisenhower had as much claim to MacArthur's legendary words as the man himself, since he was MacArthur's assistant and official speechwriter in the 1930's during their Philippine assignment. Of mild temperament and pleasing personality, Ike, as Eisenhower was fondly called, was reason to MacArthur's rhyme, in the end achieving even more than the master through quiet, almost clerical, tenacity.

Not many people know the Distinguished Service Medal was the only major US military award General Dwight D. Eisenhower ever got, and those who do know erroneously believe he got it for his role in World War II. He actually won it in World War I, although how he managed to do so remains unclear. This most popular and respected US soldier of his time never led a contingent in combat all his life, whether before becoming Supreme Allied Commander in 1943 or after. The son of pacifist parents, he had been a desk-bound petty officer on training assignments in World War I since his graduation in 1915, and that had kept him out of combat.

According to *Encyclopedia Britannica*, a big factor in Eisenhower's meteoric rise from relative obscurity was 'his ability to persuade, to mediate, and to be agreeable'. No one is sure if the only US-awarded medal of his military career was obtained using this talent, or if it was providentially given to prepare him for his future role as the highest Allied military leader in Europe. What is

193

sure is that prior to his first assignment to London during World War II, he had only been to Europe once previously to write a guidebook on American war monuments.

15. A Man, a Plan, a Continent

Myth! **General George Catlett Marshall authored the Marshall Plan, to help Europe out of the devastation caused by World War II.**

Marshall received the Nobel Peace Prize in 1953 for authoring the European Recovery Program, popularly known as the Marshall Plan, but remaining unsung is the real author, Undersecretary of State Will Clayton. Marshall may have contributed some rudimentary ideas, but it was Clayton who drafted the program in its entirety on a flight from Europe to the US, after which he promoted it vigorously in Marshall's name. Some historians offer evidence that Dean Acheson, the Secretary of State from 1949 to 1953, proposed the plan ahead of Marshall, but even Acheson may have been a latecomer. The idea of providing organized assistance for the war-devastated countries of Western Europe had long been a subject of public discussion when Marshall mentioned his version in a commencement address at Harvard University in June 1947.

The Marshall Plan pumped more than $12 billion into 16 war-torn countries over four years, avowedly to provide economic support for Truman's policy of containment to prevent the spread of Communism in Western Europe. But critics of the Plan claim American altruism had little to do with the gesture, since the real motive was to rebuild European buying power for the US market.

16. Looking for Dr. Strangelove

Myth! **The Germans were way behind the Allies in atomic research and could not have produced an operational atomic bomb even if the war had not ended.**

That Germany was on the verge of producing an operational atomic bomb when the war ended is not as far-fetched as it may sound. A team of German scientists had been actively engaged in nuclear research since 1937, and was well ahead of anyone else in the theoretical field. The Allies got wind of the project from papers and reports that the Germans themselves had published in scientific journals. The leak, incidentally, would not have happened had war broken out earlier in 1938.

At the practical level, German atomic research was also ahead of the Allies before mid-1942. The first German atomic reactor was built in Leipzig, and with the Norwegian Hydro-Electric Company at Vemork providing the Germans with Europe's only supply of heavy water (an essential ingredient in atomic reaction), experiments were well under way by May 1942.

The turning point was in June of that year when the Leipzig reactor exploded, and early in 1943, the factory at Vemork was sabotaged by a band of Norwegian commandos. These demoralized efforts at centralized direction and discouraged full-scale government support for the program. The Germans set about building a more advanced atomic reactor in the Swabian village of Haigerloch, and by the end of February 1945 were ready for the big experiment. However, the operation failed to produce a sustained atomic reaction, a result that no longer proved ironic in view of the fact that Fermi had already achieved success in the US in 1942.

Incidentally, Germany was not the only Axis power that had atomic research facilities at the end of World War II. Japanese scientists were themselves poised to delve into the secrets of the atom when the US dropped the bomb on Hiroshima and Nagasaki.

17. When the Axis Fell

Myth! Germany surrendered on VE-Day, May 8, 1945, and Japan on VJ-Day, September 2, 1945.

Contrary to its popular connotation, VE-Day was not the day Germany surrendered ending World War II. The actual surrender was made at 2:41 a.m. the previous day, May 7, in a schoolhouse at Reims. To assure Russian participation, the ceremony was repeated at the Russian Headquarters in Berlin on May 8, which has since been regarded officially as the day the war ended in Europe.

The same can be said of VJ-Day, which was the day Japan signed the formal surrender aboard the US battleship Missouri in Tokyo Bay. Japan threw in the towel and ended the war more than two weeks before, on August 15, 1945.

18. War Prison Blues

Myth! The US treated its German prisoners above Geneva Convention standards, but American POWs were not as fortunate in the hands of their German captors.

It is sometimes rumored that the largest percentage of Allied casualties in World War 2 came from the German POW camps, but in fact only four percent of the 260,000 American and British prisoners of Hitler's Third Reich died there. By contrast, more than 28 percent of the 95,000 Britons, Americans and other Allies taken prisoner by the Japanese perished in captivity. In Vietnamese hands during the Vietnam War, death was the fate of about 15 percent of the POWs, while in North Korea during the Korean War, 39 percent of American POWs did not survive.

The popular belief is that the US more than reciprocated Nazi magnanimity by treating its German prisoners extra well. But according to one historian, the best-kept secret of World War II is that at least 56,000 German POWs died while in American custody, nearly all of them from malnutrition. These were mostly German soldiers who rushed to surrender to the US Army at the end of the war because they were afraid to give themselves up to the Soviet Union. Conditions in the American POW camps were so horrific that General Eisenhower reclassified the POWs as DEFs—Disarmed Enemy Forces—to exempt them from the minimum standards of care set for POWs by the Geneva Convention.

A panel of historians belied the charge that up to a million German POWs may have died, but they did conclude "there was widespread mistreatment of German prisoners in the spring and summer of 1945. Men were beaten, denied water, forced to live in open camps without shelter, given inadequate food rations and inadequate medical care."

19. French Leave

Myth! Of the various French groups involved in the Allied invasion of Normandy, the French Resistance played the most effective role.

According to a *Time* article commemorating the 50th anniversary of D-Day, the Hollywood version of this World War II event contains more truth than the historical perspective presented by the French. The former shows British, American and Canadian troops storming the beaches and happy French civilians greeting their Allied liberators with kisses and bottles of wine. The French version, on the other hand, directs the spotlight on heroic fighters of the French underground paving the way for D-Day, oftentimes unfairly crediting to them the part played self-effacingly by non-combatant French citizens.

The French view is supported by a poll commissioned by D-Day celebration organizers, indicating that nearly 50 percent of Frenchmen believe the Resistance played a major role in preparing for the Normandy invasion. But among the others are historians who concede that local Resistance leaders shrank from urging an all-out uprising after the invasion began, partly for fear of German retribution. It would appear that the only positive action from the French underground was an anti-Nazi rebellion that occurred in Paris in August 1944 but failed to dislodge the Germans.

Direct participation by French forces in the D-Day invasion was even more dismal—it was limited to only 170 French troops, apparently because Gen. Charles de Gaulle, the Free French leader in London, was not informed of the invasion date. A French armored division under General Philippe Leclerc eventually liberated Paris in September 1944, but Leclerc, who had landed on the continent after D-Day, did not enter the city until most German defenders had already fled.

20. Death Spas

Myth! The Nazis launched the concept of the concentration camp with the establishment of their first facility in March 1933.

It is said Heinrich Himmler put up the first concentration camp when he ordered the conversion of an old gunpowder factory in the vicinity of Dachau to accommodate 15,000 Communist and socialist prisoners. However, other sources claim the Communists were well ahead of the Nazis in this regard, having had their own concentration camps since 1917 under the supervision of the dreaded Cheka (All-Russian Extraordinary Commission for Combating Counterrevolution and Sabotage). By 1922 there were 23 such camps being employed to reinforce Communist control.

Actually, concentration camps had been around long before the Nazis and the Soviets started to use them to detain or persecute political offenders. The groundbreakers were neither the right nor the left but the center—Britain, to be precise. The earliest known application was during the 1901-1902 period of the South African War, when the British confined non-combatants of the Transvaal and Cape Colony in highly secured common quarters. The concept then spread to Europe, where fascists often found a need to intern members of national or minority groups for security, political or penal reasons.

Later, even the US was not to be spared from the guilt. After the outbreak of hostilities with Japan, more than 100,000 West Coast Japanese and Japanese-Americans were placed in camps in the interior of the mainland.

VII

Armageddon In The East

On the Pacific War

*"A general is just as good or just as bad
as the troops under his command make him."*

•

Douglas MacArthur

1. East Trumps West, North Passes

Myth! **Churchill withheld advance information on the looming Pearl Harbor attack pursuant to a secret understanding with FDR at their August meeting in Placentia Bay, Newfoundland.**

Churchill's secret files discovered after his death disprove theories that he had prior knowledge of the Pearl Harbor attack. Despite several indications that Japan was about to enter the war, not one of the 1,300 documents in the trove, many obtained by breaking enemy codes, contained any information about the Japanese plan or that British sources were aware of it. British Intelligence may have learned as early as November 26, 1941, after they had cracked the Japanese naval code, that the Japanese fleet had left its home port, and, by December 2, that the critical message was 'Climb Niitakayama 1208'. However, whether Churchill knew what they knew and passed the information on to Roosevelt is undocumented.

It is a fact that Churchill was worried about the Japanese getting involved in the war and putting pressure on Britain's presence in Asia. He also did not want American strength and resources drawn to the Pacific and away from the European Theater. The British PM probably would have helped avert the projected attack had he been properly alerted, although how he would have gone about it is anybody's guess.

2. A Game of Battleship

Myth! **The first major naval victory for the US since the Japanese attack on Pearl Harbor was a battle between great ships in the vicinity of the Coral Sea.**

Earning a respectable place as one of the greatest naval fights in American military history, the Battle of the Coral Sea is considered by many to be the turning point in the Pacific War, with the US inflicting more damage than the Japanese and gaining its first major naval victory. There are more to this classic encounter than meet the eye. First, the battle was fought mostly on May 8, 1942, in the vicinity of the Solomon Islands rather than the Coral Sea. Second, it was decided by aircraft, not by artillery barrages or naval maneuvers, and in that sense was not a naval battle at all. The contending planes were launched by the Japanese and American fleets, which were more than 175 miles apart and never saw each other, much less fired upon each other.

Third, the Battle of the Coral Sea could not have provided the turning point in the Pacific War, as neither side won a clear-cut victory. More deserving of recognition was the Battle of Midway, in which the US Navy lost to the Japanese in terms of materiel but proved its ability to fight back for the first time after Pearl Harbor. It sank an aircraft carrier, the Shoho, and inflicted enough heavy damage on the Japanese to force the cancellation of their plans to carry out the invasion of Australia through New Guinea.

3. Zero Accomplishments

Myth! The battle of Leyte Gulf demonstrated the effectiveness of Japan's kamikaze squads as an offensive force in the Pacific War.

Even assuming that kamikaze as a highly unorthodox style of combat succeeded on a wide front, the claim that "if the attacks had started earlier, Japan might have won the war" easily forgets that the US had far greater resources and productivity and would eventually have rebounded with weapons like the atomic bomb.

Of the 1,228 suicide missions launched by the Japanese, only 465 zeroes became kamikazes, and their success rate—288 enemy ships damaged and thirty-four sunk—was a miniscule 7 to 8 percent of the total US Pacific fleet. Experts doubt if they could have done better, since kamikaze required the best of men and equipment, yet the pilots who flew were raw recruits and the planes were candidates for the scrap heap. Contrary to the popular thinking that the participants were fierce patriots who regarded kamikaze as the surest route to heaven, all were pressed into the special service, with no one volunteering for the job.

Oddly enough, the more effective kamikaze pilots are said to have come from the American side. At the critical battle of Midway, American aviators attacked the Japanese when it was almost certain death to do so. They suffered losses of nearly 90 percent but were instrumental in winning the battle. An admiring Japanese officer called the doomed Americans 'samurai', a term even more highly respected than kamikaze.

Incidentally, the kamikaze was not always a daredevil pilot who crashed his plane into an Allied carrier. Pledged to make the same sacrifice during the war were countless naval pilots and commanders, who used their vessels as battering weapons.

4. Going, Going, Gung!

Myth! The attack of Carlson's Gung-Ho Battalion on Makin Island in August 1942 became a strategy model for small-scale operations against the enemy in World War II.

In popular parlance, *gung ho* means "to go all out" or "to be unthinkingly enthusiastic and eager," but etymologically it is something else. As Evans F. Carlson's biographies and the 1943 film *Gung Ho!* reveal, the term was derived from *kung ho*, which Carlson thought was Chinese for 'working together'. He adopted the expression to describe the strong cooperative spirit that bound his members, not knowing that it lacked a few more words to give it the desired meaning. The 1986 movie *Gung Ho*, about a Japanese car manufacturer in America, eliminates the exclamation point but compounds the mistake by implying that the words are Japanese.

Carlson's raid, which destroyed the Japanese base and killed approximately 350 enemy troops while sustaining less than forty fatalities, wasn't really acclaimed for *gung ho* in the Chinese sense, i.e., the organizational skills it employed or the high level of discipline the raiders reportedly showed. Rather, it was for *gung ho* in the popular sense, which Carlson demonstrated with his extraordinary personal courage and endurance as the leader and his unusual democratic handling of the ranks. Strategy-wise, the operation worked against US efforts in the Pacific despite its much-publicized success. The bold move prompted the Japanese to strengthen their other Pacific strongholds—e.g., the Marshalls, Caroline, Tarawa, Marianas—which had previously been lightly fortified, converting the string of islands into an immovable defense line that the Japanese required their forces to hang on to until the last. The result was a higher cost in American lives in campaigns that followed.

5. No Swingers in Singapore?

Myth! When the Japanese assaulted Singapore from the landside, the defenders were unable to fire a single shot because their cannons rested on a fixed base pointing out to sea.

One of the more interesting trivia to come out of World War II has to do with the fall of Singapore to the Japanese in 1942. Singapore, ceded to the British by the British East India Company in 1824, assumed the status of a crown colony in 1826, but until 1942 had remained an Asian backwater in the fast setting British empire. The Japanese decided to take it anyway, and, according to a story made popular by Winston Churchill, proceeded with their plan using a bicycle corps. Unfortunately, the defenders could not employ their cannons, which were designed for reasons of economy to rest on a fixed base and fire only towards the sea. Apparently, no one expected the attack to come from the landside, which bordered on Malaya, as this was extremely difficult if not impossible because of an impenetrable jungle zone separating the two countries. However, this was the side from which the Japanese actually attacked, using foot soldiers carrying bikes on their backs and eschewing mechanized transports, large weapons and other equipment that would be hard to move through the dense growth.

Several writers, one of them Richard Miers, who in the 1950s used to be a commanding officer of the First Battalion, South Wales Borderers, Singapore, debunk the story as unmitigated Churchillian hooey. Writing in C. Northcote Parkinson's *A Law unto Themselves: Twelve Portraits* (Houghton Mifflin, 1966), Miers says, "Most of the guns had, in fact, a 360-degree traverse." The only exceptions were "those originally mounted in a battleship, which retained the dead arc of their naval mounting—

203

the arc representing the ship's own superstructure." In fact, during the invasion, many of the weapons were in action for two days, firing until the gunners were exhausted and their ammunition spent. Adds Miers: "Whoever was responsible for the fall of Singapore, it was not the officer who sited its fixed defenses nor even the officer who allocated them (sensibly enough) a high proportion of armor-piercing shell."

6. Whistling Down the Wind

Myth! The US was the first to declare war on the enemy in every conflict that it fought up to and including World War II.

Japan did make a formal declaration of war on the US even before the US could declare war on it. At 1600 EST on December 7, 1941, or some three hours after the attack on Pearl Harbor, Japan announced that it was at war with the US and the British Empire. The US Congress declared war on Japan the next day, or on December 8, 1941.

Those who nurture the impression that the US has always been first to declare war on an enemy are surprised to learn about Japan and, before it, Spain in the Spanish-American War. They are even more amazed to know that the very first country to formally initiate a state of war with the US was not a military power by Western standards. Since 1784, the U.S. government had been paying tribute to the Barbary States—Algiers, Tunis, and Tripoli, now a part of Libya—as protection against the Barbary pirates who were seizing ships and holding the crews for ransom (long antedating the Iran Hostage Crisis, when Iran arguably became the first Middle East country to receive payment from the US for the return of hostage Americans). When the Americans finally said 'no' to Tripoli's increasing demands, Yusuf Karamanli, the Qaddafi of his day, arrogantly declared war on the US on May 14, 1801. There was no action on either side and the war was never resolved. Incidentally, Tripoli's action presaged that of another Third World nation, Thailand, which declared war on the US in World War II without eliciting any response from the latter.

7. Attack of the Killer Mushrooms

Myth! The atomic bomb dropped on Hiroshima caused more loss of life and destruction than any other single event in the Pacific war.

The allegation that the atomic bomb on Hiroshima caused the most death and destruction in the Pacific War is way off the mark. The most devastating attack in that war was the air raid carried out on Tokyo on the night of March 9, 1945 by 279 American B-29s. Because high-level pinpoint bombing had failed to curtail Japanese war production, which was heavily diversified into small factories and home machine shops, it was decided to resort to the low-level incendiary bombing of the slum district Shitamachi, where much of this scattered industry was located.

Some 1,665 tons of napalm brought about incredible ruination, killing upward of 85,000 people and burning thousands of homes and buildings. The atomic bombing five months later of Hiroshima resulted in only 75,000 casualties, and the deaths at Nagasaki numbered about 30,000. The direct incineration, suffocation and scalding produced by the Tokyo attack were at least as bad as the radiation that indirectly caused most of the Hiroshima/Nagasaki deaths.

8. Atomic Power Point

Myth! The US decided to drop the newly developed atomic bomb on Japan to cut the conventional war short and prevent further losses on both sides.

The atomic bombs were dropped on Japan ostensibly to prevent a million Americans and as many as ten to twenty million Japanese from getting killed as a result of furthering the war. Experts surmise that the real reason was Truman's fear that a conventional Allied assault would only give Stalin time to enter the Pacific theater and invade the area. The President believed that, by showing off America's new military potential with an atomic strike, this would immediately discourage Stalin's expansionist designs.

Needless to state, the Soviets already knew about the new bombs through the efforts of their spies, and they were evidently not impressed because they invaded Japan anyway. By this time, the Nagasaki bombing could no longer be aborted and was carried out the following day.

Ironically, it was neither the Soviet invasion nor the Nagasaki bombing that prompted Japan to give up. According to the 1946 United States Strategic Bombing Survey, there was no need for any heavy prodding to convince Japan that it had a losing cause. As early as June 20, 1945, the emperor and leading members of the Supreme War Direction Council had secretly decided to end the war and were sending peace feelers. Unfortunately, there was some dallying over ritual and tradition, and it was not until August 15 that the unconditional terms of surrender were finally accepted.

9. Nuclear Hollow Cause

Myth! Dropping the atomic bomb on Nagasaki became imperative when Japan refused to surrender in the wake of the Hiroshima disaster.

It remains controversial whether or not Hiroshima should have been bombed, but historians on both sides tend to agree that there was absolutely no necessity for hitting Nagasaki. While the order was to drop a bomb each on two Japanese cities, the second bomb should have been reconsidered after seeing that the destruction wrought on Hiroshima by the first already proved the point.

The second bomb was not even originally planned for Nagasaki. The target was to be Kokura on August 11, which was advanced to the 9th because a storm was brewing. On the 9th, the B-29 Superfortress Bock's Car flew over Kokura three times before it decided it could not penetrate the smoke and haze that obscured the city. The plane then proceeded to its secondary target, Nagasaki, where a hole was found in the cloud cover.

No individual order was given to drop the second bomb, and no meeting was held to discuss whether it was still needed. The Nagasaki job and all the steps leading to it were taken as inseparable parts of a process. However, there were interregnums during which the matter could have been given more thought. The consensus is that the first atomic bomb on the 6th and the entry of the Russians into the Pacific theater on the 8th would have been sufficient to put pressure on the Japanese to end the war.

10. Air Today, Ground Tomorrow

Myth! During World War II, North America was never bombed from the air and no part of it ever came under enemy occupation.

Some Allied countries were able to avoid enemy bombing entirely, and for a while people thought the US was one of them. It wasn't until many years after World War II that the news came out—the U.S. mainland had been bombed from the air not once but twice!

On September 9, 1942, in what is now considered the first aerial bombing of mainland America by a foreign power, a Japanese single-engine floatplane manned by Chief Flying Officer Nobuo Fujita was launched from a submarine that had carried it across the Pacific. It flew over Oregon forests and dropped two 170-pound incendiary bombs, which were intended to start extensive fires and cause panic among the citizenry. Fujita's mission was in retaliation for Colonel Jimmy Doolittle's air raids on Tokyo. Fortunately, the forests were so wet that the bombs caused only some small, scattered fires.

A second attack by Fujita three weeks later outside Port Oxford also failed to do much damage. The general public wrongly assumed that the firebombs were carried in balloons by prevailing winds from Japan to Oregon.

A third Japanese attack on the mainland, which launched shells instead of bombs, may have been the model for Steven Spielberg's 1979 mayhem-filled film comedy *1941*. On February 23, 1942, a Japanese submarine surfaced near the town of Goleta, California, eight miles north of Santa Barbara, and hurled 15 shells at refineries owned by the Bankline Oil Company. It then disappeared, causing no injuries and only minimal damages estimated at $500. However, the rare opportunity prompted the excited I-17 captain Nishino Kozo to radio Tokyo with the news that he had left Santa Barbara in flames.

Contrary to the notion that no part of North America came under the domination of enemy forces during World War II, the Japanese invaded the Aleutian Islands in western Alaska in 1942, resulting in their occupation of three western islands—Attu, Agattu and Kiska—until 1943. The US had broken the Japanese code earlier, and had learned that the invasion was just a diversion to deflect attention from the main Japanese attack on Midway Atoll. Hence, it made little preparation for defending the islands, choosing instead to move most of the civilian population to camps on the Alaska Panhandle. American forces regained control of Attu by the end of May 1943, after taking significant casualties in difficult terrain, and Kiska in August of the same year. Arguably, this battle—called the Battle of the Aleutian Islands—marks the only time since the War of 1812 that a foreign power has occupied US territory in North America.

11. Big Ego and Small alter Ego

Myth! MacArthur coined the phrase "I shall return" and spoke it before fleeing the Japanese siege of the Philippines.

After the Japanese drove his forces from the Philippines, MacArthur expressed his vow to redeem the country in this famous slogan. As later revealed, however, the only contribution of the general to the making of the expression was the word 'I'. It was his diminutive Filipino aide, Brigadier General Carlos P. Romulo, who had suggested the line, hoping that once it's heard, it would boost sagging wartime morale in the US-held territory. Romulo's version tactfully used the word 'we', but in typical fashion, MacArthur changed it to 'I'. In another version, Romulo wanted the word 'I' from the beginning, and had to convince the Office of War Information in Washington not to pluralize it by arguing that his countrymen trusted MacArthur personally more than they trusted Americans in general.

Nonetheless, this story must remain bogged down in the realm of quasi-legends and half-truths, thanks to one Pio Andrade, Jr.

208

The 'chemist-turned-historian' challenged the veracity of Romulo's personal history in the late 1980s, when he published a documented book, *The Fooling of America, The Untold Story of Carlos P. Romulo*, exposing the alleged lies that attended the Filipino's stint in World War II.

MacArthur did speak the legendary line, but not on Philippine soil as most people imagine. Because of the confused situation when he left Corregidor on March 11, 1942, he was unable to verbalize the promise until the first opportunity came up on his arrival by train at Adelaide in Australia on his way to Melbourne. The actual words—"I came through and I shall return"—were part of the short statement of purpose that MacArthur addressed to the small crowd, mostly Australians, at the station.

12. On Borrowed Words

Myth! MacArthur originated the line, "Old soldiers never die, they just fade away."

MacArthur was reputed to be more literate and articulate than any of his contemporaries, some of whom became famous themselves just for uttering colorful words or phrases like 'nuts' or 'hell' or 's...'. But if MacArthur was not the real source of "I shall return," the most popular line attributed to him, what could we expect of his next three famous sayings?

Contrary to MacArthur's myth, he did not coin the famous axiom, "Old soldiers never die, they just fade away," nor did he even say it that way. What he really said in his valedictory before the US Congress on April 19, 1951, was, "And like the old soldier in that ballad, I now close my military career and just fade away, an old soldier who tried to do his duty as God gave him the sight to see that duty." MacArthur himself admitted in his speech that the original line was part of the lyrics of an old World War I barrack tune, a British army parody of the gospel hymn 'Kind Words Can Never Die'.

The line, "Only those are fit to live who are not afraid to die," is associated at times with the infamous GI-slapping incident involving Patton in World War II. While it is easy to imagine Patton shouting the words at the battle-fatigued soldier whom he accused of malingering, it was actually General MacArthur who spoke them at a 1935 reunion of combat veterans from the 42nd Infantry Division. We are not sure if the originator was a military man, but as with many other great MacArthur quotations, we can say it wasn't MacArthur. A few decades earlier, Theodore Roosevelt had written, "Only those are fit to live who do not fear to die," but even at that time the line already sounded suspiciously second-hand.

On April 19, 1951, MacArthur awed a joint session of Congress with the words, "In war, indeed, there can be no substitute for victory." It was yet to be revealed that seven years earlier, General Dwight D. Eisenhower had written his wife Mamie: "In war there is no substitute for victory." There was no way MacArthur could have copied the gem from Eisenhower's private mail, but no one believes Eisenhower originated the line either. Since the two had worked closely together during their early years in the military, it was more likely that both derived their inspiration from a common source.

---

13. Testing the Waters

Myth! MacArthur landed in Palo, Leyte, in October 1944, becoming the first US general to set foot in the Philippines since its occupation by the Japanese in World War II.

One of the most celebrated photographs of World War II is that of General MacArthur when he returned to the Philippines, as he had promised, in late October 1944. The American Caesar is seen with Philippine President Sergio Osmeña and General Carlos P. Romulo as they waded in knee-deep water on the beach at Palo, Leyte, in the southern part of the islands. What is not obvious is that this was only a reenactment of the actual landing, which had been made earlier on October 20, 1944 in a part of the beach located at Dulag, Leyte. The photo was taken at Palo, where the water was not as deep, partly to accommodate Romulo, who could not make the first landing because of his short height.

It is also generally assumed that MacArthur was the first to land in Leyte, but he was not. Literally stealing a march on him was Lieutenant General Walter Krueger of the US Sixth Army, who had landed ahead on the east coast of Leyte, establishing two beachheads. It was a long four hours later that General MacArthur came ashore. It was rumored that the vain general had delayed his landing in the Philippines until assured that newsreel cameras would be present to record his 'I Shall Return' march through the surf. Some of the greatest battles of the war were fought in this area, but at the time MacArthur landed there was no longer any Japanese soldier within miles.

14. Asia's Great Divide

Myth! Korea was divided into North and South at the 38th parallel in order to facilitate the demands of the Soviets and the Allies for separate spheres of control.

When first agreed on, there was no intention to segregate the northern part of the country for the occupation of the Russians, although this was the insidious aim of Stalin. The division was to facilitate the surrender of Japanese troops in Korea. Those caught on the north side of the line were to give themselves up to the Soviets, while the remainder were to yield to the Western Allies. It was not expected that as soon as the line was laid, North Korea's opportunistic Soviet puppet Kim ll-sung would establish a provisional government in the north. Thus was the Democratic People's Republic of Korea, with Kim as the premier, born. Democratization procedures in 1946 and 1947 failed because of resistance from the Soviets in spite of their promise on December 27, 1945, to create a free unified Korea. Free elections were held in South Korea under the supervision of the U.N. Temporary Commission on May 10, 1948, but by that time the two zones had become a permanent feature on the world's maps.

What may have touched off the idea that the 38th parallel was intended to divide Korea into two for the benefit of Russia was an attempt made fifty years earlier to do precisely the same thing. In 1896 Russia was attempting to pull Korea under its control even while Japan had already secured recognition of its rights in that country from the British. To avoid a confrontation, Japan proposed to Russia that the two sides split Korea into separate spheres of

211

influence along the 38th parallel. However, no formal agreement was ever reached, and Japan later took full control of Korea.

15. A Sound Heard 'Round the Rim

Myth! **The last shot fired in World War II was a torpedo from the US submarine Torsk that sank a Japanese coastal defense frigate at 2117 hours GCT on August 14, 1945.**

World War II officially ended at 2300 hours GCT on August 14, 1945, but as a practical matter the Torsk torpedo fired a couple of hours earlier wasn't the last belligerent noise heard from that conflict. There were still a number of skirmishes involving American and Japanese forces shortly after the deadline, with neither side having no notice of the war's end. There is no question that these events were still comprehended in the war, and any of the participants could have fired the last shot from the shooter's point of view.

One post-war incident would even suggest that the last shot was fired with the knowledge that the war was officially over. At 0418 hours on August 15, the USS Herman, though fully aware of the Japanese surrender a few hours before, brought down a zero on suspicion that it was a kamikaze poised on attacking the ship. It was held that as between the two participants, the war was still going on because one was not sure the other knew the war was over, and the uncertainty had created a hostile situation.

16. Unfinished War Symphony

Myth! **The Pacific war ended when Japan signed a peace treaty with the US and forty-eight other nations on September 8, 1951 in San Francisco, California.**

After the so-called Treaty of Peace with Japan, there were more territories that remained at war with Japan than made peace with her. Two of the biggest Allies—China and the Soviet Union—did not join in the signing and were technically still at war with Japan on that date and thereafter. The state of belligerency between the Chinese and the Japanese ended 27 years later, when they signed an agreement of 'peace and friendship' on August 15, 1978.

But the same cannot be said of Japan and the Soviet Union (or any of the countries that used to be part of the latter), since no formal treaty has ever been forged legally terminating the hostilities' between the two sides. Tokyo is not prepared to sign a peace treaty with Moscow unless four small islands north of Japan (called the Northern Territories by the Japanese and the Kurils by the Russians), which the Soviet Union occupied during the last few days of the war, are returned. Despite Russia's consistent refusal to repatriate the islands, the problem is expected to be resolved before the end of the decade.

17. Bushido gay Blades

Myth! **Japanese Generals Masaharu Homma and Tomoyuki Yamashita were duly tried and executed as war criminals in 1946.**

Historians say, however, that while Japanese atrocities during the war were real enough and the accused perpetrators were the overall commanders at the time, they were no more legally responsible than, say, General William Westmoreland was for leading the defeated American forces in Vietnam. There were also indications that Homma and Yamashita would have acted to prevent the abuses had they been warned of what was happening. Both had proved themselves unusually intelligent men, educated, chivalrous, Westernized and pro-Western, not to mention that they were once anti-nationalists who lost out to the extreme militaristic faction of the Japanese Army in the 1930s.

The duo's conviction was obviously railroaded to appease the egoistic General Douglas MacArthur, who had been humiliated when the Japanese made mincemeat of his forces in Southeast Asia at the onset of the war. It was MacArthur who convened the court and appointed the judges, and the trials themselves had few of the usual niceties of Anglo-American legal procedures. At their conclusion, one American correspondent informally polled the 12 journalists who had watched the proceedings, and they voted 12 to nil in favor of an acquittal.

18. Dead Men Marching

Myth! Of 78,000 American and Filipino POWs in the Bataan Death March, 25,000 died along a hundred-mile route and another 22,000 in the first two months of captivity.

The figure of 47,000 dead traditionally reported for the Bataan Death March does seem to have been exaggerated, and this event, which followed the mass surrender of American and Filipino troops to the Japanese in Bataan on April 9, 1942, may not have been as calamitous as its name connotes. The distance covered by the March measures a mere 65 miles, and the road, though mostly rural, was not as rugged as is often pictured. Official reports say only 43,000 troops—10,000 Americans and 33,000 Filipinos—manned the defenses at Bataan, and this was the same number that surrendered and joined the March. Only about 50 percent of the POWs walked at any given time, and those who did not walk were transported on trucks and suffered little. Train carried the group wherever railroad service was available. Five to ten thousand died, mostly from disease and untreated wounds after reaching the camp, and of these only 650 were Americans. The rest survived the war.

The specific atrocities committed by the Japanese guards on some of the prisoners, rather than the statistics as a whole, are what justify the term Death March.

VIII

It Was A Word War, Too

Quotes and Phrases from World War II

"Let me assert my firm belief that
the only thing we have to fear is fear itself."

●

Franklin D. Roosevelt

1. Axial Roads to War

Myth! Mussolini coined the word "Axis," while FDR came up with the term "World War II."

The conflict between the Allies and the Axis in 1939-1945 could not be called a world war in the beginning because it was limited to Europe. When the action escalated to global level in 1941, Roosevelt was still not prepared to call it a world war, preferring the more prosaic term 'The War of Survival'. Hostilities had already ended in 1945 when the American Federal Register announced that, with the approval of President Truman, Roosevelt's successor, the belligerency was to be known as "World War II."

Hungary's fascist prime minister Gyula Gömbös, who advocated an alliance of Germany, Hungary and Italy and worked as an intermediary between Germany and Italy to lessen differences between the two countries, is believed to have coined the term 'axis'. Later, Benito Mussolini put the word in vogue when, just before the war, he said that Berlin and Rome would form "an axis round which all European states animated by the will to collaboration and peace can also assemble." The statement appeared in a speech he delivered in Milan on November 1, 1936, after reaching a secret agreement with Hitler. First the Berlin Pact, then the Tripartite Pact between Japan, Germany and Italy, heeded the call of Mussolini, earning for the signatories their Axis nomenclature.

The word 'Axis' was reinvented during World War II as the name the Nazis gave to a plan they devised in July 1943 to take over Italy. They had suspected that Italy was going to defect to the Allied side as soon as the Fascist Grand Council had deposed Benito Mussolini in favor of a new government under Pietro Badoglio. When the Badoglio government surrendered unconditionally to the Allies in September of that year, the Germans immediately proceeded to execute the plan by seizing control of Rome and northern Italy, reestablishing Mussolini as head of the new, albeit puppet, Fascist regime.

216

2. Say that Again and I'll Shoot!

Myth! Hermann Goering said, "Whenever I hear the word culture, I reach for my revolver."

Because of its fascistic flavor, the saying "Whenever I hear the word culture, I reach for my revolver" has been attributed over the years to Hitler, Himmler and Goebbels, but mainly to Hermann Goering, founder and head of the Gestapo and Germany's air minister after 1937. However, no one seems to know when and where it was said, or what it means precisely.

Researchers have been able to trace its written origin to the 1933 drama "Schlageter," by an unsuccessful and little-known Nazi playwright named Hanns Johst (1890-1978), who was president of the Reich Theater Chamber. The play was about a martyr of the French occupation of the Ruhr after the First World War, and the line *Wenn ich Kultur hore . . . entsichere ich meinen Browning* was uttered by a storm trooper in act 1, scene 1. There are several versions of the English translation—Keyes cites two, i.e., "Whenever I hear the word culture...I release the safety-catch of my Browning [pistol]," and "When I hear the word culture, I uncock my revolver's safety catch"—but the German words themselves have yet to be given a sensible interpretation.

3. Here, There and Everywhere

Myth! The subject of the best-known graffito of World War II was James J. Kilroy, a shipyard inspector in Quincy, Massachusetts.

No catchphrase has equaled the popularity of "Kilroy was here" ever since it was found written on walls and on almost every other available surface during World War ll. The apparently witless graffito, often with the caricature of a face peering over a wall, dogged the American military wherever it went, raising suspicions that prankish GIs were at work. Kilroy's creator was sometimes believed to be a compulsive defacer, at other times a closet

217

socialist harboring an Oedipal fantasy (Kilroy, it was said, was a combination of "kill" and "roi").

Journalists finally traced the name to James J. Kilroy, a politician and a shipyard inspector for Bethlehem Steel Company in Quincy, Massachusetts. It seems Kilroy, beginning in 1941, chalked the words on thousands of ships and crates of equipment to indicate that he had gone over them, thus preventing unnecessary double-checking by overtime inspectors. From Quincy the phrase traveled to military bases all over the world, and amused GIs replicated the words without knowing or caring what they meant.

To debunkers, however, Inspector Kilroy poses an anachronism. Although usage of the phrase was not documented until the June 26, 1945 issue of *Kearns Air Force Post Review*, there is evidence that the Kilroy name had already appeared in a few docks and ports and on ships in late 1939 and was well established by 1942. This has cast doubt on James as the subject of the graffito, and strengthened the alternative claim that this "most widely published man since Shakespeare" is actually Sgt. Francis Kilroy, whose arrival at Kearns air base before the war begun was announced by the words "Kilroy will be here next week" scrawled on the bulletin board.

---

4. Life is a Box

Myth! The term 'basket case' originated in World War II, to describe GIs who had lost all four limbs on the battlefield.

The term 'basket case' is British slang for a quadruple amputee, particularly one who has undergone the procedure as a result of war wounds. Use of the dreadful term spread as wildly as the rumor that a good number of GIs survived the Second World War with this form of injury. That war was thought to have been conducive to the hapless condition of losing all four limbs because of its extensive use of advanced explosive weapons and effective life-saving drugs. During the 1941-45 period, it was not uncommon for a wife or mother to arrive at the town railroad station half-expecting to find her wounded soldier in a basket.

There was constant fear that the military was sending the disabled home without warning their families of their physical disfigurement.

Contrary to the popular belief, the phrase 'basket case' did not originate in World War II but in World War I, where there were more basket cases than in any other conflict. Only two individuals lost all four limbs in World War II, and they were greeted as heroes and lavished with gifts by both the government and the public. The movie *Johnny Got His Gun* (1971) has helped promote the myth of World War II basket cases, based on the wrong notion that the veteran in the Dalton Trumbo film served in that war and not in World War I.

5. Salty Reply

Myth! General McAuliffe said "Nuts!" when the Germans demanded the surrender of his forces in the Battle of the Bulge.

"Nuts" became the rallying cry of Allied troops trying to break the German siege in the battle of the Ardennes. According to the story, it started as the defiant one-word reply of Brigadier General Anthony Clement McAuliffe, acting commander of the 101st Airborne during the Battle of the Bulge, when the Germans demanded that he surrender the city of Bastogne. Field Marshal Karl von Runstedt was convinced his enemy, already encircled by five German divisions, would not hold out any longer. So on December 22, 1944, he sent some officers under a flag of truce to deliver a note from General Luttwitz of the 47th Panzerkorps demanding the surrender of the Bastogne garrison. The note was received by Major Alvin Jones and conveyed to General McAuliffe, whose remark upon reading it was, "Aw, nuts."

Other versions that have emerged despite McAuliffe's affirmation that he was indeed the source of the battle slogan sound just as credible. One is that McAuliffe's actual reply was saltier (no pun intended), but the official quote came out "nuts" because the censors wanted it that way. Another is that he did not reply at all, since the one who received the note from Jones was McAuliffe's acting chief of staff, who did not bother to show it to

219

the general. McAuliffe's staff already knew his sentiments, and took the liberty of answering back the word "Nuts" in his behalf.

"Nutsville," as the GIs later called Bastogne, was never surrendered, and McAuliffe, earning the nickname "Nuts" (deservedly or undeservedly), was promoted to major general. "Nuts" eventually became Commander-in-Chief of the United States Army Europe in 1955 and a full general on March 1, 1955.

6. Island of Doomed Men

Myth! The last message wired to headquarters by the besieged defenders of Wake Island was, "Send us more Japs."

The naval station at Wake Island, a barren atoll about 2,300 miles west of Hawaii, was considered vital to American military power in the Pacific in 1941. There were three major Japanese assaults on it, beginning with a December 7 sortie that was beaten off by only four Grumman Wildcats. The second came four days later, lasted 45 minutes, and ended with the 446 Marines on the island sinking two destroyers, damaging another destroyer, two cruisers and a transport, and killing 500 men while losing only one combatant. However, the third and final assault, on December 23, forced Wake's proud commander, USMC Major James P.S. Devereux, to capitulate.

Ironically, two weeks before the fall, a naval task force had been ordered by Pearl Harbor to reinforce Wake but was recalled before reaching the atoll because of the fear that this would weaken the line at Hawaii. No relief of any kind ever reached Wake, although legend has it that Pearl Harbor sent a half-earnest radio message to the island, asking, "Is there anything we can provide?" Devereux's gritty reply, "Send us more Japs," is mentioned in almost every popular retelling of the heroic defense of the island, but no official record of the communication exists. Some sources—the 1942 film *Wake Island*, for one—believe the last message sent out before the island was overrun by the Japanese was the rather optimistic "The issue is in doubt."

7. Fun with Joe and Jane

Myth! The term 'GI' derives from the abbreviation for 'general issue'.

'GI' emerged in World War II to become the single most important literary representation for the American soldier abroad. An anecdote recounted by William Manchester (*American Caesar*, 1978) reveals that its origin may have been the abbreviation for 'general issue', which means anything or anyone provided or issued by the US military. According to Manchester, when an army surgeon called the troops under Douglas MacArthur's command "GIs," the general sternly replied, "Don't ever do that in my presence...GI means 'general issue.' Call them soldiers."

Before this meaning became current, however, word historians say GI was already a common term for the American soldier. It came from the abbreviation for 'galvanized iron', which in the days of World War I was painted on US Army trashcans made of the material. The metaphor arose purportedly because officers loved to kick GIs around like the trashcans in the camps.

During World War II, the term became humanized when Dave Berger introduced it in his 'GI Joe' comic strip for the weekly soldier's paper Yank on June 17, 1942. Since then, GI Joe has grown more popular than its British equivalent, Tommy, although the latter, already common in Wellington's time, predates the former by at least a hundred years. However, Tommy's exposure in the post-World War II period would be greater than GI Joe's if the basis were the number of times rather than the length of the period each has seen action. Britain has had more military involvements than the US after that war, whereas the US has managed to get itself into the more protracted conflicts, such as the Vietnam War.

8. A Lose-Lose Situation

Myth! Joseph Heller invented the phrase "Catch-22" for the title of his famous 1961 novel.

'Catch-22', meaning whichever alternative you choose you are in a tight spot and are bound to lose, was introduced into the vernacular when Joseph Heller's book *Catch-22* was published in 1961. The 1970 movie into which it was made—considered one of the finest black comedies ever—centers around Captain Yossarian of the 256th US Army bombing squadron in Italy in World War II. Yossarian's main aim is to avoid being killed, so he seeks to be grounded by claiming to be crazy. However, he is stymied by a 'Catch-22' situation, which the doctor explains to him, thus: While one is indeed crazy and can be grounded, one also shows he is sane by trying to avoid combat duty.

Other forms of Catch-22 are invoked by the author to justify various bureaucratic actions, as when a character explains, "Catch-22 says they have a right to do anything we can't stop them from doing." The term appears often enough in the novel, but it wasn't really Heller who coined it. His original title was Catch-18, which he was all set to put on the cover when Publisher's Weekly informed him that Leon Uris was coming out with a novel entitled Mila 18, about the Warsaw ghetto uprising in World War ll. Afraid confusion might ensue from the use of the number 18 and harm his book when it came out, Heller agreed with his editor's suggestion to change the title to Catch-22.

9. Trump Call

Myth! **French Colonel Henri Philippe Pétain was the first to hold the line at Verdun with the words, "They shall not pass!"**

Verdun, the 1916 site of the most senseless battle in World War I, saw some 315,000 Frenchmen and 281,000 Germans dead within a period of four months. The inane defense of this fort, symbolized by the words "They shall not pass" (*Ils ne passeront pas*), made the reputation of Colonel Henri Philippe Pétain, who became Marshall at the end of the war and eventually head of the French State. Pétain, it is said, spoke the combative words to his men on February 26 of that year to express his—and the French government's—determination to hold the position.

But the first official record of the expression, or something close to it, appears in the Order of the Day for June 23, 1916 from General Robert Nivelle to his troops at the height of battle. Nivelle himself was heard to have said, "You will not let them pass" (*Vous ne les laisserez pas passer*), to General de Castelnau a few months earlier, on January 23, 1916. Obviously, Pétain was not the author of the phrase but only took credit as the more famous "Hero of Verdun."

The rallying cry was later emblazoned on the Verdun medal in the form *On ne passe pas*, and became so popular in military circles that the Spanish equivalent *No pasaran* was used on the Republican side during the Spanish Civil War. Unfortunately, Pétain compromised his image, and the famous slogan lost some of its sheen, when he agreed to be the puppet head of southern France at Vichy during the Nazi regime.

---

10. Faux Fascism

Myth! **Mussolini's highly original quotes prove he was the most articulate of the Axis leaders.**

Mussolini may not have been a great fascist leader, but he was one of the greatest quote makers—or, rather, forgers. At the height of his power, his sayings appeared in books, newspapers and magazines throughout the world, sometimes with little indication that they were stolen from other authors.

For instance, a laudatory article in Hearst's *Cosmopolitan* magazine credited to him the adage, "Fortune is a woman who must be beaten," only to turn out later that it was a Machiavellian dictum. Mussolini charmed the Chicago *Tribune* into printing the maxim, "Live dangerously," as his, although it was really Nietzsche's. The Duce appropriated dozens of paragraphs from Georges Sorel even while the *Times* of London was accusing him of misquoting the author.

It was quite a change when, in an address to the Italian Senate, Mussolini admitted that his policy to "do the maximum of good to a friend and the maximum of evil to an enemy" was not original. He said, "this formula is not by a fascist squadrist, it is by Socrates." Actually, said the *Times*, it was Plato who uttered the line, quoting Polemarcos, "the violent and bragging demagogue whom Socrates despised and silenced."

11. Prayer for the Defense

Myth! **The phrase, "Praise the Lord and pass the ammunition!," was first heard during the bombing of Pearl Harbor in 1941.**

Many sayings that were thought to have originated in World War II had the right combination of words to catch the public fancy and become the titles of popular songs. In tracing the source of one such saying, research has focused on a true incident that happened during the Japanese attack on Pearl Harbor on December 7, 1941. A naval chaplain was on board the US cruiser *New Orleans* when waves of Japanese planes appeared overhead. As men around him fired a continuous barrage at the enemy, he roused them up with a steady chant of "Praise the Lord and pass the ammunition!" The identity of this chaplain has never been clarified, but two candidates are mentioned by name in popular lore. One is Lieutenant Howell M. Forgy, born 1908, and the other is Captain W. H. Maguire, who at first could not recall having said the words but a year later thought he could have.

It is not improbable for both to have uttered the half-order-half-prayer on separate but similar occasions, since the phrase was already quite common in the military at the outset of the war. According to USMC Major Louis E. Fagan, the first recorded use of the expression was in 1689, by the Reverend Dr. Walker during the defense of Londonderry in Ulster, Ireland, against the forces of the English king James II. It was repeated during the American Civil War, but did not become a popular armed forces slogan until 1942, when it was also used as the title of a Frank Loesser song.

IX

Alarums And Excursions

On Paul Revere and the American Revolution

"If the British went out by water, we would
show two lanthorns in the north church steeple;
and if by land, one, as a signal."

•

Paul Revere

1. Revered for the Wrong Reasons

Myth! His midnight ride and the Boston Tea Party are notable proofs of Paul Revere's unselfishness and patriotism.

Most Americans would deem it almost anathema to think of Revere's motives during the War for Independence as less than patriotic. Well, Revere may have been patriotic, but not for the reasons attributed to him by standard history books. Few realize that his vaunted midnight ride, for instance, was a basically mercenary act. Revere did not volunteer his services on that occasion but rode as a paid messenger, charging the colonists a fee of five shillings 'for the night's work'.

His participation in the Boston Tea Party was not all that selfless either. The colonists' (and necessarily Revere's) motive for dumping the British tea into the harbor was to destroy the competition for John Hancock's smuggled Dutch tea. Apparently, there was a hidden intention as well to steal the tea by salvaging it afterwards.

While Revere may have shown some patriotism as a propagandist against the Crown, the chicanery and fraud that accompanied his works have indelibly tainted this folk image. His military records do not speak kindly of the man either; they reveal he was once court-martialed for cowardice and insubordination. Capt. Thomas Jenness Carnes had made accusations of unsoldierly behavior against Revere, then a lieutenant colonel, about the failed attack on British forces at Penobscot Bay, Maine in 1779. The specific charges were refusal to obey a general's orders pertaining to the use of a boat and leaving the battlefield without orders from a superior. It is said that one of the generals who pressed charges was the grandfather of poet Henry Wadsworth Longfellow, author of the poem 'Paul Revere's Ride'. Revere was relieved of his command and tried, but fortunately for him, he was acquitted.

Paul Revere is sometimes likened to Patrick Henry because of his Irish looks. The latter has long been rumored to be an Irish Roman Catholic, but this is false. The Virginia orator and statesman was of Scotch and Welsh descent, was baptized in the Established Church of England, and adhered to the Episcopal faith

226

throughout his life. Paul Revere is sometimes also thought to be Irish, but he was actually half-French and half-British.

2. Taken for a Ride

Myth! **Paul Revere asked that lanterns be hung on April 18, 1775 to signal him if the British attack was by land or by sea.**

Longfellow would have us believe Revere arranged for lanterns to be hung in the steeple of the North Church on April 18, and not on the sixteenth when it actually happened. In this regard, the poet may have made up the famous signal 'one if by land and two if by sea, and I on the opposite side shall be' merely to bolster the rhyme and meter of his verse. Experts say it made no tactical difference to the patriots which route the British took, and the signal would have been useless anyway if the British had come by both land and sea, as what likely occurred. Revere would write later that the signals in the church tower were not intended for him but for others in case he did not make it across the Charles River or over Boston Neck. The rebels wanted to know early enough if their messenger, on whom the whole project depended, was unable to surmount the initial obstacles of his journey.

3. From Horse to Verse

Myth! **Paul Revere brought the alarm to Concord on April 19, 1775.**

Longfellow felt the need to compress the facts about Paul Revere's heroism to fit them into his poem. In the process, the poet made changes that created some whopping fallacies about one of the most important events in American history.

Take the date of the ride itself. Revere actually made two rides in April 1775, the first on the sixteenth, when he rushed to Concord to warn the patriots to move the munitions from there to a

227

safer place. The second was his more famous ride to Lexington two days later, and about which Longfellow writes: "It was two by the village clock / When he came to the bridge in Concord town." It's contrary to fact, of course, because Revere never made it to Concord on this ride. He did cross the river to the Charlestown bank and get to Lexington by midnight to warn John Hancock and John Adams, who departed forthwith. But on his way to Concord, British scouts spotted Revere, now in the company of William Dawes and Samuel Prescott. Revere and Dawes were arrested and briefly jailed, while Prescott managed to escape and bring the alarm to Concord.

Upon his release, Revere went back to Lexington to rescue a trunk full of documents that Hancock had left behind. He saw no further need to go to Concord, as he had already done this on his first ride on April 16. It was Revere on the sixteenth rather than Prescott on the eighteenth who saved the supplies stored in Concord and used later by the colonists to fire the 'shots heard round the world'.

4. Cries and Whispers

Myth! At several points during his ride, Paul Revere shouted, "The British are coming!"

Longfellow's poem conjures up the dashing image of Revere shouting "The British are coming!" as he gallops "through every Middlesex village and farm." Actually, the poet makes no mention of any warning cry, and for once, he may be right. It would have been downright foolish of Revere to shout anything under circumstances that demanded the utmost stealth and secrecy. Researchers believe that if he said anything, it was probably the prosaic warning, "The regulars are out!," which he would have whispered through each door.

Readers who will swear that the memorable line "The British are coming!" appears in Longfellow's poem are also apt to say the poem's title is 'The Midnight Ride of Paul Revere'. In fact, the only title Longfellow ever used is 'Paul Revere's Ride'. The poem itself is one of several in 'The Landlord's Tale', a segment in a whole volume entitled *Tales of a Wayside Inn*.

Asked to make a statement on Paul Revere during a press tour, the American politician Sarah Palin declared that Revere "warned, uh, the British that they weren't gonna be takin' away our arms, uh, by ringing those bells, and um, makin' sure as he's riding his horse through town to send those warning shots and bells that we were going to be sure and we were going to be free, and we were going to be armed." The ensuing controversy worsened when some journalists and historians affirmed Palin's view and posted it as a "version" in Wikipedia. Palin's supporters made much of the report from archival sources that when the British intercepted Revere that night in April 1775, he had given them some information on his movements while under interrogation. However, except for Longfellow's piece, there is actually nothing written of the way our hero conducted his "ride through town," and certainly no reference to shots being fired or bells being rung while he was at it. Unless Palin's take was a metaphorical interpretation of the event rather than a literal one, it is a gross misconception of Paul Revere's famous ride.

5. This Forger was not a Smithy

Myth! Paul Revere's famous print of the Boston Massacre is true in almost every respect to the historical event.

The Boston Massacre raised an outcry from the colonists and became fodder for their propagandists. Paul Revere, for one, was a skillful engraver-printer who appeared to have captured the event in his icon entitled 'The Boston Massacre of 1770'. Or so we are told.

Revere's print of the Massacre as the first renowned picture to come out of the Revolution often serves as the main reference point for the layman's view of that event. Ironically, this graphic study of what happened on March 5, 1770 is riddled with fallacies that Revere was believed to have fabricated for propaganda purposes.

The most blatant is the depiction of British troops firing simultaneously in an orderly fashion under the command of an officer. Experts on the Massacre agree that the shooting was completely disorganized, with the muskets "(banging) almost at will." The officer, British Captain Thomas Preston, is shown with his sword raised in command and egging his troops on, yet it was proved at the trial that Preston never ordered his men to fire and was utterly surprised when they did. Although it was the word "Fire!" that could have provoked some of the soldiers to discharge their guns, historians say it was not unlikely that this was yelled by one of the mob. Witnesses attested that no shot was fired until a soldier actually had his gun knocked out of his hands by a heavy stick or other missile.

Revere's portrayal of the colonists as unarmed is contrary to official testimony that club-wielding and stone-throwing rowdies initiated the attack. One of the victims, who made a dying confession to this effect, stated that he was amazed the soldiers did not fire sooner. It was also revealed that the sentry around whom the disorders developed was so anxious to avoid trouble that he had vainly tried to retreat from his post to shelter within a building.

It is not generally known that what eventually became Revere's most famous work, fallacious as it was, was only forged from an original done by a colonial artist named Henry Pelham. The Pelham label 'An Original Print...taken on the Spot' did not prevent Revere from copying the piece before it was offered for sale, then signing it and selling it as his own. Pelham was stunned and on March 29, 1770, wrote Revere accusing him of the forgery, "one of the most dishonorable actions you could well be guilty of." Revere did not act, and by the time Pelham got his original to the public, Revere's print had become a big seller.

The Pelham rip-off was not the only fraud Revere committed for profit. When he was commissioned to do a portrait of Indian fighter Benjamin Church for a 1772 book, he did not know how Church looked and could not get a likeness of him anywhere. In desperation, Revere copied an unknown artist's portrait of English poet Charles Churchill, maintaining it was Church even though the similarity with Churchill was so obvious. Previously, Revere had taken credit for a number of copyrighted British political cartoons that he had stolen and sold under his name. An originally designed work of art by Revere is a rarity, and that is probably where its real value lies.

6. A Shooting Party

Myth! The Boston Massacre was the single tiny spark that lit the fuse of the Revolutionary War.

Most school children are made to believe it was the Boston Massacre that instigated the Revolutionary war, but serious historians cite several strong grounds in disputation. *First*, there was no real massacre to speak of, as only three colonists were killed and eight wounded. *Second*, happening as it did in 1770, the Massacre was too remote from the Lexington and Concord of 1775 to have had any strong influence on those events. There were, in fact, violent incidents before and after the outbreak that had closer links to the Revolution. *Third*, the cause of the Massacre was actually more economic than political. Redcoats numbering 4,000 in a town of 16,000 were competing for the few available jobs with the populace, and resentment on both sides erupted into violence.

The nine British soldiers who participated in the action were brought to trial. Seven (some say six) were acquitted and the others who fired directly into the crowd were convicted of manslaughter (or, as some claim, branded on their thumbs and released). Rebel propagandists led by Samuel Adams later asserted that the trial was trumped up, ignoring the fact that the patriot John Adams conducted the defense and the entire jury was American.

The propagandists also made much of the testimony that Crispus Attucks, one of the victims, was black. Attucks to this date is held up as the first black patriot of the Revolution, but no one is really sure if he was black, Indian or mulatto, and what his role was in the incident. An account describes him as a brutal brawler and leader of a gang of waterfront toughs, but it is just as likely that he was a pamphleteer's fictional creation.

The Boston Massacre may not have much meaning in the context of the American Revolution. Still, it is significant for launching not only the political career of a future US president, but also a landmark judicial decision that helped firm up the due process clause in the nascent US Constitution.

7. Avenging Spirit

Myth! **Lafayette joined the American revolutionaries because of his fervent belief in their cause for independence.**

The youngest general in US history is not American but French. The Marquis de Lafayette, who for decades was the popular symbol of the bond between France and the nascent United States, was only 20 years old when he came to America in his own ship. With a troop of soldier-adventurers, he enlisted with George Washington, who was so impressed that he made Lafayette a major general. The Marquis not only gave of himself but was also instrumental in getting his country's support for the American enterprise. He was wounded at Brandywine, fought at Gloucester, Barren Hill, Monmouth and Rhode Island, and was at Washington's side during the crucial winter of 1777-78 at Valley Forge.

Entrenched in the long history of US-French relations is the belief that this extraordinary Frenchman came to America with the pure intention of showing his sympathy for the American cause. But the more cautious historian says his royal blood and background seem inconsistent with the notion that he loved democracy and was willing to die for it in a foreign land. Shenkman, for one, thinks the real reason for his coming over was to avenge his father, whom the British had killed in the Seven Years' War. Lafayette himself revealed that he embarked on his American adventure because he thirsted for glory, which meant, according to his biographers, that he was obsessed with a desire for personal independence and self-assertion. These were no doubt fulfilled when the US showered him with gifts and honors as a token of its gratitude, and he returned home to France a hero.

During the French Revolution, Lafayette showed his royalist colors by attempting to maintain order as commander-in-chief of the National Guard. In 1791, Lafayette was on the verge of fleeing to the United States through the Dutch Republic when he was captured by Austrians and served nearly five years in prison. These are small clues, but clues nevertheless, that it was not political persuasion but his desire for personal adventure that fired up Lafayette's exploits in America.

8. Pershing Squares up with Lafayette

Myth! General Pershing stood before the tomb of Lafayette in Paris and murmured, "Lafayette, we are here."

It was July 4, 1917, or nine days after the American Expeditionary Force to World War I had landed in France, and the doughboys were honoring the Marquis for the invaluable service he rendered when he brought France to the aid of the US in its War for Independence. Attending the Paris ceremony was the head of the contingent, the redoubtable General John J. Pershing, who it is said stood erect at Lafayette's tomb and murmured, "Lafayette, we are here." The words were no doubt conveyed in time to buoy up the sagging spirit of the French, but who did the conveying is not as obvious. In Volume 1 of his book *My Experiences in the World War*, Pershing admitted he did not say the famous phrase and only wished it were his own. The general recalled that he had designated Colonel Charles E. Stanton, his chief disbursing officer, to speak for him at the tomb, and what was said there was entirely Stanton's.

A few historians say it is likely that Pershing actually uttered the statement several weeks before Stanton did, and the latter, seeing it was a *mot juste* for the coming occasion, picked it up. In any case, Burnam suggests the remark was already current at the time the American forces arrived in France, and was probably not original to either man.

9. Tea and Sympathy

Myth! The colonists staged the Boston Tea Party to protest the increase in the tax on imported British tea.

The Boston Tea Party was staged not because the tax on imported British tea was increased but because it was lowered. Although British tea had remained heavily taxed under the Townsend Act, this was of little concern to the colonists because their supply came from smuggled and necessarily less expensive

Dutch tea. However, the fiscal burden was causing the accumulation of millions of pounds of surplus tea in the warehouses of British manufacturers. In an attempt to dispose of the unsold tea and at the same time undercut the operations of the local tea-smugglers led by John Hancock, the British passed the Tea Act of 1773 eliminating the tax and allowing British tea to be priced below the cost of smuggled Dutch tea.

To demonstrate resistance to what they claim was undue interference in their economy, about sixty men dressed as Indians, with several thousand onlookers, dumped a large cargo of cheap tea from three British ships into Boston Harbor. Because the bales were tossed intact when they should have been axed open beforehand to ensure seawater contamination, suspicions have been raised that the Party was not really to protest the lowered tax but to steal the tea. Nobody knows what happened to the dumped tea, and rumors that it was recovered later as it floated in the harbor apparently have had no effect on the political significance of the event in orthodox history.

---

10. V is for Vermont

Myth! Ethan Allen organized his Green Mountain Boys to help fight for American independence and Vermont statehood.

Because Ethan Allen and his Green Mountain Boys figured prominently in the capture of the British forts at Ticonderoga and Crown Point in 1775, most people think they are authentic heroes of the American Revolution. Actually, Allen organized his famous contingent of Vermont irregulars five years before the Revolution—not to fight the British, as is generally believed, but to ward off the Yorkers, i.e. settlers from New York who were bent on taking possession of land he claimed as his own. While Allen may have ostensibly agreed later on to have his group assimilated into the colonial army to fight the British, he never deviated in spirit from his original objective.

After his victory at Fort Ticonderoga, Allen admitted to the Continental Congress that he was fighting for the independence only of his home state of Vermont. When the Congress rejected

234

this position, he went to the British to negotiate secretly for the royal recognition of his disputed land consisting of more than a quarter million acres. At one point he promised to take Vermont out of the war in return for certain land concessions, but the British wouldn't go along and the deal fell through. Critics say that despite the suggestion of Allen supporters that this was part of his strategy to secure Vermont statehood, his dealing with the British, had it been discovered, would have readily qualified as treason.

Ethan Allen's shortcomings as an authentic hero of the American Revolution, compounded by rumors about his unappealing physical features, have not detracted from the many handsome memorials that have been erected in his honor in the eastern US.

11. Bunker Hill doesn't Answer

Myth! The victory of the colonials against the odds in the Battle of Bunker Hill has become a symbol of American success in the battlefield.

The popular belief that the first organized engagement of the American Revolutionary War was won by the Americans on Bunker Hill is false on two counts. *First*, the battle was conducted on neighboring Breed's Hill, and *second*, the victory, although pyrrhic, belonged to the British.

On learning that British Lieutenant General Thomas Gage would begin fortifying the hills on Charlestown Peninsula across the Charles River north of Boston after receiving reinforcements from England, the colonists decided they would occupy Bunker Hill before the British could. Consequently, the American commander William Prescott was ordered to proceed to Bunker Hill, but for some reason he deployed his men on Breed's Hill instead.

The battle was fought on June 17, 1775, between some 1,600 American irregulars and 2,500 British redcoats. The defenders repulsed two attack waves, incurring 400 casualties in the process, and withdrew only after inflicting losses—800 wounded and 226 killed, including a notably large number of officers—comprising a third of the enemy's forces. Although the Americans were deemed to have lost the battle, they fought the rest of the war knowing that properly led, they could be matched against the best from the British military.

The encounter continues to be named the Battle of Bunker Hill, in defiance of the 221-foot-high granite obelisk commemorating it on Breed's Hill.

---

12. Revolutionary Tactics

Myth! The superiority of the American rifle over the musket and the British lack of experience in guerilla warfare accounted for the success of the American Revolution.

It is widely believed that the Americans defeated the British with the use of superior guns and guerilla tactics, but historians insist this is not really how the Revolution was won.

Many would have thought that there was some special advantage to be derived from the rifle that the colonists had developed. But it was soon learned that despite a longer range and greater accuracy compared to the smoothbore musket, the weapon was virtually useless in the clinches because it was slow and difficult to reload. Both sides actually ended up using muskets manufactured in the old country.

It is true that in the initial confrontations, the colonists fought from scattered and hidden positions, quite unlike the redcoats' formal, controlled frontal line type of assault. However, the Americans were largely ineffective, and early actions in the conflict were indecisive. The British, on the other hand, had seventy-five years of experience with 'guerrilla' methods of fighting in North America, especially during the French and Indian War.

According to the *Britannica*, modern guerrilla warfare has its genesis in the tactics employed by the Americans during the Revolution. This assertion, however, is not without challenge. Many experts maintain that what really won the struggle for the colonists was their decision to form the Continental Army early enough and have it trained in the traditional and more formal methods of European warfare. There were other factors that helped overcome the relative inexperience of the revolutionists and defeat the British on the battlefield—for instance, British ineptitude and the assistance given the colonists by the French. But it is almost certain guerilla warfare was not one of them.

13. A Straggle of Strugglers

Myth! Like most revolutions, the War for Independence was a conflict between the poor masses (the colonists) and the elite (the British authorities).

Historians say this is utter nonsense. Many of the rebels were farmers and artisans but they were not peasants, and their leaders were at least middle class, as exemplified by John Hancock, who was one of the richest men in America.

This is not to mention that the 'masses' participating in the conflict represented only 16 percent of the colonies' able-bodied males, and of this there were as many who were fighting for as against Britain. With Tories and Loyalists on both sides of the ocean playing a major role in the war, the colonial American populace was not united in its opposition to England. John Adams estimated that only about one third of the colonists were patriots, about one-third were Tories and Loyalists, and the rest did not really care who won.

Contrary to popular belief, it was not the Indians but the Loyalists who comprised the second largest contingent in the British Army. In 1780 there were 8,000 of them as against the 9,000 patriots in Washington's forces. Sometimes there were more Loyalists than patriots, the ratio changing only when many of the former fled to Canada after being attacked and publicly humiliated.

14. Whose Side were they on Anyway?

Myth! The colonists were the most patriotic of American soldiers who ever fought a war.

Those who debunk the claim that most of the colonists fighting the British belonged to the poor masses eventually lapse into a misconception themselves. They presume that these rebels, fired up by their middle class ideals, were utterly dedicated to lofty causes, such as liberty for the colonies and justice for their inhabitants. In fact, analysts say, the colonists cannot even play second fiddle to a similarly situated group—the Confederates—whom history regards as the most enthusiastic American soldiers in any war albeit they were not fighting a foreign enemy but fellow Americans. The colonists were simply not anywhere near the South's level of patriotism, since not only did many of them side with the British, but up to a third of the Revolutionary Army deserted.

Ironically, the Americans had as many of the enemy rooting for them as of their own countrymen. One historian writes: "From the beginning of tension until the final treaty of peace between Britain and the new United States of America, colonists had more friends than foes in the homeland. London—then by far the largest metropolitan center in the western world—was solidly against all anti-American measures. So were merchants, businessmen, and ordinary citizens throughout Britain." Some of England's most brilliant orators repeatedly spoke out against the king and his ministers. The star-studded roster of pro-Americans included Edmund Burke, Charles James Fox, John Wilkes, Thomas William Coke, Jonathan Shipley, and William Pitt, all of whom affected the views of substantially more than half of the ordinary folk of Britain, though not the king's.

15. For Hire by the Minute

Myth! **The American minuteman was a literate and self-reliant member of the landed middle class.**

The word 'minuteman' serves as a memorial to the vaunted reliability of this fighting man during the early stages of the Revolution, but we are told that Lexington and Concord, far from proving that reliability, exploded it. There is some question about the minutemen's actual behavior at Lexington when they came under fire. Many writers claim they "stood their ground" or

238

"confronted" the redcoats, yet their own leader, Captain John Parker, admitted that they scattered as they were told to.

There is evidence, moreover, that the minuteman wasn't much of a sharpshooter despite every school child's perception that he was a great shot. It appears more redcoats than Americans were killed and wounded in the battles only because the Americans outnumbered the British by about two to one.

Supposedly a product of the middle class, the minuteman projected the image of a self-reliant, hardy, literate, patriotic, disciplined and skillful fighter. But scholars have found that the average minuteman was actually below average—"poor, landless, out of work, and out of hope"—and that they joined the war mainly for social advancement or money. Far from being selfless volunteers, many were raw substitutes that were paid to fight by yeomen farmers who didn't want to heed the call of the militia.

16. Revolution without Retribution

Myth! Lacking a reign of terror, the American Revolution fails as a true revolution.

A reign of terror is a period during which revolutionaries carry out terroristic acts, similar to what occurred in France, England during the upheaval that dethroned Charles I, Russia and Communist China. Shenkman, citing the historian Crane Brinton, says there was more than a touch of the reign of terror in the American version, although it was not as bad as the kind that prevailed in Europe. He observes: "The extent of the barbarism can be measured in the treatment of loyalists, the Americans who stayed true to the king. They were not treated well. Countless loyalists were tarred and feathered. Thousands were forced to turn over millions of dollars in property without compensation. More than eighty thousand were driven to flee for safety to Canada, where many spent the remainder of their lives in poverty." One scholar also cited by Shenkman calculated that the American Revolution generated more latent hostility than its French counterpart, resulting in a rate of emigration of twenty-four per thousand of the population as against five per thousand for France.

239

17. A Snow Job of Historical Proportions

Myth! Valley Forge in 1777 was Washington's winter scourge.

In the words of the Britannica: "His army, twice beaten, ill housed, and ill fed, with thousands of men 'barefoot and otherwise naked,' was at the point of exhaustion; it could not keep the field, for inside of a month it would have disappeared." Quartermaster and commissary mismanagement, grafting contractors, and the unwillingness of famers to sell produce for paper money worsened the situation. Congress was too weak to help, and alleviation came mainly from a training program instituted by the Prussian Baron Friedrich Wilhelm von Steuben, which helped raise morale and discipline and generate economies.

Just as reputable as those who support this orthodox view are the historians who believe nobody starved or froze at Valley Forge. Morale was actually high and lack of food and clothing was nothing out of the ordinary. There are obviously enough records to establish that Washington was in a much worse position in 1779, when the Continental Army was nearly wiped out by one of the coldest winters at Morristown, New Jersey. Desertions and mutiny were commonplace at the latter station, but Valley Forge in 1777 or 1778 hardly experienced any. The unwelcome conclusion drawn by critics is that Washington used Valley Forge only as a ploy to get more aid from Congress.

18. Canadian Sunset

Myth! American victory in the War for Independence ended Britain's rule in all of its North American colonies.

The 1783 Treaty of Paris recognized only the thirteen colonies that rebelled as free and sovereign states. There were three more that did not rebel, namely, Canada, East Florida and West Florida. Originally settled by the French and the Spanish, they had become

British when an earlier Treaty of Paris was signed in 1763. The Spanish recovered West Florida in 1781 in the Battle of Pensacola, and two years later, sick of the whole North American enterprise, Britain swapped East Florida to Spain for the Bahamas. How the two Floridas eventually combined to become a state of the United States is another story, beginning with their cession by Spain to the United States in 1821. It is said that if Pensacola had been strengthened sufficiently to withstand Spanish attack, the entire southeastern tip of North America would not have passed to the Americans and would still be British.

X

Dissenting Voices

Quotes from the American Revolution

"Those who expect to reap
the blessings of freedom must, like men,
undergo the fatigue of supporting it."

•

Thomas Paine

1. Signing Glory

Myth! After signing in large letters on the Declaration of Independence, John Hancock said, "There! His Majesty can now read my name without glasses. And he can double the reward on my head!"

It's just a legend, but it's taught to every schoolboy as fact in order to convey a lesson in responsibility.

John Hancock, Massachusetts' representative to the 1776 Continental Congress, committed his colony to the idea of breaking from the mother country, Great Britain, by signing the Declaration of Independence on July 4 that year. As a surviving copy of the Declaration now residing in the National Archives of the Library of Congress attests, he affixed his signature with a flourish in large bold letters at the end of the document, dwarfing all the others so much that the term 'John Hancock' has since become synonymous with 'signature'. Hancock, it appears, did this in the presence of some or all of the other signers, for he was heard to say immediately after the act, *"There! His Majesty can now read my name without glasses. And he can double the reward on my head!"*

Although Hancock's display of patriotic fervor by signing the charter in dramatically large letters may have given his name eponymic significance, it is nevertheless not true that one's signature has always been known in the US as a 'John Hancock'. For instance, in the West more than a half century after the supposed incident, the phrase became altered to 'John Henry' for some unknown reason, and this is now what the cowboy calls his signature. The witticism Hancock supposedly uttered during the signing is also obviously false, inasmuch as it is premised on two popular beliefs about the July 4, 1776 event that have long been debunked (see *Snopes.com*). The first is that the declaration was addressed to King George, who was expected to be the first to read the document after all the members of Congress had signed it. Actually, the document was never sent directly to the King, but was initially published as a printed broadside for distribution to the general public; it was likely that the King only read it later in this form. The second is that Hancock signed the declaration along with several of his co-signors, as he would only have uttered the remark if he had been in the presence of others during the signing ceremony. The fact, of course, is that he was alone, except for Charles Thompson, the secretary.

The setting for the Hancock utterance is strangely similar to the one in which an equally famous—and dubious—exchange transpired between Hancock and Benjamin Franklin. On that other occasion, legend would have it that Hancock, while signing the Declaration, cautioned his colleagues, thus: "We must be unanimous; there must be no pulling different ways; we must all hang together." "Yes," replied Benjamin Franklin, "we must indeed all hang together, or most assuredly we shall all hang separately." According to Keyes, the quotes did not appear in print until more than fifty years after Franklin's death, which makes it highly suspicious that they were actually made. Moreover, Franklin's retort would be attributed in a slightly modified form to the lieutenant governor of Pennsylvania, Richard Penn, grandson of William Penn, well into the 19th century. The Penn version appeared in some 1830s accounts, and an 1840 biography eventually transferred the quote to Franklin's mouth.

---

2. Hale The Hero

Myth! **Minutes before he was executed, Nathan Hale said, "I regret that I have but one life to give to my country."**

Nathan Hale, an American soldier during the Revolutionary War, was captured by the British at Long Island and hanged without trial as a spy. It is said Hale's last words at the scaffold showed a patriot's resolve that became even stronger at the prospect of death. Paradoxically, while Hale has become famous for those words, no one is quite sure what they were. As reported in most reference books, his final message was, "I regret that I have but one life to lose for my country." A version that seems to be even more popular replaces "lose" with "give".

The first to report Hale's dying statement was General William Hull, who admitted that he had heard it only from another British officer who was present at the hanging. The inspiration for the line may have come from Act I, scene 2, of Joseph Addison's *Cato*, in which it was said: "What pity is it that we can die but once to serve our country!" It is almost certain, however, that Hale did not speak it, and that the patriot's authentic last words were much less eloquent. In a recently discovered diary, a British soldier who saw Hale die, Captain Frederick Mackenzie, wrote: "He behaved with great composure and resolution, saying he thought it the duty of every good Officer to obey any orders given by his Commander-in-Chief." Many historians today regard the second part of Mackenzie's entry as a paraphrase of what Hale really said moments before he died.

3. Ad Hoax Appeal

Myth! In his dying moments on the deck of the battered Chesapeake, Commander James Lawrence shouted to his men, "Don't give up the ship!"

One of the most famous naval battles of the War of 1812 resulted in the capture of the American vessel Chesapeake by the British frigate Shannon off the Massachusetts coast. The beaten Chesapeake was towed off to Halifax, but not before its commander, James Lawrence, lying wounded on the deck, died. The line he was supposed to have said with his dying breath is made more emphatic in some versions with the addition of the words "Sink it, blow it up!" In one retelling of the incident, Lawrence's attending physician claimed it was he whom Lawrence ordered "to go on deck, and tell the men to fire faster, and not to give up the ship."

Later, the daughter of Boston *Centinel* editor Benjamin Russell confided that the famous saying was a hoax—her father had invented the phrase and made Lawrence say it in his newspaper account of the battle weeks after the event. Actually, Russel did supply the words but had lifted them from an earlier setting, that of the American Revolution. It seems that in a 1776 engagement with the British in Boston Harbor, captain James Mugford was heard to shout while he lay dying, "Don't give up the ship! You will beat them off."

4. Sparring Moments

Myth! **When asked to surrender, John Paul Jones replied, "I have not yet begun to fight."**

The Scottish privateer John Paul Jones, gifted by the French with the refitted Bonhomme Richard, took up the US cause and engaged the British frigate Serapis in a memorable battle in English waters on September 23, 1779. The Serapis's commander, Richard Pearson, seeing he was about to win, asked Jones to give up, but the latter rejected the request with a defiant reply. Jones stood his ground, captured the Serapis at the cost of the Bonhomme Richard, and ultimately grabbed the victory from the surprised British.

An eyewitness, First Lieutenant Richard Dale, first reported Jones's retort half a century later. Jones himself had claimed, in a letter to Benjamin Franklin ten days after his victory, that his response to the English surrender request was "in the most determined negative." Unlike Dale, Jones stopped short of specifying his exact words, and so did the defeated commander Pearson, who confirmed Jones's defiant attitude only in general terms. Two decades later, Benjamin Rush recalled that a couple of years after the battle Jones had told him that what he said was, "No, Sir, I will not [surrender], we have had but a small fight as yet."

5. Taking Liberties

Myth! **At the second Virginia Convention, Patrick Henry said, "Forbid it, Almighty God, I know not what course others may take, but as for me, give me liberty or give me death!"**

There is no schoolboy in America who is not familiar with the line that has helped keep alive Patrick Henry's controversial image. The dramatic flourish makes Henry's oration in March 1775 the most memorable to come out of that blood-and-thunder period, but there is no proof he actually said it. Some historians suspect William Wirt, Henry's first biographer, made them up as one of the liberties he took when he reconstructed Henry's speech decades after it was delivered. Wirt saw fit to base his reconstruction on the recollection of John Tyler and George Tucker, who were delegates at the Convention. However, both Washington and Jefferson, who were also present during the proceedings and had their own records of what went on, did not think any of Henry's words were worth mentioning. Douglas Southall Freeman (cited by Keyes) writes in his biography of Washington that Henry's historic oath is most likely apocryphal, "probably far more Tucker, Tyler and Wirt, chiefly Wirt, than Henry."

Whether genuine or not, Henry's oration has a fiery elegance that betrays the image of a fiercely independent aristocrat from Virginia. In reality, Henry was a failure in both business and farming but would later acquire a license to practice law with the help of influential friends.

6. Reneging on a Dare

Myth! Speaking before the House of Burgesses, Patrick Henry, responding to shouts of "Treason!," exclaimed, "If this be treason make the most of it!"

In late May 1765, Patrick Henry rose in Virginia's House of Burgesses to denounce the hated Stamp Act and defend the colonies' right to tax themselves. The most remembered line in his speech is the peroration: "Caesar had his Brutus, Charles the First his Cromwell, and George the Third may profit by their example." The speaker of the House interrupted at this point with the cry of "Treason!," and Henry responded: "If this be treason make the most of it!"

Believing that Henry's speech was not duly recorded, biographer William Wirt reconstructed it half a century later based on consultations with House members John Tyler and Thomas Jefferson. But in 1921, it was discovered that a Frenchman had witnessed the debate and had kept a journal confirming that Henry made the speech but had already ended it when the speaker castigated him for "speaking treason." According to the journal's description, instead of replying with his famous last line, Henry stood up to ask for pardon and even affirmed his loyalty to the King. It seems one of the most admired lines in the repertoire of American patriotic quotations never existed.

Historians say this was not the first time Henry apologized for an utterance, and that what the Frenchman had recorded was entirely in keeping with this overindulged American's character. Neither was it the only time, other than when he supposedly delivered his controversial "Give me liberty or give me death" peroration, that he would be credited with a pseudo-historical line. In a 1956 piece in *The Virginian* (and reprinted in the American Mercury) discussing Henry's last will and testament, the author commented: "It cannot be emphasized too strongly or too often that this great nation was founded, not by religionists, but by Christians; not on religions, but on the gospel of Jesus Christ!" Unbelievably, the comment has since become entrenched in popular belief as having come from Henry himself.

7. Eye Contact

Myth! **Faced by the British at the Battle of Bunker Hill, Colonel Putnam of the revolutionaries told his troops, "Don't fire until you see the whites of their eyes."**

Israel "Old Put" Putnam, a "brave, intrepid and very industrious soldier though not a great one," was a farmer who left his plow to join the colonials when the shooting started in Lexington. Becoming a colonel in the Connecticut militia and later a general, he was with the troops that fortified Breed's Hill on the night of June 16, 1775, and on the next day he led some troops at the Battle of Bunker Hill. His moment of glory when he shouted his famous order was all too brief, for with victory in sight Old Put failed to reinforce an American position. This caused his troops to break ranks, and he was nearly court-martialed.

The only direct evidence that the utterance was made is the claim of one combatant that he heard it from Putnam. An 1849 history of the battle listed a similar order coming from Putnam's side, but did not specify the officer who gave it. Because of Old Put's unfortunate debacle, there is a tendency among popular historians to put the heroic words in the mouth of a stauncher figure, Colonel William Prescott, another American commander at Bunker Hill. However, whether it was Putnam or Prescott who said it is of little importance, for it is almost certain neither originated it. The words "By push of bayonets, no firing till you see the whites of their eyes" were heard from Frederick the Great in 1757, and earlier, in 1745, Prince Charles of Prussia was reported to have said, "Silent till you see the whites of their eye..."

8. Better Seen than Heard

Myth! Confronted by 700 British regulars, Captain John Parker shouted to his minutemen, "Don't fire unless fired upon, but if they mean to have a war, let it begin here."

Captain Parker is said to have given the order moments before the first firefight of the American Revolution erupted between the British and the colonists. He was addressing the seventy-seven local armed citizens—called minutemen because they were pledged to take the field at a 'minute's notice'—who had taken positions on a site in Lexington to resist the British advance on the provincial congress' arms depot at Concord. But someone fired a shot anyway—'the shot heard 'round the world'—eliciting a British volley that killed eight minutemen and wounded ten.

In a deposition given after the incident, Captain Parker recalled: "I immediately ordered our Militia to disperse and not to fire." These are not the words tradition insists he spoke that day, and which are now carved on the pedestal of Parker's statue in Lexington. The legendary quote—"Don't fire unless fired upon, but if they mean to have a war, let it begin here"—was not composed until 1868. It was a complete recast of the original, made at the instance of Parker's grandson to erase any doubt that Parker had ordered his men to deploy rather than to withdraw from the fight.

Incidentally, Parker was a tubercular who died from the disease five months after the incident that made him famous. His statue by Henry Hudson Kitson, standing like a handsome sentinel on the town green, is called The Lexington Minuteman because it was originally intended to represent the ordinary American patriot. But it has now become generally accepted as Captain Parker despite the fact that no known likeness of him survives today and no one is sure what this hero really looked like.

---

9. A Half-done Toast

Myth! **Coming to his turn to offer a toast, Stephen Decatur rose and shouted, "My country, right or wrong!"**

It is said that Stephen Decatur, a naval hero who brought the 1804-1805 war with the Barbary pirates to 'the shores of Tripoli', once attended a long night of heavy drinking at a banquet held in his honor in Norfolk, Virginia. At one point, the guests were so fired up by patriotic enthusiasm that they started toasting to the nation's success and glory. When it came to his turn, he stood up and shouted the line for which he is most remembered.

After further distinguishing himself in the War of 1812, Decatur was killed in a duel in 1820. Unhappily, historians believe the line that made him famous is not wholly authentic. One version of the real quote is, "Our Country! In her intercourse with foreign nations may she always be in the right; but our country, right or wrong." Another version replaces the phrase "but our country, right or wrong" with "and always successful, right or wrong."

John Quincy Adams once said, "My toast would be, may our country be always successful, but whether successful or otherwise, always right." Adams may not have taken his cue from Decatur, but Missouri Senator Carl Schurz surely did with his 1872 gem, "Our country right or wrong. When right, to be kept right; when wrong, to be put right."

---

10. Taxing Trial

Myth! **Arguing at a 1761 Boston trial, firebrand lawyer James Otis said, "Taxation without representation is tyranny."**

James Otis raised the cause of the colonials against British oppression to a high level by allegedly saying, "Taxation without representation is tyranny." Serious historians prefer to give the credit to the patriot John Adams, who authored the writing in which the phrase was found. The line was not contained in any contemporaneous document, but surfaced only in 1823. That year, Otis biographer William Tudor wrote that Adams had sent him a letter in 1818 recalling that Otis denounced "the tyranny of taxation without representation" at a 1761 Boston trial where colonial merchants represented by Otis petitioned the Massachusetts Superior Court to refuse applications by customs officials for search warrants on ships and warehouses. Adams did not make clear whether he was quoting Otis directly or merely paraphrasing him, or simply stating in general terms what he remembered of the dim past. Tudor nonetheless commented, "From the energy with which he (Otis) urged this position that taxation without representation is tyranny, it came to be a common maxim in the mouth of everyone."

What is clear is that Otis couldn't have said the words at the time and place he was supposed to have said them. Taxation was barely an issue to the colonists in 1761, and was not even relevant to the trial at which Otis spoke. It did become an issue later, but not before the passage of the Sugar Act of 1764 and the Stamp Act of 1765 by the British Parliament. Only then could Otis have become a radical oppositionist to the British tariffs, and written that everyone should be "free from all taxes but what he consents to in person or by his representative."

11. God, Congress and a Gun

Myth! Asked by whose authority he was demanding the surrender of Fort Ticonderoga, Ethan Allen answered, "In the name of the Great Jehovah and the Continental Congress!"

After the American Revolution broke out, Ethan Allen joined forces with Benedict Arnold in his successful bid to capture Fort

251

Ticonderoga for the colonists. According to Allen in an account he wrote four years after the event, it was in the early morning of May 10, 1775 when he pounded on a door and roused a half-dressed British subaltern from sleep. Hearing his demand for the surrender of the fort, the commanding officer asked by whose authority he was acting. Allen answered, "In the name of the Great Jehovah and the Continental Congress!"

Some historians think the incident is possible, if not probable, because of "the total unpreparedness of the British." But others assert that, even if Allen's story were true, the line was a lie because he "had no commission from either of those high authorities." Benedict Arnold was the only American on the expedition who held an actual commission from the Continental Congress. As for Allen's reference to the Almighty, he was an atheist and not predisposed to mentioning God except in an irreverent way. Most biographers believe the rough-and-tumble Allen would have neither the inclination nor the ability to wax eloquent at such a critical moment, and would more likely have said, "Come out of here, you damned old rat." The British commander, belying Allen's version, said: "[He] told me his orders were from the province of Connecticut."

XI

A House Divided

On the American Civil War (Part 1)

"It is well that war is so terrible—
lest we should grow too fond of it."

•

Robert E. Lee

1. Why they Fought

Myth! **The slavery issue was the prime cause of the Civil War, with Southerners fighting to protect their ownership of slaves and Northerners seeking to obtain their freedom.**

The ignorance, says a writer, is so pervasive about the war being over slavery that people are surprised to learn that the great majority of white southerners who fought in the war held no slaves.

Popular history has propagated the idea that North-South rivalry came to a head because the slavery question had become so hot and the parties had developed strong political and social attitudes towards the institution. The two sides are shown as having taken extreme positions, one calling for the abolition of slavery and the other for its preservation. In reality, abolition was no longer the vogue in the North when the adversaries made their call to arms. The abolitionist movement had peaked in 1830 and had ceased to be active in the 1850s. When the South seceded, almost no one in a prominent position in the North seriously considered abolishing slavery outright, and even Lincoln did not dare do so in his Emancipation Proclamation.

What actually caused Southern animosity and sparked the war was the movement to limit slavery to the places where it already existed. The South saw the restriction as a threat to its way of life, to the freedom of pro-slavers to choose their institutions, and to the economic competitiveness of the sector. Southern leaders feared that the expansion of free territories would be a further distortion of the balance of power between the two sides and would bring the South more and more under the control of the North and its free blacks.

2. A Second Call to Arms

Myth! **Secessionist Edmund Ruffin fired the first shot of the Civil War at Fort Sumter on April 12, 1861.**

254

Civil War buffs who regard Fort Sumter with the utmost respect will be disappointed to learn that the first shot in that conflict was not fired on April 12 but three months earlier, on January 9, 1861. A Union ship—the *Star of the West*—was steaming toward the Fort with supplies when it was fired upon by a rebel battery located on nearby Morris Island. It fled back without sustaining any casualties, but not before two of the seventeen volleys fired connected. That the war did not then begin in earnest may have been because the South was still preparing an army and preferred to bide its time.

Most historians date the beginning of the war to the Fort Sumter confrontation in April because President Lincoln issued a 'state of insurrection' proclamation three days later. Actually, it was not Edmund Ruffin, as some people believe, but Captain George S. James who signaled with the first shot on that occasion, and Ruffin only followed suit from one of the many Confederate batteries that responded. On the Union side, history gives the honor to Abner Doubleday. But for those who regard the *Star of the West* episode as 'the first overt act of the war', the Morris Island cadet George Haynesworth, who made the opening salvo for the rebels, is the overall record holder.

Lincoln has been blamed for giving the South no recourse but to start the Civil War, in much the same way that FDR has been accused of manipulating the Japanese into attacking Pearl Harbor and starting the Pacific War. But Kenneth C. Davis, noting that the accusation against Lincoln was made generally by historians sympathetic to the Confederate cause, demolishes their arguments with the facts. Davis writes: "First, South Carolina had already fired the first shots against a federal ship (the *Star of the West* three months earlier) and, by taking the other federal forts and arsenals, had begun the war. Jefferson Davis was ready to fire on Sumter before hearing of the relief expedition, as soon as Lincoln refused to meet with Vice President Stephens (of the Confederacy) and the other Confederate delegates. Davis had also written to General Braxton Bragg at Pensacola, ordering him to take Fort Pickens. Bragg was not ready, otherwise the war might have begun off the coast of Florida." In effect, it was the South, through these hostile actions, that gave Lincoln no choice but to accept the war's inevitability.

255

3. Clash of the Iron Giants

Myth! **The North's Monitor beat the South's Merrimack at Hampton Roads, Virginia, on March 9, 1862, in the first battle involving an ironclad.**

History tells us the first battle involving an ironclad was at Hampton Roads, near Norfolk, Virginia, on March 9, 1862. But this is history viewed from the winning side. Objectively, the conflict began on March 8, 1862, when the rebels encountered the Union blockade fleet on the Elizabeth River in Virginia. The rebel *Virginia*, an ironclad, took an early lead by inflicting heavy damage on the Union fleet, which included the *Cumberland*, the *Congress* and the *Minnesota*. The *Virginia* then withdrew, confident that it had won the battle, only to encounter the *Monitor* at Hampton Roads the next day.

Hampton Roads is foremost in the popular mind as the place where the *Monitor* won to make a turning point for the North. But in fact, neither side gained any appreciable advantage in the Hampton Roads engagement to influence the general outcome. The two ships fought for more than four hours, each retiring from the battle with the impression that it got the better of the other. Later, her crew scuttled the *Virginia* to prevent capture, while the *Monitor* sank in a gale the same year.

The Southern protagonist at the battle that ended the era of wooden fighting ships is sometimes called *Merrimack* (or *Merrimac*), the old name assigned to the Confederate vessel when it was first built by the Union. The wooden frigate had been set afire and scuttled in the spring of 1861 at Norfolk, to prevent if from falling into the hands of the rebels when the naval station there was abandoned. The Confederates, lacking time and money and otherwise unable to match the Union's ship-building potential especially for the new iron ships, came upon the sunken, partially burned *Merrimack*, and immediately saw the possibilities. They raised the hull, replaced the upper decks with armor-shielded sides, added guns, and renamed it the *C.S.S. Virginia*. It was under this name that the new pride of the South spread devastation throughout the Union fleet before being stalemated by the *Monitor*.

256

4. Patches of Black

Myth! The Union's 54th Massachusetts was the first black regiment organized to fight in the Civil War.

Contrary to what the highly acclaimed film *Glory* (1989) would make us believe, the 54th Massachusetts was not the first black contingent to fight in the Civil War but only the first colored regiment to serve on the Union side. That it was "America's first unit of black soldiers during the Civil War," as movie critic Leonard Maltin observes, is correct only in the sense that America was the Union.

Oddly enough, the earliest black group to figure in the conflict took the side of the pro-slave South. Two years before the Union recruited the 54th Massachusetts in January 1863, nearly 1,000 blacks in New Orleans enlisted freely with the Confederacy in 1861 to form the First Louisiana Volunteer Regiment, called the Native Guards. They were the first Civil War unit of black soldiers ever, and also the first to be all black from the officers down to the last man. Unlike the Louisiana group, the 54th Massachusetts was under the command of white officers, one of whom was ably portrayed in *Glory* by the young star Matthew Broderick.

5. When the Rivers ran Red

Myth! The Battle of Shiloh was the bloodiest battle of the Civil War, and the second was the one at Antietam, Maryland, the following September.

The Battle of Shiloh on April 6 and 7, 1862, was also the occasion for Lincoln's celebrated defense of General Grant, who had nearly lost the fight due to negligence. Though it was Grant's counterattack that carried the day, he was severely criticized afterward, prompting Lincoln to remark, "I can't spare this man; he fights."

257

Shiloh happens to be the Hebrew word for 'sanctuary' and was originally used for the Old Testament location of the Ark of the Covenant. That it is also the name of one of the bloodiest battle sites in the annals of the American Civil War would be ironic were it not for the fact that the fight was actually waged in Pittsburg Landing, Tennessee. Except for the presence of Shiloh Church near the center of hostilities (which could account for the name), the town itself had no relevance to the event as it was too far away to witness any of the fighting.

The battle gave the North one of its greatest victories despite the loss of thirteen thousand men to the South's eleven thousand. Be this as it may, Shiloh is not the bloodiest ever fought in the Civil War; it had been so for only five months, after which an even greater horror, the Battle of Antietam, occurred in Maryland. Antietam was a small village at the mouth of Antietam Creek, along the entire length of which the fiercest battle ever to occur on North American soil raged on September 17, 1862. Like Shiloh, however, Antietam is a misnomer because most of the battle was fought in another town adjoining the creek—Sharpsburg, which accounts for its sometimes being called the Battle of Sharpsburg.

6. Stoned Martyrs

Myth! **The Fort Sumter engagement produced the first casualty of the Civil War.**

What is generally regarded as the first battle of the American Civil War was practically no battle at all, and there were no casualties, not even one wounded. The Union army under Major Anderson surrendered Fort Sumter in Charleston to Confederate General Pierre Beauregard after a one-and-a-half day siege. Although the first death at the Fort and of the war occurred on this occasion, it was not due to the skirmish. Anderson and his men had been allowed to leave the harbor on Union supply ships, and they had fired a cannon in a salute to the Stars and Stripes as a final tribute to the Union. The gun exploded and killed a Union soldier outright and fatally wounded another—the only deaths caused in this initial period until more fatalities resulted for the Union in the next incident at Baltimore.

258

Some historians have formed the belief that Baltimore produced the first true casualties of the Civil War, but this view must be taken with caution as well. What happened in Baltimore may have been a mere fracas in which four members of the Massachusetts militia were stoned to death by a mob consisting of Confederate sympathizers. The action was not military in nature, firearms did not cause the losses, and the attackers were not affiliated with any regular military unit. Nonetheless, the chaotic times and the lack of organization on the Confederate side all but erased the distinction between the civilian aggressors and so-called Southern "irregulars," and this has made it easier to qualify the Union victims as casualties of war.

7. Dixie Draws the Line

Myth! The Mason-Dixon Line was designed to be the geographical boundary between the free states and the slave, or 'Dixie', states.

Because the Mason-Dixon Line has been traditionally the boundary between North and South, it is often supposed that it was deliberately laid out to divide the so-called free states of the North from the slave states of the South. It wasn't. The line started as a short 244-mile-long regional border set between 1763 and 1767, or nearly a hundred years before the Civil War began. The English surveyors-astronomers Charles Mason and Jeremiah Dixon drew it to settle a boundary dispute between the Calvert family proprietors of Maryland and the Penn family proprietors of Pennsylvania. The two families had been at odds for nearly a century and they finally agreed to abide by whatever line Mason and Dixon would establish as the Pennsylvania-Maryland boundary.

In 1820, the Missouri Compromise sought to divide western lands into slave and free by running the Mason-Dixon Line in latitudinal fashion further along the Ohio River and the 36'30" parallel west of the Mississippi. This extended boundary, with everything below it becoming 'the south' and every point above it 'the north', became the new Mason-Dixon Line. This despite the fact that it had nothing to do with Mason and Dixon, who had kept strictly to their original assignment and never bothered with the

259

Midwest. Today, people perceive the Mason-Dixon Line more as a long stretch from the Atlantic to the Pacific than as the short boundary separating Pennsylvania from Maryland and part of West Virginia.

According to popular belief, the term 'Dixie' was derived from the Mason-Dixon Line in order to refer to the region of the slave states and the US South. But two other known derivations of 'Dixie' appear to be better substantiated by the evidence and are therefore preferred by etymologists. The first is of Northern vintage, and traces the word to a successful 1859 New York minstrel show about 'Dixie's Land.' This was a farm in Manhattan to which some slaves sent to Charleston by the farm's owner, a character called Johann Dixie, gave the name. The curtain call finale contained the song, "I Wish I Was in Dixie's Land," which grew popular in the North and was Abraham Lincoln's favorite. Contemporaneously, it was a hit in the South, where it became the unofficial national anthem of the Confederacy despite its blatant reference to a well-known bastion of the North.

The second derivation is from the little-known fact that New Orleans was the hometown of the so-called 'dixies', or $10 banknotes, in the 1830's. The Citizen's Bank and Trust Company of New Orleans had issued the highly elaborate bank notes, with the French *dix*, meaning ten, imprinted on them, to discourage counterfeiting. It was not long after that wags began to call New Orleans 'Dixie Town' and the entire South 'Dixie Land'.

8. Degrees of Separation

Myth! Slaves in the South were not treated as humanely as free blacks were in the North.

Heightening the myth of the Mason-Dixon line is the notion that at the time of the Civil War, the South was synonymous with slavery and the North with freedom. Shenkman, citing a number of historians, tells us this is baseless. The South before the war was anything but solidly proslavery, at times nurturing more groups opposed to the institution than did the North. Some of these were abolitionists who very nearly succeeded with their objective. In the Virginia legislature of 1832, after a two-week debate, fifty-three legislators voted to abolish slavery against seventy-three who wanted to keep it. A motion to condemn slavery as an evil lost by just seven votes. Redneck politicians like John Calhoun were dominant in the region, but there were also notable Southerners, such as Hinton Rowan Helper and Cassius Marcellus Clay, who were vehemently opposed to slavery for political, economic or moral reasons.

An example where the freedom-slavery dichotomy between North and South was not clear-cut was West Virginia, which undertook the Union cause below the Mason-Dixon Line. On the other hand, denial of the vote and of job and housing opportunities to Negroes was not uncommon in many Union states, both during and after the war. A writer notes that in what was supposed to be an oppression-free North, "(c)ustom, extralegal codes, and sometimes mob law served to relegate the Negro to a position of social inferiority and impose a harsh rule of segregation."

9. Trade Winds of War

Myth! Trading between North and South was closely regulated during the Civil War.

Those not familiar with the intricacies of the American Civil War generally presume that, coincidental to military action, North and South imposed economic sanctions against each other and used naval blockades to inhibit trading between the states and with other countries. The industrial North did seem capable in this regard, and consequently in stifling economic activity to some degree in the South.

However, while it is true that the South's economy could barely support its war effort, this was not due to blockades and other forms of trade restrictions by the North. There was, in fact, lively trading between the adversaries during the conflict, and it was never clandestine. Merchants from both sides of the Mason-Dixon line were authorized by their respective governments to trade with each other whenever if would be of benefit. Since the South had a surplus of cotton but lacked opium for the wounded, and the North had opium but no cotton for its garments, these two items became the most actively traded.

10. Two under the Shade

Myth! The American Civil War ended when Lee formally surrendered to Grant under an apple tree.

All forms of media have burnt into America's collective memory the myth of Robert E. Lee relinquishing his sword to Ulysses S. Grant, and the latter returning it to Lee, in a ceremony held on April 9, 1865 under an apple tree near the Appomattox Courthouse. The simple yet elegant act is seen as heralding the end of the American Civil War.

One of the concessions a magnanimous Grant gave to all rebel officers who surrendered in April 1865 was the right to keep their swords and side arms. This has been the rationale for the widely held belief that after Lee handed his sword to Grant to symbolize the surrender at Appomattox, the latter immediately gave it back to Lee. But Grant himself debunked the story, saying that "the much talked-of surrendering of Lee's sword and my handing it back to him…is pure romance." The political cartoonist Thomas Nast corroborated Grant somewhat in a contemporary drawing showing the Union general with his saber, and Lee and the other rebel officers standing beside him without their own.

The image of Lee and Grant under an apple tree beside a courthouse when they performed the surrender ceremony lives on in the traditional use of the apple tree design on jewelry and other items commemorating the Civil War. In reality, the surrender was made inside a private dwelling in the Appomattox Courthouse (the name of the locality in which the residence stood and not of a government building, as is commonly supposed). The only apple tree involved was the one that figured in a side event before the surrender. On his way to the surrender site, and learning that Grant had not yet shown up, Lee had decided to wait at the foot of an apple tree, seating himself on some rails that were placed there by his assistants for his convenience. The tree, however, could not have had any relevance to the ceremony, as it was at least half a mile away.

Most people have the impression that the American Civil War finally ended with Lee's surrender to Grant on April 9, 1865. In fact, it was the surrender of Confederate General J. E. Johnston to

General Sherman nine days later that marked the formal end of Confederate resistance.

XII

O Brother, Where Wert Thou?

On the American Civil War (Part 2)

"Although a soldier by profession, I have never
felt any sort of fondness for war, and I have never
advocated it, except as a means of peace."

•

Ulysses S. Grant

1. What about Bob?

Myth! **Jefferson Davis and Abraham Lincoln appointed their respective first choices, Robert E. Lee and Ulysses S. Grant, to head the Confederate and the Union Army.**

Robert E. Lee's famed role as commander of the Confederate army in the Civil War overshadowed a longer if not more distinguished career previously pursued in the US military. Comparatively little is written of the thirty-five years Lee spent with the Federal army, some of it as commander of the West Point Military Academy. Few people know that because of this record, Lincoln preferred Lee to Grant and actually offered the Union command to Lee first. But while Lee was an anti-slaver at heart and an oppositionist to secession, he felt he would not be able to execute the commission faithfully without taking up arms against his beloved home state of Virginia. So he declined the appointment, resigned from the US Army, and on the same day accepted a commission in the Confederate Army.

It was Lee who faced Grant most of the time and would eventually surrender the Confederate Army to Grant's Union forces in April 1865. Ironically, Lee was only a co-equal of the many Confederate generals under President Jefferson Davis for the better duration of the war. Davis finally named Lee to succeed him as commander-in-chief in February 1865, only two months before the war ended at Appomattox.

A much lesser light, General Albert Johnston, fared better than Lee after refusing Lincoln's offer of second-in-command of the Union Army in 1860. President Davis immediately rewarded Johnston, till then a US Army commander, with the position of second-ranking general in the Confederate Army.

2. Conflict of Interests

Myth! **True to their causes, the South's Robert E. Lee kept slaves while the North's Ulysses S. Grant did not.**

265

General Robert E. Lee of the pro-slavery South came from a slaveholding family, but there is no proof he ever owned a slave himself. In the late 1840s, Lee insisted that the slaves his wife inherited from her father be released, and they were.

Ironically, the same thing cannot be said of his counterpart from the freedom-loving North, General Ulysses S. Grant. In addition to the four slaves his wife Julia brought into the marriage in 1848, Grant bought a slave from his father-in-law, a Missouri plantation owner, in 1858. Although Grant freed his slave a year later, he did not stop using slaves as field hands during the four years he worked his farm. Julia Grant's slaves were freed only at the end of the Civil War, when it became politically expedient to do so.

Mrs. Grant was an apologist for slavery all her life, and her husband stood up for her. The South's foremost general was different. Lee nurtured genuine anti-slavery sentiments, and this was clearly demonstrated when he wrote that "slavery as an institution is a moral and political evil."

3. The Bomber was Bombed

Myth! Grant drank inordinately while he was in the Army.

"Tell me what brand it is, and I will send a barrel to the other generals." This was supposedly President Lincoln's response to complaints that Ulysses S. Grant drank too much whiskey. The story became popular during the lifetime of both luminaries, and an amused Lincoln regretted having to deny it personally. According to W. E. Woodward, the President thought the false quote might have been a spin-off of an outburst by George II of England when the king was confronted with the news that General James Wolfe was mad. "If General Wolfe is mad," George allegedly said, "I hope he bites some of my other generals." Actually, the Lincoln anecdote was the creation of Charles G. Halpine, writing under the name Miles O'Reilly, who reported that the President had said it in an imaginary banquet.

Many biographers believe the incident could not have

266

happened anyway, since Grant's reputed drunkenness while in the Army is completely untrue. In *Grant Takes Command* (1969), the respected historian Bruce Catton says one John Rawlins, who thought he saw Grant whooping it up with his aides one wet evening, started the myth. The real story is that Grant arrived on the scene late, having gone there to break up the party when he found out about it, and he did precisely that by telling off the rousers in "blistering" language. Catton is corroborated by many reports that while Grant drank a lot when he was unemployed in Illinois, he was never intoxicated after he joined the Army.

4. Fire, Burn!

Myth! **General William Sherman, nicknamed Old Tecumseh after the famous Indian chief, was the Northerner most hated by the South for his callous burning of Atlanta, Georgia.**

It's hard to believe that the Union general Southerners loved to hate was himself a Southerner. William Tecumseh Sherman, who carved a 6-mile-wide wake of utter destruction from Atlanta to Savannah, Georgia, on his inexorable 'march to the sea', had been superintendent of a military academy in Louisiana when that state seceded from the Union. He resigned and was commissioned as a Union infantry colonel, eventually becoming a general in Lincoln's forces.

Sherman earned the undying enmity of Southerners for something he didn't really do. They saw Atlanta's destruction in November 1864 from photos taken by Civil War correspondent George Barnard, and immediately took for granted that Sherman was the perpetrator. What Barnard didn't say—because he thought everyone already knew—was that Confederate general John B. Hood, not Sherman, had caused much of the desolation to prevent anything of use from falling into the hands of the enemy. Some newspapers would later note that Sherman's army didn't even pass through Atlanta until five days after the conflagration had started. Those who set the fires included soldiers and civilians hoping to get some booty under the cover of the flames.

A similar fate befell Columbia, South Carolina, on February 17, 1865, when fires of mysterious origin almost completely destroyed the city. Although Sherman's forces were blamed, evidence pointed to departing Confederate soldiers as the real culprits.

Sherman was called 'Old Tecumseh' by his troops supposedly after the Shawnee Indian prince (c.1768-1813), and most people assume this was how Tecumseh became part of his name. Actually, Tecumseh was not a nickname or a second name, but the general's first name from birth, with William only added later on.

---

5. To Hell and Back

Myth! General Sherman authored the line, "War is hell," and the message, "Hold the fort! I am coming!," which he semaphored to a besieged Union depot in Georgia.

The epigram "War is hell" is actually a distillation, through folk editing, of certain words General William Tecumseh Sherman spoke at the Ohio State Fair in Columbus on August 11, 1880. Appearing before a group of Northern veterans, the Union stalwart cautioned, "There is many a boy here today who looks on war as all glory, but, boys, it is all hell. You can bear this warning voice to generations yet to come. I look upon war with horror, but if it has to come I am here." Sherman was heartily applauded for this patriotic posture, but it is the anti-war sentiment encapsulated in the three-word line he never spoke that is most remembered.

Few people know that this was not the first and only time the general expressed his antipathy for war. In several conflicts for which he became famous, Sherman managed to make remarks that essentially meant war was hell. When Atlanta was under siege, for example, Sherman wrote that city's mayor: "War is cruelty, and you cannot refine it." And in an earlier battle, he reportedly said, "War is barbarism." Ironically, in later years, he became so absent-minded that he forgot he ever said anything like "War is hell."

In another Sherman anecdote, the general was on his famous march to the sea in October 1864 when informed that Confederate guns were besieging the key supply depot of the Union army at Allatoona Pass, Georgia. "Hold the fort! I am coming!," he

268

reportedly semaphored from nearby Kennesaw Mountain to Gen. John Murray Corse, the depot's commander. Historians confirm the event, but their recollection of Sherman's actual words is somewhat different. Apparently, what he sent were two messages: "Hold out; relief is coming," and "Sherman says hold fast. We are coming." The newspapers dramatized Sherman's determination to come to the aid of the beleaguered defenders by merging the import of both messages in a single dispatch. The unitized version became a Union-rallying cry and later the first line of a religious revival song published in 1874.

---

6. Rebel Yell

Myth! **Southerners originated the phrase 'damn Yankees' to deride Northerners during the Civil War.**

The expression 'damn Yankees' was a natural for the Civil War, and was probably most widely used during that period. This may imply that it originated in that war, but it did not, whether as an insult applied by Southerners to Northerners or as an affectionate reference to Northerners by Union sympathizers who were not themselves from the North.

The word 'Yankee' itself has had an unclear origin for the last two hundred years, although etymologists have run it down to three possibilities. The first is American Indian, based on a myth popularized by James Fenimore Cooper, if not wholly invented by him, that a tribe from Massachusetts could not properly pronounce the word 'English'' or 'Anglais''' and had to make do with the corrupted 'Yankee'. The second theory, an extension of the first, is that the British appropriated the word from the Indians, who were using it against them during the French and Indian Wars, and then shifted its application away from themselves and to the American colonials during the Revolution. According to the third, and likeliest, explanation, Yankee was derived from the name of a Dutchman whose name sounded like Yanky or Jankee, the diminutive for Jan or John. In 1945, H. L. Mencken wrote that Yankee came from Jan and Kees, signifying John Cheese. In its original form the term was Jan Kaas, and in that form it has been a nickname for a Hollander in Flanders and Germany for a great

269

many years. In the US, the word became a tag for the Dutch settlers of the New England states until the Dutch turned around and used it on the English settlers.

Later, 'Yankee' came into general use in the colonies to designate a disliked neighbor to the north. By the Revolutionary period the English were using it to spite the American colonials. It was about this time that the whole phrase 'damn Yankee' emerged, though not as a British put-down of the American rebels. Members of General Philip Schuyler's revolutionary army, called 'Yorkers', felt that 'Yankee' wasn't derogatory enough for certain New Englanders known as 'northern provincials', so they tacked on the word 'damn' for effect.

During the Civil War, the Southerners used 'Yankee', sometimes with 'damn' and at other times without, in contempt of all Northerners. American soldiers overseas gave the word some dignity during the two World Wars, but it has since lapsed back to its old pejorative sense, particularly in Third World countries where "Yankee go home!" has become a fashionable slogan.

7. Cabin in the Cotton

Myth! Harriet Beecher Stowe's *Uncle Tom's Cabin* was a faithful depiction of life in the South before the Civil War.

Uncle Tom's Cabin, or Life Among the Lowly, was regarded as "the book that made the Great War," and Lincoln himself was reported as an ardent admirer who greeted the author with the words, "So you are the lady that wrote the book that started this war." Apparently, Stowe had opened the eyes of Northerners to the sufferings of blacks under bondage in the South, and the story and the shocking language in which it was told had raised a storm of indignation in the Union and provoked feelings of antipathy that ignited the Civil War.

But critics say the belief that *Uncle Tom's Cabin* gave a faithful portrayal of everyday life among slaves in the South is unfounded. The "life among the lowly" that Stowe depicted was inaccurate, her characters were unreal, and the events she described were over-dramatized and exaggerated. The writer hadn't the foggiest idea why and how the nation would be affected when she began to publish the story as a serial in the anti-slavery *National Era* of Washington, DC She had intended it to be just a commercial piece of fiction, and only later, with the limelight already on her, did she declare that her purpose was to make it factual. Contemporary historians ultimately agreed that the whole book was fictional, with very minimal true-to-life elements. Obviously, Stowe could not have given a fair portrayal as promised because she had practically no first-hand knowledge of the South and had never lived there.

8. Judah's War

Myth! Jefferson Davis was the 'brains of the Confederacy'.

Mark Twain described Jefferson Davis as 'The Head, and Heart, and Soul of the Mightiest Rebellion of Modern Times'. This meant Davis was the political leader of the Confederacy, which is not the same as saying he was its thinker or planner. The unofficial nickname 'brains of the Confederacy' belonged to Judah Philip Benjamin, a noted lawyer, US Senator, and Attorney General, Secretary of War and Secretary of State in Davis' cabinet.

Judah's parents—Philip Benjamin, an English Jew, and Rebecca de Mendes, a Portuguese Jew—had attempted to immigrate to New Orleans in 1811. But after learning that the British were blockading the mouth of the Mississippi, they lived a few years on the island of St. Croix in the British West Indies, where Judah was born. Judah was four years old in 1815 when the family moved to the United States and settled in Charleston, South Carolina. Before graduating from Yale College, he moved at seventeen to New Orleans, where he studied law and was admitted to the bar in 1834. What is interesting from the evidence—or from the lack of it—is that Benjamin and his father, both of British nationality, never became citizens of the US or of any state of the Confederacy.

271

9. Torpedo Bay

Myth! Naval Commander David Farragut, under torpedo attack while leading his fleet into Mobile Bay, shouted, "Damn the torpedoes—full speed ahead!"

Commander Farragut was following instructions on August 5, 1864, to take the port of Mobile, Alabama, from the Rebels during the Civil War. A Confederate 'torpedo' struck the lead ship, an ironclad, causing the ship after it to stop and the rest of the line to slow down. Afraid this would cause fear and confusion in the fleet, Farragut climbed the rigging of his flagship and supposedly bellowed out his famous order. Farragut captured the port in three hours, and for his achievement was promoted at war's end as the country's first admiral.

Modern Americans are reminded of this naval hero by his statue in Washington, DC, with the famous words carved underneath. But those words may have to be recarved in light of the disclosure that what Farragut really said was "Damn the torpedoes! Captain Drayton, go ahead. Jouett, full speed." Another version is even longer: the additional phrase "Four bells!" appears between the first and second lines.

We are further told that what was called a torpedo in Farragut's day was totally different from our concept of that weapon today. The British engineer Robert Whitehead perfected the first self-propelled underwater torpedo only in 1868, and the first boat that would carry it did not appear until 1877. Before that, "torpedo" was the term used for floated mines, which in the battle of Mobile Bay were beer kegs filled with powder.

10. A Cut Line

Myth! An enemy bullet felled Union General John Sedgwick before he could finish saying, "They couldn't hit an elephant at this distance."

Major General Sedgwick is sadly remembered as the Union commander whose last word on earth was split right in the middle by a Rebel bullet. This West Point graduate and veteran of the Mexican War and several Indian campaigns was leading the Sixth Army Corps against Confederate forces at Spotsylvania, Virginia, in the spring of 1864. On May 9, the general was peering over a parapet to view the enemy lines, seemingly unconcerned about sniper fire. When told to keep his head down, he laughed off the warning, saying, "They couldn't hit an elephant at this dist—." The sentence couldn't be finished because at that very moment, a bullet hit him squarely on the jaw, killing him on the spot.

Later, an aide wrote a book that exposed some of the details as myth. His prosaic account described how the general was sitting under a tree, talking with one of his staff about the upcoming battle, when he noticed some of his troops were incorrectly positioned along the lines where the next fight would commence. He got up and strode out to the front to adjust the lines when a Rebel sharpshooter started firing from somewhere out of sight. The Union soldiers began ducking, but the general just laughed and said, "What, what, men! This will never do; dodging for single bullets! I tell you they could not hit an elephant at this distance." He paused, and was in the act of resuming conversation with the staff officer by his side when the sniper bullet hit.

11. Klansman's Credo

Myth! **When asked what his military credo was, Confederate general Nathan Bedford Forrest replied, "To git thar fustest with the mostest."**

The singularly phrased slogan quickly achieved legendary status—and unexpected additional fame for the tough Rebel general. It sounded precisely the way Northerners would have wanted to hear it from Forrest, who was a former slave trader from southern Tennessee. But Southerners found the enunciation strange and the syntax unnatural. According to one biographer, the construction was a "literary carpentry" that Forrest, whose only achievement outside the military was his founding of the Ku Klux Klan after the Civil War, would not have been capable of.

In various writings and memoires, Forrest's Confederate colleagues and Union officers who had talked with him referred to his credo in its refined form: "To get there first with the most men." The general was ill-educated even by contemporary standards, but he was not ignorant or illiterate. More likely, what he said was "Git thar fust with the most men" in accordance with the diction of the time, but the key words became corrupted in the process of mythification.

XIII

Old World Woes

On Europe's Wars

*"Once more unto the breach,
dear friends, once more."*

•

Henry V

1. The Valley of Decision

Myth! The Light Brigade's entire force of 600 men perished in their heroic charge at the Battle of Balaklava.

Alfred Lord Tennyson's 'The Charge of the Light Brigade' describes the suicidal attack of a British cavalry contingent during one of the most famous battles of the Crimean War (1853-56). The poem draws a pathetic image of the action with the unforgettable line, "Into the valley of death, rode the six hundred".

But historians say Tennyson resorted to too much poetic license in his effort to romanticize "a foolish battle in a foolish war." He fudged numbers when he suggested that 600 made the charge and all died in the action. In fact, there were 675 cavalrymen who joined in the assault, of whom only 113, or 17 percent, died, while another 134 were wounded or captured. What may have given Tennyson the idea that the maneuver ended in a complete massacre is that all or nearly all of the horses used in the onslaught did not survive. Some 475 horses perished outright and more than a hundred others had to be killed later.

Doctoring the count in the interest of harmony and syntax is one thing, but passing off an incident as a fine example of British heroism, when it should be one spotlighting the moral ineptitude of the British in the Crimean War, is another. The best of British soldiery, brave and patriotic as they were, carried out a foolish and suicidal charge, a grave faux pas that marred the fine military tradition of the Empire. The commander Lord Raglan had wanted to prevent the Russians from taking captured Turkish artillery. Misinterpreting the order, the runner, Captain Nolan, conveyed it to two levels of command—Lord Lucan, overall commander of the cavalry, and Lord Cardigan, commander of the Light Brigade—before anyone realized there was an error. The commanders, who were quarreling at the time, were too proud to communicate directly with each other, and allowed the order to be implemented without challenge.

Tennyson wrote a second, less popular, poem describing another unfortunate attack by a British contingent of three hundred in the same battle. Its title: 'The Charge of the Heavy Brigade'.

2. Out of whole Cloth

Myth! The Bayou Tapestry, depicting how King Harold lost an eye in the Battle of Hastings, was embroidered in France by the wife of William the Conqueror.

William the Conqueror landed his force and marched to Hastings on England's southeast coast, where he quickly built a timber castle as a base. A few days later, the battle portrayed on the famous Bayeux Tapestry raged, coming to a close when the Norman archers rained arrows on the Anglo-Saxons.

The Tapestry has perpetuated the myth that one such arrow landed in King Harold's eye, and due to this mishap he was easily slain by the Normans. It had been settled as early as 1068 that Harold's death was caused solely by wounds inflicted by four Norman nobles hacking at him in the heat of battle. Later, some historians, finding this description too bland, took a cue from the Tapestry and concluded that the scarred and bewildered gallant plucking an arrow from his eye in the cloth's controversial scene is Harold. Experts insist Harold is not this figure but another one in the same scene seen falling to the right of a Norman horse and being attacked by its rider with a sword.

Another curious circumstance about the Bayeux Tapestry is its name. While implying that it is a tapestry made in Bayeux, France, the artifact is in reality a very long embroidered hanging done in the British Isles with colored wool on a plain background of bleached linen. A half-brother of William the Conqueror, Bishop Odo of Bayeux, commissioned the item and had it made between 1067 and 1070 somewhere in England, where Odo was then residing. No less than William's queen Mathilde was supposed to have worked on the embroidery, but most French historians consider this part of the myth.

The Bayeux Tapestry is not the only relic that contains false information about a European battle. One famous engraving shows the French, under white-plumed, 21-year-old duke D'Enghien, driving off the Spanish in the Battle of Rocroi on May 19, 1643. This was the French's first great military success in decades, a triumph rivaling England's rout of the Armada in 1588. General Beck of the losing side may be seen in flight, but in the actual event, he did not arrive until the next day and missed the battle completely. Historians say he could have turned the tide against the French had he been on the scene in time. The duke's cavalry, so completely fatigued by their relentless rush, was at the point of collapse when the Spanish commander Don Francisco de Melo surrendered because he had run out f cannonballs.

3. Down into the Sea in Ships

Myth! The defeat of the Spanish Armada by a superior English navy precipitated the decline of Spain as a power.

According to most popular reviews of the events that led to the defeat of the Spanish Armada, the English, although outnumbered, had more heroic and competent sailors who were inspired by Queen Elizabeth's leadership. The verdict generally is that the tragic outcome of the venture started Spain's decline as a colonial power.

Analysts disagree on several points. Firstly, it was the English assisted by, among others, the Dutch, that outnumbered the Spaniards, and not vice versa. The handicap was doubly compounded when a surprise storm wiped out a third of the Spanish force (although the English contended this happened after, not during, the battle). Secondly, contrary to what the standard texts state, England's navy was poorly maintained and its sailors untrained, a situation that Spain was unable to turn into an advantage because of the inefficiency of its own lumbering ships as they tried to negotiate the narrow channel. Providing the real clincher for the English were Elizabeth's commanders, who knew the Spanish secret plan of attack and lost no time laying a trap for the over-confident aggressors.

According to the same sources, the biggest fallacy is to think that the Armada's defeat destroyed Spain's standing in the hierarchy of colonial powers. For in fact, though Spain may have been humbled by the experience, it only took a very short period of adjustment before coming out stronger than ever. Between 1588 and 1603, Spain recovered more treasure from the colonies than in any other prior fifteen-year period. The navy, after some

278

revamping, emerged from the debacle to become a leaner and more effective instrument of exploration and conquest.

4. Color Clashes

Myth! The Thirty Years War was fought between the Red Roses and the White Roses for an uninterrupted period of thirty years.

The Thirty Years War is popularly perceived as a single continuous conflict with a well-defined beginning and ending and lasting precisely thirty years. It was called 'The Wars of the Roses' in the belief that the red rose and the white rose were used as symbols by the warring sides.

The thirty-odd-year civil strife that agitated England in the late fifteenth century was not really as well defined as tradition would later make it. *First*, the period did not consist of a single conflict, as most people believe, but of various clashes that had identities of their own. *Second*, it is not clear if the wars started in 1455 with the battle of St. Albans or in 1460 with the Battle of Northampton, where the Yorkists took the deranged Henry VI prisoner. Nor is it certain if they ended in 1487 at the battle of Stoke or in 1485 at Bosworth, where Henry VII wedded Elizabeth, daughter of King Edward IV of England, to unite both Houses.

Third, the red rose is generally seen as the principal badge of the Lancastrians, and the white rose as the main Yorkist symbol. In truth, the white rose was only one of several Yorkist badges that included Richard III's white boar, which was the better known of these icons toward the end of the wars. Richard's rival Henry VII made the red, or Tudor, rose popular, but not until after his victory at Bosworth Field in 1485. Henry VI, the chief Lancastrian, had not used the symbol at all.

Lastly, many modern scholars consider the term 'The Wars of the Roses' anachronistic and unhistorical because it came up only 300 years after the last battle had been fought. It was used by David Hume for the first time in 1762 in his *History of England*, and was later noted in Scott's *Anne of Geierstein*.

279

5. From Holy Cause to Holocaust

Myth! In three of the four Crusades, exemplary knights devoted to the Christian ethic prevailed over Moslem armies.

There were six full-scale Crusades, contrary to the popular belief that there were only four. Three more are officially designated Crusades and numbered as such even though they were no more than short-lived wars. A tenth Crusade called the Children's Crusade, an unnumbered disaster occurring between the Fourth and Fifth Crusades, was waged by thousands of Christian children who were sold into slavery or died of hunger and disease before reaching the battlefields.

While the Crusades are often touted as proof of the historical superiority of Christians over Muslims in warfare, this is only true in the movies. The First Crusade, begun by European Christians in 1095 and culminating in their recapture of Jerusalem from the Muslims in 1099, was the only successful one. The Muslims, wresting back Jerusalem in 1187, won the Second Crusade. The Third Crusade ended in a tie, with the Muslims keeping Jerusalem at the sacrifice of many innocent followers who were massacred by Richard the Lion-Heart. In the Fourth Crusade the Christians sacked Constantinople, but it was otherwise inconclusive. So also was the Fifth Crusade, which saw the Muslims retaining Egypt after the Christians were forced to flee by the rising floodwaters of the Nile. There were no winners or losers for the Sixth Crusade and the three small ones that followed, although the Muslims gained a permanent advantage when, in 1291, they took back their former bailiwick Akko (now called Acre), which had become the last Christian stronghold in Muslim territory.

Tradition portrays the Crusades as holy wars waged by grimly devoted Christians against Muslims to protect if not promote venerated dogmas. That picture has now been scrapped by modern historians with the finding that "the Crusades were no more religious wars than political, social, or economic wars, with the spoils always going to the conqueror." The knights, after 'purifying' themselves before each adventure through the most sacred Catholic ceremonies and rituals, including papal benedictions and Holy Communion, became murderous, superstitious and adulterous brigands in the fields. Their incursions into the forbidden territory of Islam was ostensibly to establish the superiority of the Christian ethic and possibly convert the infidel, but much of it was done in the spirit of pursuing political and materialistic ends. The peasants themselves were a rabble of aimless fanatics, "singing pagan songs, indiscriminately mutilating the citizenry (young and old), raping and beheading women, laying unmerciful siege to villages and towns, and slaughtering souls with Church-sanctioned impunity."

6. Billion People Market

Myth! The British fought the Opium Wars to stop the Chinese from exporting opium to the West.

One who has only casually heard about the Opium Wars, the popular name given to the 1839-42 conflict between China and Britain and the 1856-60 war between China and an Anglo-French combine, assumes they were fought to keep China from exporting opium to Western countries. This is wrong, and so also is the premise that China was a producer of opium and was planning to develop it as a major export product after corrupting its own people with the drug.

What is true is just the reverse. China's purpose behind the Wars was to defend its trade restrictions against the British, who were smuggling opium into the country from British India, and to enforce its drug laws to protect its citizenry. In 1839 the Chinese government attempted to put a stop to the trade and confiscated all opium warehoused at Canton by British merchants. When the British refused to surrender some British sailors who had killed a Chinese villager in a drunken brawl, hostilities broke out. The British were quickly victorious, and the Treaty of Nanking was signed on August 29, 1842, forcing China to lease Hong Kong to the British and to open five other ports to trading and residence.

The importation of opium was totally legalized with China's capitulation for the second time in the 1856-60 war. When the Chinese refused to ratify the 1858 Treaty of Tientsin, Peking was captured and the emperor's summer palace put to the torch. The Chinese then signed the Peking Convention, after which British merchants began to flood China with opium, resulting in the addiction of about 90 million Chinese at the end of the 19th century. Several countries followed Britain and forced unequal terms of trade on China, completing the latter's humiliation and contributing to the Taiping Rebellion (1850-1864), the Boxer Rebellion (1899-1901), and the downfall of the Qing Dynasty (1911).

7. A Game of Diplomacy

Myth! Refusing to offer a bribe to French negotiators, Charles Pinckney said, "Millions for defense, but not one cent for tribute."

Charles Cotesworth Pinckney (1746-1825), minister to France in 1797, should not be confused with his cousin Charles Pinckney (1757-1824), a prominent politician who made important contributions to the U.S. Constitution. The minister became famous in his own right for refusing to offer a bribe to French negotiators, causing the conflict known as the XYZ Affair.

In the late 18th century, the French tried to exert all pressure on the US to give its support against England, but the US insisted on being neutral. In 1798 a mission headed by Pinckney was asked by certain French agents (later identified as X, Y and Z) to pay a quarter of a million dollars just to be heard by the foreign minister Talleyrand and to soothe ruffled French feelings. Pinckney supposedly summed up his displeasure in the words, "Millions for defense, but not one cent for tribute."

The diplomat vigorously denied he ever made the statement, claiming that what he really said was "It is no. No! Not a sixpence!" According to a report in the American Daily Advertiser dated June 20, 1798, it was Robert Goodloe Harper, a prominent South Carolina legislator, who originated the "millions for defense" quip. Harper included the line in a toast he made to John Marshall, one of the envoys sent over to France to help Pinckney negotiate with the French, in the course of a dinner given by Congress in Marshall's honor.

It is worthwhile noting that, to Pinckney's credit, he did not react the way he was expected to considering American past performance. In the early years, the US paid tribute regularly to other countries to avoid war, as when it gave $10,000 to Morocco in 1786, an annual tribute of $21,600 to Algiers beginning in 1795, and a sizeable gift to Tripoli under a treaty in 1797.

8. One Fine Day

Myth! The longbow made its debut as a major weapon of war in the Battle of Agincourt.

In one of the greatest fights in the Hundred Years War, "a small, sick and exhausted English army under King Henry V won an astounding victory over a seasoned French host at least three times as large." When the dust of battle cleared, between 7,000 and 10,000 French, compared to fewer than 500 English, had been killed. This was in Agincourt, where the longbow is said to have figured prominently as a weapon of war and to have been the key to the English victory.

However, there is as little truth that the longbow was first used on an impressive scale in Agincourt as that it was a uniquely English weapon and the single major factor in the victory. The weapon was quietly introduced into European warfare at the instance of the Germans and Scandinavians ca. 500 AD, and 500 years later it was playing a prominent role in Wales, although it is not known if it was developed there independently or if it was borrowed elsewhere. The Welsh built such a reputation around its use that, for a time, 'Welsh archers' using 'Welsh longbows' were being fielded out as mercenary or loyal support to other European armies. At the Battle of Falkirk in 1298, Edward I defeated William Wallace (of *Braveheart* fame) largely due to a devastating hail of arrows from Welsh archers against the Scots. This was apparently when the English began to be awed by the power of the weapon, having seen a combatant receive a wound from a longbow arrow that had penetrated his chain mail, passed through his thigh, the chain mail on the other side of his leg and a wooden saddle, and wounded (or killed) the horse. Although the incident is believed to be myth or to have happened elsewhere, the Welsh longbow emerged from the battle as a breakthrough weapon for

283

the English, since then becoming specialized as the 'English longbow'.

Contrary to popular belief, the Battle of Agincourt did not produce the most impressive win using the longbow, that distinction going to the earlier Battle of Crécy (1346) also during the Hundred Years War. In Crécy, the English army of Edward III defeated the French, killing 4000 knights, including two kings, two dukes and three counts, while limiting English losses to only 50 men. Historians warn, however, that the weapon would probably not have been as effective had it not been helped along by weather conditions. In both Crécy and Agincourt, according to eyewitness reports, a hail of powerful arrows crushed an enemy that could hardly defend themselves because of the rain or mist hampering their sight.

The warning comes as a vindication to Hollywood for allowing British actor and director Kenneth Branagh to redo the Agincourt spectacle despite a critically acclaimed first version by the masterful Laurence Olivier. Because Shakespeare's *Henry V* provides no clue, Olivier, a known stickler for the written original, chose to shoot the battle scene in brilliant sunshine. Branagh was a reputed Olivier successor but decided to show a dismally wet scene to comply with most historical accounts saying that it had not stopped raining for 11 days when the Anglo-French battle occurred in 1415. According to the critics, the multi-awarded Olivier knew he was stretching history somewhat by shooting the battle scene in clear weather. He had invested in a visually stunning climax at Agincourt and wanted to make sure the cinematographic advantage gained from filming outdoors would not be lost in a murky setting.

9. Tortured by Questions

Myth! The Catholic Church launched the Inquisition in Spain to ferret out and destroy Protestants and heretics.

Technically there were at least five inquisitions with rather distinct objectives—medieval, Roman, Spanish, Portuguese, and Venetian—and they were not all Catholic in orientation. The most exaggerated is the Spanish Inquisition, which was not a single unified historical event, as most people believe. Some 25,000 fell victim to its machinations over a period of three and a half centuries (1478-1834), during which many more witches, estimated at several hundred thousands, were summarily killed, mostly by Protestants. The killing in the 16th and 17th centuries of 30,000 witches in England alone triggered an exodus of pilgrims to the New World.

Not many know that the Spanish Inquisition was entirely separate from the Roman Catholic Church's Inquisition, which was started about 1230 by Pope Gregory IX and became part of the Holy Office as the Congregation for the Doctrine of the Faith in 1965. The Spanish was broader and less religious, although it was also directed against Catholics suspected of heresy. Members of other churches fell prey because of the hazy line between their orthodoxies and what the Catholic authorities considered heretical.

Contrary to popular belief, the Spanish Inquisition did not originate in Spain, but began in southern France and spread later to other Catholic bastions. More significantly, the perpetrator was not the Church but the government in connivance with clerics. The condemned were turned over to the civil authorities to face civil justice, resulting in abuses when the state used the system as a means of political repression.

10. Cold War in Siberia

Myth! The US and Russia never clashed in battle.

While Russia had been the assiduous foe of the US in that long drawn-out ideological conflict called the Cold War, it is the only major power that has not engaged the Americans in actual battle. Or so it may appear. Historians have described in detail at least two major skirmishes in the past between Americans and Russians, with casualties on both sides.

In 1918, with the end of World War I still months off, several of the Allied nations sent troops into Russia. The purpose of the British and the French was to push Moscow back into the war against Germany after it had signed a separate peace with the Kaiser. The US, on the other hand, sent five thousand troops to northern Russia ostensibly to stiffen local opposition to the

Germans, and another nine thousand to Siberia to help keep open the Trans-Siberian Railroad in what looked like a rescue operation for cornered Czech troops. But the real reason for the American intervention was to help topple the Communists in the civil war that had broken out between the ruling Bolsheviks, or 'Reds', and the counterrevolutionary 'Whites'. The encounters that followed caused many American casualties, five hundred in the north Russian campaign and thirty-six in the Siberian operation. It wasn't until April 1920, or 17 months after Germany surrendered, that the last U.S. soldiers in Red territory returned home.

11. Years of Living Dangerously

Myth! The Hundred Years War raged for a hundred years, beginning with the Battle of Sluis and ending with the Battle of Castillon.

This long-drawn war fought mostly on French soil between France and England occurred sporadically and was not a truly unified conflict because of the varied personalities and issues involved. Underlying it, however, was the basic struggle for supremacy between the two countries exacerbated by territorial disputes, problems of succession, and greed for plunder.

In 1337, Philip VI confiscated the English duchy of Guyenne, marking the beginning of the war, although the first real action would not be seen until the naval battle off Sluis in 1340. Memorable clashes at Crécy, Poitiers, Agincourt and Orléans immortalized the names of Edward the Black Prince, Richard III, Joan of Arc, Henry V and Charles VII. In between were two treaties—Brétigny in 1360 and Troyes in 1420—as well as numerous truces. Gascony, Aquitaine and Calais were lost and regained before 1453, on which date the British were once more expelled, this time for good, from Guyenne at the battle of Castillon. Only then were the hostilities considered permanently ended.

Like the War of the Roses, the Hundred Years War was given its name long after people had forgotten what it was all about or how long it lasted. It actually raged for much more than a hundred years—to be exact, 116 years based on the cease-fire at the battle of Castillon, 138 years based on the Truce of Picquigny in 1475, or 221 years based on the final British withdrawal from Calais as the last contested French soil. Or 464 years, if it is considered that no peace treaty was ever signed and the English did not withdraw their claim to the French throne until 1801!

12. Marathon Man

Myth! After running from Marathon to Athens to report the news about the battle, the courier Pheidippides collapsed and died.

The Athenians under Miltiades were fighting the Battle of Marathon in 490 BC against a Persian force sent by Darius when the former decided to order the runner Pheidippides (or Philippides) to deliver a request for help to Athens's allies in Sparta 140 miles away. Pheidippides covered the distance to Sparta in a day and a night, and with hardly any pause he ran back to Marathon in the same amount of time to rejoin the battle as an infantryman. The Athenians won despite the odds, and news of the victory was brought to Athens from the battlefield by an unnamed soldier-courier who, unfortunately, fell dead on his arrival after running 23 miles in a few hours. It is said that with his last breath, the dying messenger shouted, "Victory, victory," as he staggered into the central marketplace of Athens.

This was how Lucian of Samosata, a composer of satirical essays of the second century AD, wrote the original story without revealing its source. Later writers mythified the historical facts by confusing the identities of the two runners, and almost every retelling of the incident now mentions Pheidippides as the one who collapsed and died. Historians say the fallacy, whether or not intended, has done no harm and has in fact given everyone in the story his due. Most are agreed, however, that of the two feats of endurance described by Lucian, Pheidippides' is the more impressive and significant, and would be even more so if the second runner had survived. Since he did not, "the latter, probably by his dying, became a greater hero under Pheidippides' name, and his deed served as the basis of the modern marathon."

287

13. Ride a Pale Horse

Myth! The posture of the horse on most equestrian monuments in the US and Europe is determined by the fate of its rider in the last battle he fought.

There is a widespread belief, made even more popular by trivia collectors on the Internet, that sculptors particularly in the US and Europe follow a code or pattern for equestrian statues of generals. Apparently, someone made the observation, years after the last monument was erected, that if the horse had one hoof raised, the rider had been wounded in the battle, and if the horse had two hooves raised, the rider had been killed. Where all four of the horse's feet were on the ground, the rider survived the war and died of natural causes. From the pattern that emerged, it became obvious that the posture of the horse had something to do with the fate the rider met in the particular battle or event represented.

Debunkers don't agree that such a code or pattern has been deliberately instituted, saying that it's all a coincidence. Ed Zotti (*Know It All*) goes a step further and asserts that the pattern is not even true for many existing monuments. He sums up the whole thing as a myth spread by someone who didn't think twice after noticing a few isolated cases. Says Zotti: "I dug out pictures of 18 horse statues in places from Chicago to St. Petersburg (the one in Russia), then tried to find out how the riders died. Result: zip. The riders died every which way, and for the most part it had nothing to do with how the horses in their statues were standing."

Disasters

I

A Disaster Of Titanic Proportions

On the Titanic

"There are worse things that could have
happened to me than just a scar on my thigh."

•

Molly Brown

1. That Sinking Feeling

Myth! The 1912 sinking of the Titanic is the worst disaster in maritime history.

As would later come out, the death list of the Titanic was only one-fifth that of the unarmed German vessel Wilhelm Gustloff, which a Russian torpedo sank off Danzig in the Baltic Sea in 1945. The Gustloff tragedy, though resulting in the death of 7,700 people, mostly women and children, never got the same attention in the US and Britain as the Titanic sinking. Possibly, this was because the victims were Germans, enemies of the Allies at the time, and quite unlike the Titanic's passenger list, did not include the rich and famous. This is not to mention that the Gustloff's dead, most of them civilians, were barely noticeable among the 50 to 60 million casualties of World War II.

The Gustloff sinking arguably had military overtones and occurred in wartime, but this still doesn't make the Titanic incident the worst *civil* maritime accident in peacetime. That ignominy belongs to the collision between the 2,215-ton Philippine ferry Doña Paz and the 629-ton oil tanker Victor in the Philippine Sea on December 20, 1987. The tanker exploded, and with both vessels sinking in flames, passengers were forced to jump into a sea covered with burning oil and infested with sharks. Upwards of 4,000 people were believed to have perished, perhaps even more as the ferry was heavily overloaded. The ferry's captain had turned over the bridge to an inexperienced seaman so he could drink beer and watch video with his officers!

2. Tipping Point

Myth! The main culprit in the sinking of the Titanic was an iceberg.

For all the 80 years that the Titanic lay serenely in its North Atlantic grave, the entrenched belief had been that no ship would have much of a chance after hitting an iceberg like the one that struck the 'unsinkable' behemoth. But evidence collected from the wreckage of the luxury liner over a period beginning in 1985, when it was discovered, showed that the doomed ship might have survived the catastrophic collision—or at least would have stayed afloat longer—had it not been for reasons intrinsic to the vessel and its operation. A chemical analysis of the ship's steel had detected an intolerable amount of sulfur—a key ingredient for brittleness at low sea temperatures—indicating that what was apparently rated as high-grade steel when the ship was built was really inferior material. Top quality modern steel has very low sulfuric content, and is generally not expected to shatter or break in water above 130 degrees below zero F, a limit well under the 28 degrees F prevailing at the time of the accident.

According to a scientific report released in 1994, the impact with the iceberg was probably not strong enough to crack the hull directly and produce a 350 foot gash, as was originally theorized. It was more likely that the iceberg damage occurred below the waterline. Common sense dictates that the eyewitness accounts of a gash above the waterline should have been discounted if not dismissed outright, since it was a dark moonless night and extremely difficult to see. Indeed, what the forensic examination showed was not a gash but six narrow non-contiguous openings in the starboard side of the forward hull about 10 feet above the ship's bottom. The openings, of which the longest was about 36 feet, appeared to follow the hull plate, suggesting that the iron rivets along the plate seams popped open and gave way to the splits. Since the rivets were also high in sulfur and very brittle under water, it was likely that shearing stress from the hull plate as it bent initially during the collision caused them to fail. To compound the problem, the stamping process used to create the holes in the hull plates to accommodate the rivets gave rise to microscopic cracks in the steel, and reduced the structural integrity of the steel plate at the rivet hole. This explained why the Titanic had completely gone under in only 2 hours and 40 minutes after it began to take on water.

The consensus is that these six openings may have been all that was needed to bring down the Titanic, and the matter was fully deserving of an answer from the ship's owners and representatives. In response, the ship's naval architects and engineers were quick to bring up a point that would place at least part of the responsibility on the Titanic's management and operation. They surmised that, had the vessel been traveling at a slightly slower rate of speed, the rivets would probably not have sheared and caused the splits, or that there would have been fewer openings in the hull. The iceberg's impact would not have been strong enough to produce the kind of damage done, and the consequent spiral of events culminating in the tragedy could have been averted.

3. Lord was their Witness

Myth! The S.S. California was in the vicinity of the Titanic but failed to come to its rescue.

It's still written about in books and shown in the movies: a mysterious ship hovered about while the Titanic was in its death throes, then quietly slipped away without picking up a single survivor. The blame has been placed squarely on the shoulders of Captain Stanley Lord, the commander of the S.S. California, the ship that investigators claimed was the one the passengers and crew of the Titanic saw looming in the distance as the latter sank. Lord (not to be confused with Walter Lord, who wrote one of the most lucid accounts of the Titanic disaster without ever being at the scene) denied the accusation, claiming he had been 23 miles away, had seen nothing, and couldn't have responded soon enough if he had. He went to his grave in 1962 carrying the stigma that the condemnation of the authorities and the public attached to his name.

Recently, however, a Norwegian sea captain, Hendrich Nœss, revealed in his autobiography that the mystery ship might not have been the California but his own. Nœss was first officer on the Norwegian seal hunting ship Samson, which was illegally taking seals just 10 nautical miles away when it sighted the Titanic firing rockets. Although it could have easily taken aboard all the crew and passengers of the distressed liner, the Samson mistook the Titanic for a revenue vessel out to make an arrest, and with no radio to receive SOS signals, it hastily left the scene. In 1926, the Norwegian press printed Noess' story but the non-Norwegian media ignored it.

4. The Casualty List was no Cameron Trick

Myth! Many died in the Titanic sinking due to a lack of life preservers.

There were many fallacies that followed in the wake of the Titanic tragedy, among them that the crew had kept perfect discipline, that most male passengers had given up their lifeboat seats to women, and that icebergs had never been seen that far south before. But one that has caused the ship's owners as much embarrassment as the claim of unsinkability is that the Titanic sailed without adequate logistic provisions commensurate to its physical and operational dimensions.

Early newspaper reports of the Titanic sinking came out with a casualty list that included 1,513 lives lost (and 827 saved) out of 2,340 people on board. Official figures eventually confirmed the dead, but lowered the number of survivors to 711 out of 2,224 registered passengers and crew. Self-anointed analysts were quick to observe that so many life preservers could have saved those who perished, not knowing that the Titanic had 49 ring buoys and 3,560 life belts or jackets but could not use any of them in freezing water. Originally designed for 32 lifeboats, the ship had 20 for a total capacity of 1,178 persons. With lifeboat space for at least half the passengers and crew, the Titanic carried more life saving equipment than was required by the British authorities. At the time, the minimum number of lifeboats on a vessel was determined by its gross tonnage rather than its human capacity.

That the Titanic's safety features complied strictly with government regulations brings up the more relevant issue why only 711 survived when 1,178 people (54% of those on board) could have been saved. Experts say this was because the 'women and children first' policy in force during the life saving operations created inefficiencies, including delays in passenger downloading and the premature launching and underutilization of lifeboats. Undoubtedly, had the lifeboats been filled to capacity, all 534 women and children could have been saved, with enough room left over for an additional 644 men.

Others suggest it could have been worse—the Titanic was traveling well below capacity because of widespread premonitions of its fate, which caused untold hundreds to cancel their reservations. In truth, there were no such premonitions, and due to its 'unsinkable' reputation the Titanic was in fact overbooked, with very few cancellations. This much Cameron's movie confirms when it shows Leonardo DiCaprio and friends playing cards for the few remaining tickets just before the voyage.

---

5. Sea Dirge

Myth! **A five-man band played 'Nearer, My God to Thee' as the Titanic sank.**

The Titanic tragedy provided an opportunity for a number of untypical heroes to do their gigs. A quietly spectacular display of bravura came from five members of the ship's band, which played a religious anthem as the huge vessel sank.

When news of the incident reached England, the Daily Chronicle noted that the hymn played was 'Nearer, My God to Thee', calling it "a fitting ending to a solemn and terrible tragedy." Lloyd's Weekly News concurred by printing the text in full with the score. There was no evidence, however, that the five-man band played 'Nearer, My God to Thee' during those critical hours other than the fact that the Sarah Adams hymn was a popular inspirational hit at the time.

Many historians, including Walter Lord, author of the definitive *A Night to Remember*, state that no survivor could recall ever hearing the Adams strain during that fateful night. Some did confirm that the ship's band, which had been playing ragtime, changed the tune abruptly when the bridge began to submerge, but the new piece was the *Songe d'Automne* ('Dream of Autumn') by the French composer Francois Barthelemon. Before the song was finished, the huge ship turned and slipped beneath the surface, taking the bandsmen with it.

Despite the clarification, most portrayals of the tragic event in American and British media have continued to feature the Adams hymn. This has piqued some critics, particularly those who are not fully convinced that the ship's band played a role during the sinking. Hard-liners have in fact taken the position that the whole story is a mere embellishment by popular writers to perk up the account of the disaster.

6. Futility Hounds a Voyage

Myth! Morgan Robertson based his novel *Futility* on the Titanic event.

We are not at all surprised to learn that some of the best works of fiction are based on true-to-life occurrences. But what if a novel was written long before an event on which it is based happened?

The best-known example of this phenomenon—called *promesia*, or 'memory of the future'—is Morgan Robertson's short novel *Futility* (1898), published 14 years before the sinking of the Titanic. The novel tells the story of a ship named Titan, which was filled with fabulously wealthy passengers, many of whom were killed when the vessel sank in the Atlantic one April night after hitting an iceberg. Like the Titanic, the Titan was triple-screw, measured between 800 and 900 feet long, weighed between 65,000 and 75,000 tons, and carried a maximum load of 3000 passengers. Both ships were the largest in the world and reputedly unsinkable, sailed the same route, could reach 25 knots, and impacted with the iceberg at a speed of 23 to 25 knots. The Titan lost most of its 2,500 passengers because it had only 24 lifeboats, compared to the 20 of the Titanic.

Incredibly, *Futility* was not the only fictional predecessor of the Titanic event. Earlier, in December 1892, the distinguished journalist W. T. Stead published a novel—*From the Old West to the New*—about a ship named Majestic coming to the rescue of a liner that struck an iceberg and sank. By an ironic twist of fate, Stead was on board the Titanic on its maiden trip, and became one of its casualties. Odder still was the fact that the name of the Titanic's captain was E. J. Smith, the same name Stead gave to the Majestic's captain!

II

Groundbreaking In San Francisco

On Great Earthquakes

"Logarithmic plots are a device of the devil."

•

Charles Richter

1. Earthshaking Events

Myth! **Registering at 8.3 on the Richter scale, the 1906 San Francisco earthquake is slightly higher than Japan's 1923 Kanto earthquake at 8.2.**

Japan's Kanto earthquake of 1923 is rated 8.2 on the Richter scale, but as with many other great earthquakes of the past, this 'reading' is like a retrofitted estimate. The Richter scale, or more precisely the Gutenberg-Richter magnitude scale, was invented only in 1935 by the American seismologist Charles Richter in association with the German Bruno Gutenberg. Although we say 'invented', the scale is not in the strict sense an instrument or piece of equipment one sees in a seismology laboratory. An earthquake is defined by the amount of energy released and the potential for damage caused at the surface by ground motion, and the Richter scale is simply a system or way of measuring both.

Because its numbers range from 0 to 9, it is popularly believed the device operates by an arithmetical progression of 1 on a scale of 10. This is false. In the first place, the Richter scale has no upper limit. Although there have been no recorded earthquakes of Richter 10 or above, and geologists are confident there will be none, the scale takes into account that nature can do whatever it wants and is therefore open-ended. Neither is the lower limit Magnitude 0. Smaller earthquakes happen all the time, and the smaller they are the more frequently they occur. But the least that can be detected is only around magnitude -3.

In the second place, the progression is not arithmetic but logarithmic, so that Richter 8, for example, is not twice intensity 4 but incredibly more. To measure ground motion, each Richter number is increased by the power of 10 for every notch that it goes up, which means that magnitude 8 in relation to magnitude 4 is $10 \times 10 \times 10 \times 10$ or 10,000 times as powerful. If the amount of energy released were the basis of measurement, the power of progression would not be 10 but an astounding 32. Thus, an earthquake of magnitude 8 has 1,048,576 (or 32 to the 4th power) times as much energy as one of magnitude 4.

The Alaska Science Forum also reveals that an earthquake's Richter magnitude does not change with distance from its source. The ground effects, known as earthquake "intensity," die away

298

with distance, but the magnitude as a function of the energy released at its source does not. Thus, "an earthquake of, say magnitude 5 is a magnitude 5 earthquake no matter where on the globe it occurs."

2. It Moves

Myth! During the great Kanto earthquake, some of Tokyo's streets opened up and literally swallowed people and vehicles.

Almost a century of Hollywood hype and media exploitation has conditioned the popular mind to believe that an earthquake of some magnitude can literally be an earth-shattering and engulfing experience. As a prominent movie critic once observed, no earthquake movie worth its box office ratings has failed to feature a yawning abyss that suddenly appears in the ground, cars and people and sometimes even buildings falling into the chasm, and the hole closing up moments later, burying everything in it. The typical viewer thinks this sequence is possible in real life, as there is nothing predictable about what an earthquake can do. Yet there is no evidence whatever that anything like this has ever happened. Early reports from Tokyo on the great Kanto earthquake of 1923 included descriptions of "huge chasms opening up in the streets, swallowing up people, even tram cars, then closing on them like a giant mouth." Later investigations showed these were exaggerations designed by the media to sensationalize the event. Regardless of supposed eyewitness accounts of these incidents in the great earthquakes of the past, they are discounted by experts who think that while earthquakes may open cracks in the earth, it is highly improbable for any further movement to put it as it was before. More likely, a person or vehicle falls into a ditch or chasm that is already there when the earthquake happens, and the ground around him collapses.

The Alaska Science Forum says a magnitude 8 earthquakes translates into only about an inch and a half of actual back-and-forth vibration for about 60 miles, and will not cause unusual displacements other than those resulting from the cumulative effects of sustained shaking and from localized ground failure.

3. Flames on Barbary Coast

Myth! The San Francisco earthquake of 1906, the greatest of its kind to hit the US, caused the almost total destruction of that famous City by the Bay.

The earthquake that struck the western coast of California on April 18, 1906 produced two major tremors extending all the way from Los Angeles to Winnemucca, Nevada, some three hundred miles east. Buildings were demolished, hundreds of electrical wires fell, gas lines broke, and streets were ripped up. It is generally assumed that the earthquake was what caused most of the damage to the city of San Francisco. It was not. Of the nearly 1000 deaths and the $420 million damage wrought on 28,000 buildings, some 15,000 of them homes, more than half were due to the fire that followed. Casualties and damages from the conflagration were actually underreported so as not to upset eastern bankers and ruin the city's credit rating. Three days of fire scorched a track over three miles wide through the city, and more destruction was caused deliberately to create firebreaks, which finally stopped the fire.

There is another reason why native San Franciscans call the disaster the San Francisco Fire of 1906 when most others call it the Great Earthquake of San Francisco. Even at 8.3 on the Richter scale, it wasn't much of an earthquake compared to the December 16, 1811, shocker out of New Madrid, Missouri.

4. The Sound Resonates as the Missouri Breaks

Myth! The US has not experienced an earthquake higher than 8.3 on the Richter scale.

The Missouri tremor measured 8.7 on the Richter scale, and was followed by smaller but no less serious quakes for more than a year afterwards (1,874 shocks were registered during the first three months alone). There were few casualties, but it is said that if the same disturbance were to occur today, it would do ten times the damage of the San Francisco earthquake (including the ensuing fire) owing to the increased population of the area. The rumblings were felt over nearly a million square miles as far north as Canada. The ground rose and fell and the earth opened up in deep cracks. Huge tidal waves swept across the Mississippi River, which changed course in a matter of two weeks in the wake of the aftershocks.

Although considered the greatest earthquake to strike the US mainland, the Missouri phenomenon is still not the biggest to happen in the North American continent. The really enormous one (after it was upgraded from 8.5 to 9.2 on the Richter scale) was the quake that hit Prince William Sound, Alaska, on March 27, 1964. Lasting nearly five minutes, it was also the second most powerful ever measured by seismograph and the second largest earthquake in the recorded history of the world. This shocker has elicited relatively little attention despite its unprecedented extent because, like Missouri in 1811, Prince William Sound was sparsely populated and the death toll was not more than 117.

5. California Split

Myth! California will eventually slide into the Pacific Ocean because of the constant collision between the Pacific and the Atlantic Plates.

The vision that California will at some point in time slide into the Pacific Ocean, and will do so sooner in a great earthquake, is pure fantasizing by those who would love to live there but can't afford to. For those who have the means, however, there's no harm keeping their fingers crossed.

It is claimed the Pacific plate on which California sits is being pushed west by the Atlantic plate due to the constant collision between these major earth crusts. Actually, the plates do not collide but slide past each other in a lateral motion along what are called fault lines or zones. On the San Andres fault, which runs on land through western California from the Gulf of California in Mexico to just north of the small coastal town of Manchester, the Pacific plate is heading northwest and rubbing against the

301

relatively immobile Atlantic plate, taking part of the California coast, including Los Angeles, with it.

But while it is true California is moving up towards Canada and beyond, computer projections plotting the location of the plates place Los Angeles in the vicinity of Anchorage not earlier than in 50 million years at present rates of movement. In the slightly shorter term, say 15 million years, "Los Angeles, if it still exists, will be a suburb of San Francisco." In the San Francisco earthquake of 1906, the western side of the San Andreas Fault moved twenty-one feet northwest. This is probably the most that can be expected from a great earthquake, and proves that California is never going to sink into the ocean regardless of how many more earthquakes manage to pull the state out of its geological moorings.

6. Lava from Java

Myth! **The eruption in the last century of Krakatoa, one of Indonesia's monster volcanoes, is the biggest in the world.**

In fact, it was only the second biggest in Indonesia, although it was probably the loudest in the world in modern times. This August 1883 event reduced an entire island to about a quarter of its former size, producing a shock that traveled around the world several times and an explosion heard 3000 miles away in Australia. Most of the estimated 36,000 people who were killed were drowned by the enormous tsunamis that ensued.

The explosion of Tambora on Sumbawa Island in April 1815 holds Indonesia's record as the biggest. In that year alone, an estimated 150 million tons of ash were discharged into the atmosphere out of a total of 220 million tons spewed over a seven-year period. On the other hand, Krakatoa managed only some 50 million tons. The energy of the Tambora blast was estimated to be the equivalent of all the nuclear stockpiles during the 1980's. About 50,000 people living on nearby islands were killed and as many as 90,000 overall died from the volcano's wider effects.

Unbelievably, scientists put Krakatoa's explosion at only one-fifth the size of the eruption of Thera, or Santorini, in the Aegean

302

Sea, which permanently destroyed the centers of Minoan civilization sometime between 1650 and 1500 BC. It is said that, if the numerous disasters recounted in the Bible and the sinking of the continent of Atlantis mentioned by Plato had any scientific explanation, it could only be the Thera phenomenon.

According to one critic, the 1969 Bernard Kowalski movie *Krakatoa, East of Java*, puts the eruption in awesome perspective, but the Cinerama format and other production values are apparently not enough to compensate for the weakness of the script. Purists are also unhappy about the movie's misleading title. While Tambora is east of Java, Krakatoa (sometimes called Rakata or Krakatau, but never Krakatowa, as the name is spelled on some movie posters) lies in the Sundra Strait, at latitude 60 11' S. and longitude 1050 26' E., putting it west—not east—of Java. Krakatoa would be east of Java if one were traveling between the two points taking the longer way around the globe. The producers probably thought the original title had stretched the matter too far and simply renamed the film *Volcano.*

7. Fire in the Sky

Myth! Pompeii was completely buried in molten lava and life in the city was wiped out when Vesuvius erupted in AD 79.

There are several fallacies about Vesuvius' eruption in AD 79, all influenced by the E. Bulwer-Lytton classic *The Last Days of Pompeii* (which was based on Dion Cassius' writing a century and a half after the event) and by a lay interpretation of the museum artifacts of the disaster. First is that Pompeii, including the neighboring cities of Herculaneum and Stabiae, were destroyed by molten lava; second, the population was totally overwhelmed in a moment by Vesuvius; and third, all the residents perished.

According to the more credible evidence provided by Pliny the Younger, who wrote about his experiences and those of his uncle Pliny the Elder, it rained pumice stone, burning rocks and millions of tons of ash for seven days. On the last day were enormous quantities of steam and water, which proved to be noxious, forming a poisonous cloud that spread and killed those present.

Then came a great flood of water that dashed down the mountainside, and mixed mud and ashes into a volcanic paste that quickly covered the cities and dead bodies. The residents had ample warning to evacuate the area, and many did escape. Of about 20,000 Pompeians, the actual death count was only 2,000 souls (16,000 in all three cities).   A previous eruption of Vesuvius—in A.D. 63, during the reign of Nero—produced a great earthquake that very nearly destroyed the whole of Pompeii and Herculaneum, and probably killed more.

8. High Scale Rumble

Myth! An earthquake in the 7.0-7.9 range of the Richter scale occurs anywhere in the world every five years.

According to the experts, an earthquake in the 7.0-7.9 range of the Richter scale can decimate an entire population. Luckily, one doesn't hear about it too often.

People are generally not aware of the many life-threatening earthquakes around them each year. While media reports a few sensational ones, most end up as dormant figures in the labs of the National Earthquake Information Center, which is the official repository of earthquake data in the US.

It's probably better that some people don't know, because the overall picture can be upsetting. Around the world, there is on the average one great earthquake (8.0 on the Richter scale) a year, one major quake (7.0-7.9) every two months, and ten destructive (6.0-6.9) quakes every month. Some 6,000 lesser earthquakes annually (4.0-4.9) are potentially dangerous, with the number going up to an unbelievable 49,000 each year in the 3.0-3.9 range, which are shocks that are not alarming but can be felt.   Microseismic disturbances, or those that show up as miniature amplitude lines on graph paper—there are 300,000 for the barely perceptible (2.0-2.9) and 600,000 for those measurable only with instruments (2.0)—are nothing to worry about, but they still prove it's a very unstable globe we live on.

We might mention at this point that when newspapers report a great earthquake "decimating" a whole town or village, we can't be sure if this means all or only some of the residents died. The

304

popular sense of "decimate" is to wipe out completely, but its true meaning is derived from the fearful practice of dictators and conquerors in the past of killing a tenth of the population to prove that they meant business.

III

Signs Of The Apocalypse

On Other Major Disasters

"Me, if I can blow up the world in the first
ten seconds, the show is a flop."

•

Irwin Allen

1. Flu on the Fly

Myth! A flu bug originating in Spain in 1918 produced more casualties in World War I than did all of its armaments combined.

Some epidemics occurring worldwide cause more casualties than great wars. That's when it's officially called a pandemic. By reputation, the worst ever is the bubonic plague of 1346-61, appropriately nicknamed the Black Death, while a flu bug that supposedly originated in Spain in 1918 is only the next worst.

In actuality, however, the Black Death is not "the worst epidemic the world has ever known," as it is sometimes called, and neither is any of the other great outbreaks of bubonic plague in history. Although deaths from this malady, mostly in Europe and Asia, have already reached more than a hundred thirty million, each individual occurrence has not exceeded a death rate of more than two million a year.

The Black Death is a rash compared to the flu pandemic that raged for eighteen months, killing from 22 to 25 million, or more than twice the nine million military casualties of the four-year World War I. It started in the spring of 1918 and by the middle of 1919 had infected some 200 million people—roughly a tenth of the human race at the time. Because the epidemic—the most widespread and deadly in modern times—began during the period of the conflict, it stirred up false suspicions and uninformed talk linking the disease to all kinds of dangerous chemicals that the Germans were believed to have introduced into the trenches.

Contrary to common belief, the real killer was not the flu bug but the bug that brought the accompanying pneumonia; the two traveled in tandem. Nor was the bug born in Spain. The name Spanish Flu came about for no real reason other than that this country was one of the most affected, although the bug had already ravaged more than half the world before it reached Spain. The Spaniards thought that German troops, weakened by hunger and lack of proper clothing, had bred the disease and the bacteria had come to Spain in the strong coastal winds during the winter. Actually, the first known situs of the outbreak was an American military base—either Fort Riley or Camp Funston in Kansas—in March 1918. From there it was brought to France by American

307

troops that formed part of the mopping up operations in World War I, then to Spain and later China.

2. Return of the Rat Pack

Myth! Called the Black Death because of its devastating nature, the bubonic plague that hit Europe in past centuries was transmitted by the bites of rats.

The London Plague, while held in awe as one of the greatest outbreaks of bubonic plague, was nothing more than an epidemic that confined itself to the Greater London area in 1665-66. It did produce 100,000 deaths, but this pales in comparison with the 27 million victims of the Black Death in medieval Europe in 1346-61. The Black Death itself was nothing compared to Justinian's Plague in the 6th century, which killed upward of 100 million people in fifty years. Incidentally, the color black had nothing to do with the devastating nature of the visitation, but came from the dark skin hemorrhage (ecchymosis) that afflicted the victim.

People in the present century heave a sigh of relief, confident that the disease is no longer active and not likely to recur. Little do they know that the plague is still prevalent in unsanitary tropical countries, and limited outbreaks do occur occasionally in the western United States. In fact, thirteen million have died worldwide since 1894.

The plague was at first believed caused by the bites of rats, until a pathogenic finding showed that the disease was transmitted by the bites of infected rat fleas. This detail has unfortunately given rise to the misconception that the bacterium is not directly communicable from one human to another (England was laughed at when it banned kissing as a way of curtailing the London Plague). It is not realized that the disease usually attacks the victim's lungs, becoming a pneumonic form that spreads directly from person to person through breath and sputum literally swarming with bacilli.

3. Bugs in their Bonnets

Myth! Germs have never been used as a weapon of war in North America.

Germ warfare is not a new concept, only the methodology has changed. Unbelievable as it may seem to most Americans, it was not only used in the North American continent, it started there.

Devised by the British more than 200 years ago as a weapon against the American Indians, it was effected by the transmission of disease through infected supplies left at the scene of battle or sold to the unwary braves. The tactic was first used in 1763, when British forces in Pennsylvania found themselves yielding to the onslaught of the Indian chief Pontiac. The British commander, Sir Jeffrey Amherst, who had a special hatred of Indians, conceived the idea of infecting them with smallpox-infested clothing. Seeing that the disease was already rampant among his men, Amherst ordered the ranks to 'lose' blankets and handkerchiefs belonging to the sick to the enemy. By the following spring, smallpox had stricken several tribes in the area.

The practice spread to South America, particularly Brazil, where white settlers began practicing genocide against the Indians of the interior. Their weapons, among which were the usual 'gifts' of smallpox-infested clothing, contributed significantly to the deaths from disease of as many as 6 million Brazilian Indians since the sixteenth century.

4. How to Plug a Plague

Myth! The Great Fire of London added hundreds of casualties to the London Plague of 1666, but eventually caused the latter's disappearance by incinerating the major sources of the germ.

John Dryden commemorated 1666 in his poem "Annus Mirabilis" as the year that saw the end of the London Plague. The poet, like many others, thought the Great Fire of London, which ravaged most of the city at this time, became the main agency for the plague's disappearance by incinerating many of the likely sources and harboring places of the germs. But historians point out this was unlikely, since most of the slum quarters where the disease had festered escaped the disaster. Moreover, the plague actually disappeared in all major areas, whether hit by the fire or not.

The blaze destroyed a lot of property, giving way to the Renaissance architecture we see in London today, but contrary to popular belief, it did not add many more victims to the epidemic. The disease wiped out 100,000 of the city's population, as against six that were killed by the fire. Four perished directly in the smoke and flames, namely, a simpleton girl employed at the baking shop where the fire started; an old woman who was caught seeking refuge in St. Paul's Church; an old man who returned to his house to retrieve some bedding; and a watchmaker who thought he could wait out the fire in his house. Another two who were drunk fell into the river and drowned when they ran from a burning building.

5. Keep a Watch on that Burner

Myth! **A French watchmaker named Robert Hubert started the Great Fire of London.**

When Robert Hubert, a French watchmaker from Rouen, confessed to the crime, neither the judges nor any present at the trial believed him guilty. But the Old Bailey jury did, and he was hanged. Soon after, it was conclusively proved that he had not even arrived in London until two days after the fire broke out.

The fire had started at Thomas Farriner's bakehouse in Pudding Lane, Thames Street, on Sunday, September 2, 1666, jumped to the neighboring houses, and raging till Wednesday, September 5, spread "from the Tower to the Temple and from the Thames to Smithfield." Farriner denied any fault, insisting it was a clear-cut case of arson. Hubert's confession, one of dozens received by the authorities from various sources, said he did it because he was "weary of his life, and chose to part with it in this way." After he was hanged, Londoners, including Farriner, claimed it was sabotage perpetrated either by the Catholics or the French. What

310

is now accepted as by far the most likely explanation is that Farriner's apprentice had left a bundle of twigs to dry in the oven overnight, and they had overheated and burst into flames.

6. Just A Bag of Air

Myth! The era of the giant airships ended with the crash of the Hindenburg.

Contrary to popular belief, the crash of the Hindenburg on May 6, 1937 at Lakehurst, New Jersey, was not disastrous in terms of human lives lost. In fact, of 97 on board, only 13 passengers and 22 crewmembers died. Footage of the tragedy, which was fortuitously filmed and permanently preserved for posterity, showed many survivors walking away from the accident practically unaided.

The Hindenburg was one of the largest airships ever to fly—it was four times larger than the corporate blimps flying today—but it was a zeppelin, not a blimp. A blimp is just a large gasbag with no framework, whereas a zeppelin has a hull formed by a rigid metal framework.

The ill-fated Hindenburg was made lighter than air by gas cells filled with hydrogen. This was unfortunate, since America's own short-lived affair with airships proved the only safe gas was helium. It was initially felt that America hastened the downfall of the zeppelin program by refusing to export helium to Germany, which had no supply of its own. The truth, however, is that it would not have mattered, since Germany, with a few revisions in the ship's design, could have continued to use hydrogen safely. According to Reader's Digest (*The Truth About History*), "the world might believe that the Hindenburg disaster was caused by a hydrogen leak, but we now know it was the varnish that sealed the canvas which caught fire."

Although the crash is remembered in most history books as the event that ended the era of the giant airships, it actually was not. After the crash, the LZ series, which were as big as the Hindenburg, if not bigger, continued to fly for commercial passenger purposes and in surveillance missions conducted by the Luftwaffe. They were later destroyed or salvaged for their metal on the orders of Luftwaffe chief Herman Göring, who saw that the aircraft was becoming more a liability than an asset in the war.

7. When the Wall Crashed

Myth! The stock market crash of October 1929 triggered the Great Depression.

Most popular treatises on the subject of the stock market crash of October 1929 leave readers with the impression that it was this phenomenon that triggered the Great Depression. But economists who prefer to be more analytic tend to be wary about establishing a cause-and-effect interdependence between the two.

First, although the roots of the Great Depression were already taking hold in the latter half of 1929, it was a full nine months after the market crash before it was broadly acknowledged that it was under way. Second, both the Crash and the Depression, being cyclical events, were just waiting to happen. For more than a century, America had suffered periodic economic downturns that struck the nation approximately every twenty years. Each of the years 1829, 1837, 1857, 1873, and 1893 saw the beginning of a major recession; 1913 would have seen the first one in the twentieth century had this not been averted by the beginning of World War I, which brought about a need for goods and quickly revived the flagging economy. Following the pattern, the 1929 stock market crash and the subsequent Depression were right on schedule.

Third, the Crash was itself a manifestation of the economic conditions that pushed the US over the edge and into the depths of the Depression. These conditions included the gross imbalance between the agricultural and the industrial sector, the extension of excessive credit to domestic and foreign borrowers, the steady decline of wholesale prices, the fantastic overpricing of corporate stock and even the existence of crime and corruption nationwide. The 2008-09 Depression, believed to be worse than the one of 1929, was likely caused by similar economic conditions and not by a stock market crash, which did not happen.

312

8. There's Something about Mary

Myth! **Typhoid Mary infected more than 1,000 cases during her public life, causing the deaths of many.**

Typhoid fever is an acute, highly infectious ailment caused by a bacillus transmitted chiefly by contaminated food or water. Mary Mallon earned the nickname Typhoid Mary because she was a carrier of the disease in more than 1,000 cases reported in the New York area in the early 1900s.

An occurrence of typhoid fever at Long Island in 1906 was traced to the 36-year-old Mary, who had worked as a household cook in one of the upper class neighborhoods there. Sanitation engineer George Soper got on her trail, and learned that Mary had practiced her profession for many years, changing jobs frequently, and that at least one case of typhoid fever had emerged in every place where she had worked. Caught several times over a period of eight years, she refused to be examined until Soper succeeded in removing her to a hospital, where it was confirmed that she was indeed a typhoid carrier. She escaped the hospital, changed her name, and took to the kitchen again. But when an epidemic was reported at the hospital, a new search turned up Mary, who was then placed in permanent quarantine beginning in 1925. She was committed by the New York City Health Department, despite an appeal to the U.S. Supreme Court, to an isolation center on New York's North Island where she died in 1938 of a stroke.

It was believed that as a carrier, Typhoid Mary was immune to the typhus bacteria but could pass on the disease to other people. Actually, she was not an immune carrier, as she herself suffered from the disease although missing most of its symptoms. She appeared not to be aware of her infection, and even if she were, she would recover from time to time and believe she was all right. But from the date she first contracted the disease, she continued to harbor the germs.

Although the typhoid bug caused infection and death in at least seven epidemics in New York, the actual historical imprint left by "Typhoid Mary" seems exaggerated. She may have caused several outbreaks of the disease, at least seven of them, but none was of any major proportion. She was responsible for only fifty-one original cases and three deaths in her entire career, not the 1,000 or so commonly attributed to her.

9. Knight Templar

Myth! The Great Fire of London convinced Christopher Wren to take up architecture, in which he was eventually knighted for his achievements.

Despite being an astronomer and geometrician of great distinction, Sir Christopher Wren is remembered chiefly as the architect of St. Paul's Cathedral in London as well as of 52 parish churches in the same city and the royal buildings of three reigns. It is said that Wren, who had neither the academic training nor the experience for architecture, turned to that field suddenly and by accident. The Great Fire of London in 1666 had just reduced St. Paul's into a fiery ruin, and Wren saw an opportunity to put into practice what he saw during his visit to Paris the year before.

This is myth, of course, for what really happened was that, even before the fire, Wren had already noted the almost complete absence of serious architectural endeavour in England. Thus, in 1662, when he was 30, he offered to design the Sheldonian Theatre at Oxford. Bishop Sheldon was obviously pleased and started consulting Wren about London's battered, and in parts nearly derelict, St. Paul's. At Oxford in the spring of 1666, he made his first design for a dome for the cathedral. The central tower being well on the way to collapse, Wren proposed its entire demolition and the building of a new central space at the crossing of nave, choir and transepts, surmounted by a drum rising to a dome. The design was accepted in principle on August 27, 1666. One week later, London was on fire, and the event hastened the opportunity for Wren to rebuild the entire Church.

Unlike what most people think, the new Cathedral was Wren's masterpiece and monument but it was not the real reason for his knighthood. The honor was bestowed in 1673, three years before the construction started, and was mainly for his scientific endeavors.

10. Chicago when it Sizzles

Myth! The biggest fire to hit the US in the nineteenth century destroyed nearly the whole of Chicago.

In describing the Great Chicago Fire of 1871 as "the greatest calamity of the nineteenth century," most history books fail to consider that on the same day, a bigger and deadlier fire just across the boundary was consuming Peshtigo, Wisconsin.

The Peshtigo fire devastated the entire city, an area proportionately larger than what was destroyed in Chicago, and killed 1,500, or twice more than the number that perished in the Chicago conflagration. A series of small fires started by loggers, railroad workers and farmers to burn debris had ignited the forest, which was completely dry from three months of drought, and fanned by a fierce wind had erupted into a firestorm. The hurricanes of flame literally dropped from the heavens, whirled through nine towns and 400 square miles of Wisconsin territory, and burned more than four million acres of timber and prairie lands. The blaze is the deadliest fire ever on the North American continent, but the simultaneous fire in Chicago caused it to be virtually ignored. Aid did not come to Peshtigo for weeks because it was first directed to the Windy City. In the end, Chicago was rebuilt with hardly any scar from the fire, but Peshtigo remains ghostly, with barren wastelands greeting the visitor to this day.

11. Firestarter

Myth! A cow started the Great Chicago Fire of 1871 by tipping over a lantern in Mrs. O'Leary's barn.

The Great Chicago Fire of 1871 would have been just a statistic in most disaster lists had it not been for its purported origin, which made it into a legend. The holocaust killed 200 to 300 (with about the same number missing), rendered 90,000 homeless, and destroyed over seventeen thousand buildings in a five-mile-long path of destruction at an estimated cost of two hundred million dollars.

One building ironically left standing was the home of Mrs. Catherine O'Leary, who was at first rumored to have triggered the accident in anger over the untimely termination of her relief payments. As it turned out, she wasn't even on relief, although it was established that the fire did start at the barn behind her house on De Koven Street. Later, a news dispatch carried the story that the cause of the accident was an animal—Mrs. O'Leary had kept a cow in the barn, the cow had kicked over a kerosene lantern, and the flame had swept over a pile of hay.

The sensational news made it around the world and continued to appear in print—until it was revealed that a young newspaperman named Michael Ahern had invented the cow and the lantern in order to boost his paper's circulation. An official board of inquiry created by the Chicago Fire Department investigated the fire but never found the real cause.

12. Most Allen Movies end in Disaster

Myth! **Many of the great Hollywood disaster films that Irwin Allen produced are based on actual events.**

Two films starring Michael Douglas invited controversy because they opened in the same year that unfortunate events similar to those featured in their plots occurred in the real world. The first, *The China Syndrome*, followed in the heels of the atomic leak at the Three Mile Island nuclear plant in Pennsylvania in March 1979. The second, *Wall Street*, premiered just two months after the stock market collapsed in October 1987. The producers argued that there was absolutely no intention of profiting from these debacles because filming had actually started before the fact. This obviously meant that, by some providential turn, the scripts served as the basis for the disasters and not the other way around.

Movies that make uncanny predictions of future disasters are apparently not unusual, as the czar of the genre, Irwin Allen, has himself demonstrated many times. Most people think Allen's movies are about real disasters, but in fact, it is the disasters that seem to follow the scenarios of his movies. For instance, in 1972 the decommissioned luxury ship Queen Elizabeth capsized after catching fire in Hongkong Harbor; in *The Poseidon Adventure* shown that year, an ocean liner is capsized by a tsunami. At the time *The Towering Inferno* was premiering in 1974, three skyscrapers in Brazil caught fire, killing 170. And in 1980, Allen's film about a volcanic eruption, *When Time Ran Out*, coincided with the eruption of Mount St. Helens in Washington. In each case, the actual event could not have given Allen the idea for his script because it happened after production had already begun.

13. City Heat

Myth! The worst fire to hit New York City was in 1904, causing at least a thousand casualties.

What New Yorkers believe to be the worst fire in the history of their city would have been so had it happened on land and caused directly the 1,021 deaths imputed to it. But the situs of the tragedy was water and the cause of deaths for most was drowning.

The excursion steamboat "General Slocum" was churning up the East River with a Sunday school outing on the sunny Wednesday morning of June 15, 1904, when it caught fire. The accident simply couldn't be avoided, what with a decrepit vessel, an incompetent crew and grossly inadequate safety equipment. The captain, a reckless old man, was later convicted of ordering the burning vessel to North Brother Island instead of turning it toward the Manhattan shore three hundred yards away. The casualties were mostly women and children who jumped into the river in blind panic.

In other record books, the worst fire to hit New York City was the one that destroyed a Brooklyn theater on December 5, 1876, trapping and incinerating 295 of the audience.

14. Smokey Says No

Myth! Most forest fires are caused deliberately or through negligence.

317

Come the dry season, we are reminded to keep our fire-making propensities in check, particularly when we are in or near a forest, as a simple act of neglect like flicking a cigarette butt can cause a disaster of major proportions. Fortunately for those who are hardheaded or hard of hearing, this warning, well intentioned as it is, is not supported by the facts.

Statistics prove that the source of combustion for most forest fires is not man but nature itself, with lightning as the main culprit. Of the few fires caused by humans, the person responsible is less likely to be a careless camper or a tourist visiting in the woods than loggers, farmers or even the United States Forest Service. This federal agency, which is in charge of overseeing the safety of the country's vast woodlands and prairies, does a lot of slash-burning as the cheapest way of waste disposal to rid the area of cut or broken limbs, uprooted shrubs, and residues of logging operations. But quite often, the burning is brought out of control by the dry air and the wind, and a forest fire results.

***

LIST OF TOPICS IN THIS VOLUME

HEROES & VILLAINS

Days of Guns and Bosses
    Bringing Out the Dead Files
    The Forest for the Trees
    Brotherhood of Hoods
    Blood and Wine
    Touch Me Not
    Shooting from the Mouth
    Red for Danger
    Your Friendly Hoover Man
    The Last Wave
    Barrow & Parker, Bank Specialists
    The Caged Bird Wouldn't Sing
    Halloween Perennial
    Tweedy Man in Nasty Situation
    Big, Maybe, but Stainless, No
    Bank Jobs and Cash Flows
    Top Goon

The Long Arm Of The Law
    The World is his Beat
    Le Jeune Air
    Changing Lanes
    Treading the Yards
    London Nightsticks and Bobby Pins
    Les Condés de France
    Years of the Pig
    Rough Stuff in the Blue Lodge

Way Of The Gun
    The Far Country
    Five in the Body, One in the Foot
    Tastes Like Dirt
    The Deadliest Guns are Live
    Off the Wall and Into a Hole

Precocious Young Guns
Bat Strikes Out
Roving Hood of the West
The Coach that Turned into a Bank
Why Wyatt was at the Fight
It Wasn't OK, Doc
The Path to Dusty Death
Tinhorn Star
Craven Idol
Calamity was a Woman
A Hand to Die For
Bison Bill and the Indians

Tramps And Thieves
Something Wrong with the Count
Hatchet Job
Surly Czar
Hardcore Practitioner
Nobody Loves Lucy
Having a Ripping Time
Mad Monk
Out for Blood

Cloak And Dagger
Cracker Jacks at Work
Spies in the Closet
Crosswords of the Times
The I in Intrepid
They Talked to the Wind
Moles in the Field
Laughing his Way to the Gallows
Square Pegs in the Oval Office
A Column too Many
Stirrings Underground
Returning a Coat?
Mission Implausible

Days Of The Jackals
He loved Twinkies but hated Milk
Reruns of an American Tragedy
Cry of the Wolf

The Name on the Bullet
End of a Long Story
A Short Film About Killing
The Unlucky Stars of India
A Medieval Murder Mystery
Death on the Dot
Leading Death by the Nose
Hands of Fate
Addressing the State of the President
With a Friend like Harry
For King and Country
The Mighty Queen
Somos Diferentes
Caught in Charlotte's Web
Fall Guy

Abraham And John

A Parallax View
Escape Sequence
Time Triplets
Four Scores and Twenty Years Ago
Four from the Cold Files
Dear Secretary
Bullet in the Head
The Mirror has two Faces

P As In Pirate

Say 'Aar', not 'Arrrgh'
They Smoked and Chewed Tobacco at the Same Time?
Didja Hear About the Parrot...?
Ocean Viewing in 2D
Depp Ears
Mapping their Future
Where'd he Get those One-legged Johns?
Dead Man Walking
Flagging Concerns
The Gin tasted Rummy
Hook and Blood in the Movies
Sir Harry Meets Billy the Kidd
Ain't he a Jolly Rogue?
When beached Sharks Lose their Teeth

His last Grand Stand

The World In Flames
Words of War
Tripped by a Wire
Hell on High Water
Never second Gas the Enemy
Those Rampaging Huns
The Archduke of Hazards
Angels in the Battlefield
Immortal Sergeant
Peace with no Beginning, War without End
Pyrrhic Defeat
Hour of the Dove
Last Action Hero

Red Curtain Down
The 'N' is for Nyet
Mayday or May Day?
The Guns of November
Some Parts are Stronger than the Whole
Ice Palace
Red is Beautiful
Jack in the Wall
How to Sight a Kremlin
Colorable Differences
To Each his Own

Europa Europa
Blitzkrieg—This is no Drill!
Nothing to Fear But...
Know thine Enemy
Escape Artistry
The Story of G.I. Joe
Running on Empty
The Longest Day
Things that Go 'Blam' in the Night
Bull in a China Shop
Blitz Spirit and Heinz Sight
Panzers on a Short Leash

A Puzzle Wrapped in an Enigma
Suppress that Bulge!
Too Late the Hero
A Man, a Plan, a Continent
Looking for Dr. Strangelove
When the Axis Fell
War Prison Blues
French Leave
Death Spas

Armageddon In The East

East Trumps West, North Passes
A Game of Battleship
Zero Accomplishments
Going, Going, Gung!
No Swingers in Singapore?
Whistling Down the Wind
Attack of the Killer Mushrooms
Atomic Power Point
Nuclear Hollow Cause
Air Today, Ground Tomorrow
Big Ego and Small alter Ego
On Borrowed Words
Testing the Waters
Asia's Great Divide
A Sound Heard 'Round the Rim
Unfinished War Symphony
Bushido gay Blades
Dead Men Marching

It Was A Word War Too

Axial Words to War
Say that Again and I'll Shoot
Here, There and Everywhere
Life is a Box
Salty Reply
Island of Doomed Men
Fun with Joe and Jane
A Lose-Lose Situation
Trump Call

324

DISASTERS

Lord was their Witness
The Casualty List was no Cameron Trick
Sea Dirge
Futility Hounds a Voyage

Groundbreaking In San Francisco
Earthshaking Events
It Moves
Flames on Barbary Coast
The Sound Resonates as the Missouri Breaks
California Split
Lava from Java
Fire in the Sky
High Scale Rumble

Signs Of The Apocalypse
Flu on the Fly
Return of the Rat Pack
Bugs in their Bonnets
How to Plug a Plague
Keep a Watch on that Burner
Just a Bag of Air
When the Wall Crashed
There's Something about Mary
Knight Templar
Chicago when it Sizzles
Firestarter
Most Allen Movies end in Disaster
City Heat
Smokey Says No

SELECTED READINGS

Adams, Cecil, *The Straight Dope*, New York: Ballantine Books, 1986

Adams, Cecil, *More on the Straight Dope*, New York: Ballantine Books, 1988

Agel, Jerome and Glanze, Walter D., *Cleopatra's Nose, The Twinkie Defense, & 1500 Other Verbal Shortcuts in Popular Parlance*, New York: Prentice Hall Press, 1990

Alterman, Eric, *When Presidents Lie,* London: Penguin Books, 2004

Aron, Paul, *Unsolved Mysteries of History,* New York: Barnes & Noble Books, 2000

Aron, Paul, *More Unsolved Mysteries of History,* New York: Barnes & Noble, 2004

Aron, Paul, *Did Babe Ruth Call His Shot?,* New Jersey: John Wiley & Sons, 2005

Barham, Andrea, *The Pedant's Return,* New York: Bantam Books, 2006

Barthel, Manfred (translated by Howson, Mark), *What the Bible Really Says*, New York: Wings Books, 1992

Battle, Kemp P., *Great American Folklore*, New York: Barnes and Noble, 1992

Boardman, Barrington, *Flappers, Bootleggers, "Typhoid Mary" & the Bomb*, New York: Harper & Row, 1968

Boller, Jr., Paul F., *Presidential Anecdotes*, New York: Penguin Books, 1981

Boller, Jr., Paul F. and Davis, Ronald L., *Hollywood Anecdotes*, New York: William Morrow, 1987

Boller, Jr., Paul F. and George, John, *They Never Said It*, New York: Oxford University Press, 1990

Boller, Jr., Paul F., *Not So!,* New York: Oxford University Press, 1995

Boorstin, Daniel J., *The Discoverers*, New York: Random House, 1983

Boorstin, Daniel J., *The Creators*, New York: Random House, 1992

Breuer, William B., *Daring Missions of World War II,* New Jersey: Castle Books, 2001

Breuer, William B., *Deceptions of World War II,* New Jersey: Castle Books, 2001

Brokaw, Tom, *The Greatest Generation,* New York: Random House, 1998

Brown, Anthony Cave, *Bodyguard of Lies*, London: W. H. Allen & Co. Ltd., 1977

Brown, Peter H. and Pinkston, Jim, *Oscar Dearest*, New York: Harper & Row, 1987

Botting, Douglas & the Editors of Time-Life Books, *The Pirates*, Virginia: Time-Life Books, 1978

Bullis, Don, *The Old West Trivia Book*, California: Gem Guides Book

328

Company, 1993

Carnes, Mark C. (ed.), *Past Imperfect,* New York: Henry Holt and Company, 1996

Cole, Sylvia & Lass, Abraham H., *The Dictionary of 20th-Century Allusions*, New York: Ballantine Books, 1991

Cowley, Robert (ed.), *What Ifs? Of American History,* New York: G.P. Putnam's Sons, 2003

Craughwell, Thomas J., *Urban Legends,* New York: Barnes & Noble, 2000

Crofton, Ian, *Brewer's Cabinet Of Curiosities,* London: Weidenfeld & Nicolson, 2006

Davis, Kenneth C., *Don't Know Much About History*, New York: Avon Books, 1992

Davis, Kenneth C., *Don't Know Much About Geography*, New York: Avon Books, 1993

Davis, Kenneth C., *Don't Know Much About Mythology*, New York: Harper, 2005

Davis, Kenneth C., *Don't Know Much About World Myths,* New York: HarperCollins, 2005

Davis, Kenneth C., *Don't Know Much About Anything,* New York: Harper, 2007

Del Re, Gerard & Patricia, *History's Last Stand*, New York: Avon Books, 1993

Dickson, Paul & Goulden, Joseph C., *Myth-Informed*, New York: Putnam Publishing, 1993

Diefendorf, David, *Amazing...But False!,* New York: Sterling, 2007

Donald, David Herbert, *Lincoln*, London: Jonathan Cape, 1995

Durant, Will, *Caesar and Christ*, New York: Simon and Schuster, 1944

Durant, Will, *The Age of Faith*, New York: Simon and Schuster, 1950

Durschmied, Erik, *How Chance And Stupidity Have Changed History,* New York: MJF Books, 1999

Eastman, John, *Retakes*, New York: Ballantine Books, 1989

Editors of Time-Life Books, The, *Visions and Prophecies*, Virginia: Time-Life Books, 1988

Editors of Time-Life Books, The, *Feats and Wisdom of the Ancients*, Virginia: Time-Life Books, 1990

Evans, Harold, *They Made America,* New York: Back Bay Books, 2004

Evans, Ivor H., *Brewer's Dictionary of Phrase and Fable*, New York: HarperCollins, 1991

Farquhar, Michael, *A Treasury of Deception,* New York: Penguin, 2005

Farquhar, Michael, *A Treasury Of Foolishly Forgotten Americans,* New York: Penguin, 2008

Feldman, David, *Why Do Pirates Love Parrots*, New York: Collins, 2007

Filler, Louis, *The Muckrakers*, Chicago: Henry Regnery Company, 1968

Flexner, Stuart Berg, *Listening to America*, New York: Simon & Schuster, 1982

Flexner, Stuart and Doris, *The Pessimist's Guide to History*, New York: HarperCollins, 2000

Fox, Robin Lane, *The Unauthorized Version*, New York: Vintage Books, 1993

Funk, Charles Earle, *Thereby Hangs A Tale*, New York: Harper & Row, 1985

Gardner, Martin, *The Magic Numbers of Dr. Matrix*, New York: Dorset Press, 1990

Gardner, Martin, *Science Good, Bad and Bogus*, Buffalo: Prometheus Books, 1989

Garrison, Webb, *Behind the Headlines*, Harrisburg: Stackpole Books, 1983

Garrison, Webb, *A Treasury of White House Tales*, Nashville: Rutledge Hill Press, 1996

Gentry, Curt, *J. Edgar Hoover*, New York: W.W. Norton & Co., 1991

Goldberg, M. Hirsch, *The Book of Lies*, New York: Quill / William Morrow, 1990

Gore, Chris, *The 50 Greatest Movies Never Made*, New York: St. Martin's Griffin, 1999

Gottlieb, Agnes Hooper et al., *1000 Years, 1000 People,* New York: Barnes & Noble, 199

Graham, Lloyd M., *Deceptions and Myths of the Bible*, New York: Citadel Press, 1975

Greenberg, Gary, *101 Myths of the Bible,* New York: Barnes & Noble, 2000

Greig, Charlotte, *Conspiracy,* New York: Barnes & Noble, 2003

Gribbin, John, *The Scientists,* New York: Random House, 2002

Griffin, Lynne & McCann, Kelly, *The Book of Women*, Maine: Bob Adams, 1992

Haining, Peter, ed., *A Sherlock Holmes Companion*, New York: Barnes & Noble, 1994

Hamilton, Edith, *Mythology*, Boston: Little, Brown and Co., 1942

Handford, S.A. (transl.), *The Fables of Aesop*, London: Penguin Books, 1964

Hardwick, Michael, *The Complete Guide to Sherlock Holmes*, New York: St. Martin's Press, 1986

Hay, Peter, *Movie Anecdotes*, New York: Oxford University Press, 1990

Haycraft, Howard (ed.), *The Art of the Mystery Story*, New York: Grosset & Dunlap, 1946

Haycraft, Howard, *Murder for Pleasure*, New York: Carroll & Graf Publishers: 1984

Hayward, James, *Myths & Legends of the Second World War*, Stroud, Sutton Publishing, 2003

Hendrickson, Robert, *World Literary Anecdotes*, New York: Facts on File, 1990

Hendrickson, Robert*, American Literary Anecdotes*, New York: Facts on File, 1990

Hendrickson, Robert, *British Literary Anecdotes*, New York: Facts on File, 1990

Herbert, A. P., *Uncommon Law*, London: Methuen & Co., 1964

Hersch, Hank and Bechtel, Mark, *Classic Rivalries,* New York: Sports Illustrated Books, 2003

Holden, Anthony*, Behind the Oscar*, New York: Plume, 1993

Holland, Barbara*, Hail to the Chiefs*, New York: Ballantine Books, 1990

Holt, Patricia Lee, *George Washington Had No Middle Name*, New Jersey: Citadel Press, 1988

Innes, Brian, *Fakes & Forgeries,* New York: Reader's Digest, 2005

Isaacson, Walter*, Pro & Con*, New York: G. P. Putnam's Sons: 1983

Jackson, Robert*, Unexplained Mysteries of World War II*, New York: Gallery Books, 1991

Jeffers, H. Paul, *History's Greatest Conspiracies,* New York: Barnes & Noble, 2004

Jennings, Peter & Brewster, Todd, *In Search of America,* New York: Hyperion, 2002

Johnsen, Ferris, *The Encyclopedia of Popular Misconceptions,* New York: Carol Publishing, 1994

Johnson, Paul, *Modern Times*, New York: Harper Collins, 1991

Jones, Judy and Wilson, William, *An Incomplete Education*, New York: Ballantine Books, 1987

Kahn, David*, The Code-Breakers*, London: Weidenfeld and Nicolson, 1967

Kerr, Philip, ed., *The Penguin Book of Lies*, London: Viking Press, 1990

Keyes, Ralph, *"Nice Guys Finish Seventh,"* New York: Harper Perennial, 1993

Kick, Russ, *You Are Being Lied To,* New York: MJF Books, 2001

Kick, Russ, *Everything You Know Is Wrong,* New York: Barnes & Noble Books, 2002

Lane, Sheldon, ed., *For Bond Lovers Only*, New York: Dell Publishing, 1965

Lass, Abraham H., Kiremidjian, David & Goldstein, Ruth M., *Dictionary of Classical, Biblical, & Literary Allusions*, New York: Ballantine Books, 1988

Leighton, Isabel, ed., *The Aspirin Age*, 1919-1941, New York: Simon and Schuster, 1965

Lindskoog, Kathryn*, Fakes, Frauds & Other Malarkey*, Grand Rapids: Zondervan Publishing House, 1993

Llewellyn, Sam, *Small Parts In History*, New York: Barnes & Noble, 1992

Lloyd, John & Mitchinson, John, *The Book Of General Ignorance,* New York: Harmony Books, 2006

Loewen, James, *Lies My Teacher Told Me*, New York: Simon & Schuster, 1995

Loewen, James, *Lies Across America*, New York: Touchstone, 1999

Lorie, Peter, *Superstitions,* New York: Simon & Schuster, 1992

Macrone, Michael, *By Jove!,* New York: HarperCollins, 1992

Macrone, Michael, *Brush Up Your Shakespeare!,* New York: Harper Collins, 1990

Magee, Bryan, *The Story Of Philosophy,* New York: Barnes & Noble, 2006

Manser, Martin, *Melba Toast, Bowie's Knife & Caesar's Wife*, New York: Avon Books, 1990

Matthews, John, *Pirates*, London: Carlton Books, 2006

McCullough, David, *Truman*, New York: Simon & Schuster, 1992

Montagu, Ashley and Darling, Edward, *The Prevalence of Nonsense*, New York: Dell, 1969

Moore, Laurence, *Lightning Never Strikes Twice*, New York: Avon Books, 1994

Morrow, Ed, *The Grim Reaper's Book of Days*, New York: Carol Publishing Group, 1992

Most, Glenn W. and Stowe, William W. (eds.), *The Poetics of Murder*, New York: Harcourt Brace, 1983

Nash, J. Robert, *Darkest Hours*, New York: Simon & Schuster, 1977

National Insecurity Council, The, *It's A Conspiracy!*, Berkeley: Earth Works Press, 1992

Opie, Iona & Peter, *Classic Fairy Tales*, New York: Oxford University Press, 1980

Page, Michael & Ingpen, Robert, *The Time-Life Encyclopedia of Things That Never Were*, Virginia: Time-Life Books, 1988

Panati, Charles, *Panati's Extraordinary Origins of Everyday Things*, New York: Harper & Row, 1989

Panati, Charles, *Sacred Origins Of Profound Things,* New York: Penguin, 1996

Pappas, Theoni, *The Joy of Mathematics*, California: Wide World Publishing / Tetra, 1989

Pappas, Theoni, *Mathematical Scandals*, California: Wide World Publishing/Tetra, 1997

Pearson, John, *James Bond*, London: Colins Publishing, 1986

Perkes, Dan, *Eyewitness to Disaster*, New York: Gallery Books, 1985

Platnick, Kenneth B., *Great Mysteries of History*, New York: Dorset Press, 1987

Poirier, René (transl. by Crosland, Margaret), *Engineering Wonders of the World*, New York: Barnes & Noble, 1993

Poundstone, William, *Big Secrets*, New York: Quill, 1983

Poundstone, William, *Bigger Secrets*, Boston: Houghton Mifflin Company, 1986

Poundstone, William, *Biggest Secrets*, New York: William Morrow & Co,. 1993

Powell, Michael, *Forbidden Knowledge,* Massachusetts: Adams Media, 2007

Randi, James, *Flim-Flam!,* New York: Prometheus, 1982

Rawson, Hugh, *Devious Derivations*, New York: Crown Publishers, 1994

Reader's Digest, The, *Great Cases of Interpol*, Hong Kong: Reader's Digest, 1982

Reader's Digest, The, *Facts & Fallacies*, New York: The Reader's Digest Association, 1988

Rees, Nigel, *The Nigel Rees Book of Slogans & Catchphrases*, London, Unwin Paperbacks, 1984

Rees, Nigel, *A Word in your Shell-like, London: Trafalgar Square, 2007*

Roberts, Andrew (ed.), *What Might Have Been,* London: Phoenix, 2005

Robertson, Patrick, *The Guinness Book of Movie Facts & Feats,* New York: Abbeville Press, 1991

Rogers, Tom, *Insultingly Stupid Movie Physics,* Naperville: Sourcebooks Hysteria, 2007

Rosenbaum, Ron, *Travels with Dr. Death*, New York: Penguin Books, 1991

Rosenberg, Bernard & White, David Manning, eds., *Mass Culture: The Popular Arts in America*, London: Collier-Macmillan, 1964

Rowan, Richard Wilmer, *33 Centuries of Espionage*, New York: Hawthorn Books, 1967

Rowse, A. L., *William Shakespeare*, New York: Harper & Row, 1963

Sanders, Dennis & Lovallo, Len, *The Agatha Christie Companion*, New York: Berkley Books, 1989

Sanello, Frank, *Reel v. Real,* New York: Taylor Trade Publishing, 2003

Shenkman, Richard & Reiger, Kurt, *One-Night Stands with American History*, New York: Quill, 1982

Shenkman, Richard, *Legends, Lies & Cherished Myths of American History*, New York: Harper & Row, 1988

Shenkman, Richard, *Legends, Lies & Cherished Myths of World History*, New York: Harper Collins, 1993

Shirer, William L., *The Rise and Fall of the Third Reich*, New York: Exeter Books, 1987

Stewart, Desmond and the Time-Life Editors, *Early Islam*, New York: Time-Life Books, 1972

Tamarkin, Bob, *Rumor Has It,* New York: Prentice Hall, 1993

Thornton, Willis, *History: Fact & Fable*, New York: Dorset Press, 1992

Tiballs, Geof, *The Olympics' Strangest Moments,* London: Robson Books, 2004

Tuleja, Tad, *Fabulous Fallacies*, New York: Harmony Books, 1982

Vankin, Jonathan and Whalen, John, *Based On A True Story,* Chicago: Chicago Review Press, 2005

Walker, Barbara G., *Woman's Encyclopedia of Myths and Secrets*, San Francisco: Harper & Row, 1983

Wallace, Robert and the Editors of Time-Life Books, *World of Leonardo*, New York: Time, 1966

Wallace, Robert and the Editors of Time-Life Books, *World of Rembrandt*, New York: Time, 1968

Ward, Philip, *Panama Hats, Crocodile Tears and Other Common Fallacies*, New York: Barnes & Noble, 1993

Wecter, Dixon, *The Hero in America*, Michigan: The University of Michigan Press, 1963

Weir, Stephen, *History's Worst Decisions,* New York: Metro Books, 2009

West, Nigel, *A Thread of Deceit*, New York: Random House, 1985

Whitehouse, Arch, *Espionage and Counterespionage*, New York: Doubleday, 1964

Wiley, Mason and Bona, Damien, *Inside Oscar*, New York: Ballantine Books, 1988

Williams, Hywel, *Days That Changed The World,* London: Quercus, 2006

Wills, Gary, *What Jesus Meant,* New York: Penguin Books, 2007

Winter, Gordon and Kochman, Wendy, *Secrets of the Royals*, New York: St. Martin's Press: 1990

Wise, David and Ross, Thomas B., *The Invisible Government*, New York: Bantam Book, 1964

Wright, Mike, *What They Didn't Teach You About The 60s,* California: Presidio, 2001

Zich, Arthur, and the Time-Life eds., *The Rising Sun* (World War II), Alexandria: Time-Life Books, 1978

———*Mysteries of Mind, Space & Time*, Westport, Conn: H. S. Stuttman Inc., 1992

———*The New Encyclopedia Britannica*, 15th Ed., Chicago: Encyclopedia Britannica, 1994

———*The Truth About History,* New York: Barnes & Noble, 2007

www.ingramcontent.com/pod-product-compliance
Lightning Source LLC
Chambersburg PA
CBHW072347290526
45794CB00001B/35